# Perfect
# Poultry

## Other Books by Family Circle

*Recipes America Loves Best*
Family Circle *Hints Book*
*Great Meals on a Tight Budget*
*Delicious Desserts*
Family Circle *ABZ's of Cooking*
Family Circle *Holiday & Special Occasions Cookbook*
*One Dish Meals*
*The Best of Family Circle Cookbook*

# PERFECT POULTRY

More Than 200 Recipes and Dozens of Tips
for Making Delicious Meals
with Chicken and Turkey

The Editors of

**FamilyCircle**

Foreword by Jean Hewitt

**Times**
BOOKS

## SPECIAL PROJECT STAFF

PROJECT EDITOR • *Heather Allen*
FAMILY CIRCLE FOOD EDITOR • *Jean Hewitt*
FAMILY CIRCLE ASSOCIATE FOOD EDITOR • *David Ricketts*
FAMILY CIRCLE GREAT IDEAS EDITOR • *Marie Walsh*
TYPE SUPERVISOR • *Wendy Hylfelt*
TYPESETTING • *Vickie Almquist*
SPECIAL ASSISTANTS • *Helen Russell and Joanne Hajdu*
COVER PHOTO • *Gordon E. Smith*
ILLUSTRATION • *Lauren Jarrett*

PROJECT MANAGER • *Annabelle Groh*
PRODUCTION EDITOR • *Margaret Chan-Yip*

All rights reserved under International and Pan-American Copyright
Conventions. Published in the United States by Times Books,
a division of Random House, Inc., New York, and simultaneously
in Canada by Random House of Canada Limited, Toronto.

The contents of this work were previously published in
*Family Circle* and *Family Circle Great Ideas*.

**Library of Congress Cataloging in Publication Data**

Main entry under title:

Perfect poultry.

Includes index.
1. Cookery (Poultry)    I. Family Circle (Mount Morris, Ill.)
TX750.P47          1985          641.6'65          85-40274
ISBN 0-8129-1210-1

*Designed by Giorgetta Bell McRee/Early Birds*

Manufactured in the United States of America

9 8 7 6 5 4 3 2

First Edition

*Dedicated to the readers of*
**Family Circle** *Magazine*

# CONTENTS

FOREWORD *by Jean Hewitt*  **ix**

INTRODUCTION: Cooking with Poultry  **3**

  **1.** Roasts  **17**
  **2.** Fried and Sautéed Chicken  **33**
  **3.** Barbecued and Broiled Chicken  **49**
  **4.** Stews, Ragouts and Braised Dishes  **71**
  **5.** Casseroles, Baked Dishes and Pies  **87**
  **6.** Appetizers  **109**
  **7.** Soups  **127**
  **8.** Salads and Sandwiches  **147**
  **9.** Party Dishes  **171**
 **10.** Quick-to-Fix Dishes  **199**
 **11.** International Dishes  **221**

INDEX  **245**

# FOREWORD

For versatility of preparation, healthful eating and ease on your food budget, it's hard to beat chicken and turkey. Increased consumption of both birds in recent years shows that more consumers are becoming aware of the good things they have to offer. All year round *Family Circle* prints dozens of good-tasting, good-looking recipes calling for chicken and turkey.

In this book, Special Editor Heather Allen has given attention to recipes using chicken and turkey parts and the many methods of cooking them—from barbecuing and broiling to sautéing and simmering. Either pick up the parts from the meat case or, if you prefer, follow the step-by-step directions for cutting up whole birds and boning chicken breasts that are included in this book.

In addition to the sections on different techniques, almost half of this book is devoted to chapters on chicken and turkey appetizers, soups, salads and sandwiches, party dishes, quick-to-fix meals and international favorites. And throughout the book there are tips, hints and facts about chicken and turkey that will make it easy to purchase, store, cook and serve the birds for any occasion. Happy Cooking!

—Jean Hewitt

# Perfect
# Poultry

# INTRODUCTION

For thousands of years, chickens have been served on dinner tables around the world. Early Egyptians and Chinese prized them as a delicacy and developed methods of breeding and raising them. They were also highly esteemed by the ancient Persians, Greeks and Romans, who introduced them into Britain. Chickens preceded Christopher Columbus to the New World.

Turkeys are natives of the American continent. There is strong evidence that Indians had domesticated the birds well before the Pilgrims arrived in Massachusetts and included them on the first Thanksgiving menu.

However, it wasn't until well into the twentieth century that commercial methods of raising, processing and marketing chickens enabled American families to enjoy the birds more often than on Sundays or holidays. Today, chicken is served at least once a week in 70 percent of American households, and its per capita consumption has almost doubled in the last twenty years.

No doubt, one reason chicken is so popular is that it is very kind to the budget. Since 1969, the price of chicken has actually declined by

42 percent relative to the rate of inflation. Another reason is its extraordinary versatility.

Chicken could be served every single day of the year in a different dish. Its mild flavor blends well with fruits, vegetables, grains, herbs and spices in a wonderful variety of soups, stews, casseroles, salads and other dishes. There seems to be no limit to the ways that chicken (and turkey) can be cooked and served.

In the following pages, you'll find chapters covering the basic methods of cooking poultry—roasts with stuffings, fried and sautéed chicken, broiled and barbecued chicken, top-of-the-stove stews and oven casseroles and baked dishes. Also included in the book are recipes for appetizers and soups, salads and sandwiches as well as dishes for parties and quick-to-fix meals. In the final chapter, there is a selection of well-known international favorites, such as Chicken Cacciatore and Arroz con Pollo.

Chicken and turkey are not only delicious, they are also highly nutritious. Both birds are an excellent source of complete protein, with considerably less fat and fewer calories than other meats. In addition, they contain thiamine, riboflavin, niacin, iron and other nutrients. An outline of the nutritional value is shown in the chart below.

## NUTRITIONAL VALUE OF POULTRY

| 4-ounce portion, no skin or bones | Calories | Protein (grams) | Fats (grams) | Carbohydrates (grams) | Sodium (milligrams) | Cholesterol (milligrams) |
|---|---|---|---|---|---|---|
| Chicken, fried breast | 232 | 22.4 | 11.3 | 3.1 | * | 63 |
| Chicken, fried drumstick | 242 | 20.7 | 15.5 | 1.4 | * | 90 |
| Chicken, roasted, light meat | 188 | 35.3 | 3.8 | 0 | 72.5 | 99 |
| Chicken, roasted, dark meat | 199 | 31.8 | 7.2 | 0 | 97.5 | 99 |
| Chicken livers | 187 | 30 | 5 | 3.5 | 68 | 86 |
| Turkey, light meat | 187 | 35 | 4.1 | 0 | 87 | 81 |
| Turkey, dark meat | 216 | 31.9 | 8.9 | 0 | 105 | 106 |

* No reliable data.

# *HOW TO BUY*

Most poultry in supermarkets today is government inspected for quality and wholesomeness, and carries the inspection shield. Although there are grades A, B and C, nearly all chickens found in markets today are Grade A (top quality). More than half of all chickens raised in this country leave the processing plants already cut up and packaged, with the company's name and Grade A shield printed on the wrappings. The expiration-date label on the outside of the package is a crucial key to freshness and should be carefully checked whenever poultry is purchased.

Most chicken, which is sold chilled, is displayed in the retail stores' fresh meat cabinets, but whole turkeys and larger chickens are more often sold in frozen form and are displayed with other frozen foods in a separate freezer case. Consumer demand for convenient home storage and preparation, plus a preference for specific parts, has encouraged companies to market birds to suit a variety of needs. Chicken is available in the following forms:

## Whole Birds

● *Roaster*
Weighs between 4½ and 6 pounds and is usually about 10 weeks old with tender flesh, soft, smooth-textured skin and enough fat to brown well at moderate roasting temperatures.

● *Broiler/Fryer*
Around 2½ to 3½ pounds in weight and 7 to 8 weeks old. Some heavier broilers can weigh up to 4½ to 5 pounds.

● *Stewing Chicken*
Mature bird, usually a year or more old, weighing around 4½ to 6 pounds. The bird is plump, flavorful and meaty but tends to be tough and requires long, slow cooking.

## Parts

● *Halves*
Useful for broiling or barbecuing and for one-person meals.

● *Quarters*
Usually sold four in a package. Allow one quarter for each person.

- *Breasts, thighs, drumsticks, wings*
Packed by specific parts or a combination of parts in a wide variety of quantities from two pieces to several pounds, suitable for a large family or party. Boneless breasts and thighs are also available.

Turkey is available in the following forms:

## Whole Birds

- *Roaster*
Traditionally an impressive bird for a festive occasion—weighs anything from 8 to 30 pounds. Today, the size does not effect the tenderness of the flesh. The larger the bird, the less it costs per pound, making it an economical choice for parties. Self-basting birds cost more but can save a lot of time and labor.

- *Roaster/Fryer*
Generally young, tender bird weighing 4 to 9 pounds. One is an ideal choice for a small family or for barbecuing on an outdoor rotisserie. Two are a perfect substitute for a large bird when refrigerator and oven space is restricted.

## Parts

- *Breasts, thighs, drumsticks, wings and drumettes (large wing sections)*
Usually packaged by specific part, in quantities from two pieces to several pounds. Breasts, whole or halves, are available with or without the bone, and also sliced. For turkey lovers they offer festive eating at everyday prices.

- *Ground Turkey*
Marketed in rolls, fresh or frozen. It offers a versatile low-calorie source of protein. It is ideal in meatloaves, patties, baked dishes and casseroles.

# AMOUNT TO BUY

The amount to buy will depend on the number of people to be served, the size of servings and the recipe, among other factors. Allow ½ pound of chicken or turkey per serving when roasting, broiling, frying or stewing. Most people can eat two chicken drumsticks or thighs, one turkey drumstick or thigh or half a chicken breast. Consider a single serving as being approximately three ounces of cooked meat without bone or skin.

*Note:* Although prepackaged chicken and turkey parts are now readily available, sometimes it is preferable to cut up the bird yourself. A whole chicken or turkey usually costs less than parts and "on special" can be very economical. Also, a last-minute switch from one recipe to another (for example, from a roast to broiled chicken) may necessitate cutting up the bird.

The following illustrations show how.

# HOW TO CUT UP A CHICKEN

**Step 1. Breaking the joints** Using a sharp knife, cut through the skin between the body and thighs; bend the legs away from the body to break the joints.

**Step 2. Removing the legs** Turn the bird on its side. Remove the leg and thigh from the body by cutting from the tail toward the shoulder between the joints.

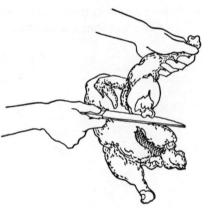

**Step 3. Separating the thighs and drumsticks** Locate the knee joint by bending the thigh and drumstick together. Cut through the joints of each leg.

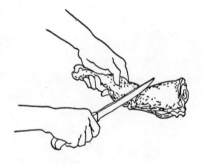

**Step 4. Removing the wings** With the chicken on its back, remove the wings by cutting down through the skin at the base of the wing and through the joint.

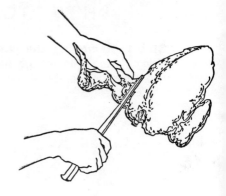

**Step 5. Separating the backbone from the carcass** Place the bird on its back; put the knife in the cavity from the tail end. Cut through the rib cage on one side next to the backbone. Repeat on the other side of the backbone.

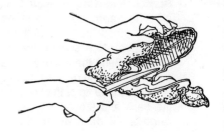

**Parts** Backbone (for soups), thighs, drumsticks, wings and breasts are now ready to use in recipes that require chicken parts. To skin and bone breasts, see page 12.

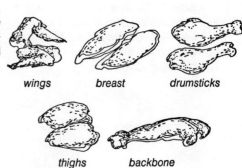

wings          breast          drumsticks

thighs          backbone

Instructions courtesy of the National Broiler Council.

# HOW TO CUT UP A TURKEY

**Step 1. Removing the wings**
Using a sharp knife, remove the tip
and second joint of the wings.

**Step 2. Removing the legs** Cut the
skin between the leg and body
(keeping the knife close to the leg),
leaving as much skin on breast as
possible. Bend the leg outward and
down to snap the hip joint. Continue
cutting with the tip of the knife along
the back and around the cavity to
remove all dark meat. Cut the
connective skin so the legs can be
removed. Repeat on the other side.

**Step 3. Cutting the ribs** Insert a
knife into the body cavity at the wing
joint and cut through the ribs along
the line of rib cartilage. Repeat on
the other side.

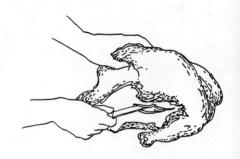

**Step 4. Separating the back from the breast** Cut under each shoulder blade from the point of rib separation to the base of the neck. Pull the breast up as you cut.

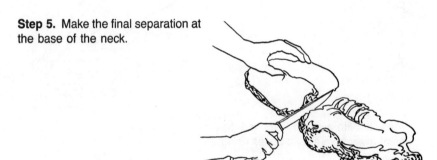

**Step 5.** Make the final separation at the base of the neck.

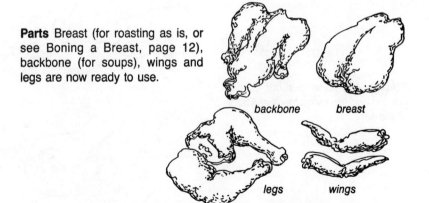

**Parts** Breast (for roasting as is, or see Boning a Breast, page 12), backbone (for soups), wings and legs are now ready to use.

backbone        breast

legs        wings

Instructions courtesy of the National Broiler Council.

# HOW TO BONE A CHICKEN BREAST

**Step 1.** Split the breast into halves; cut the wishbone in two at the V of bone.

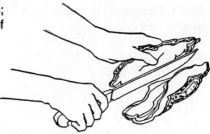

**Step 2.** Slip your fingers between the skin and meat; gently, but firmly, pull off the skin.

**Step 3.** With a sharp knife, cut the meat away from the rib bones using little strokes.

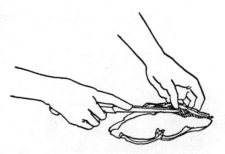

**Step 4.** Continue boning, cutting around and removing the small bone at the top.

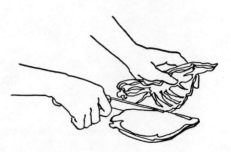

# HOW TO STORE

## In the Refrigerator

Fresh, chilled, tray-packed poultry can be kept, in the coldest part of the refrigerator, for up to two days. Birds purchased in bags or loose wrapping paper should be completely repacked in clean plastic wrap or wax paper before refrigerating. Giblets should be wrapped and stored separately.

Cooked poultry should be wrapped loosely and put into the coldest part of the refrigerator as soon after a meal as possible. Stuffed birds should have the stuffing removed and stored in a sealed container separately from the remains of the bird. Carcass and stuffing should be kept in the refrigerator no longer than two to three days.

## In the Freezer

Uncooked and cooked poultry can be stored for several months in the home freezer at 0°F or lower. Generally, uncooked birds retain flavor and texture during freezer storage better than cooked ones.

The maximum length of time that frozen raw poultry maintains its quality in the home freezer depends on its initial quality, the kind of packaging and wrapping used and storage temperature. However, at 0°F or lower, whole chickens and turkeys should keep for up to 12 months and parts from 6 to 9 months. Giblets should be used within 3 months.

Cooked slices or pieces of chicken or turkey will keep one month when not covered by broth and 6 months when covered with broth. Cooked poultry dishes and pieces of fried chicken can be frozen for up to 4 months and poultry gravy or broth between 2 and 3 months.

# HOW TO THAW

## Conventional Method

While frozen poultry parts and whole birds without giblets can be cooked without thawing, plenty of extra time should be allowed. Commercially frozen stuffed poultry *must* be cooked without thawing.

Whole birds can be thawed in the refrigerator and will take 12 to 16 hours for a bird under 4 pounds and 24 hours or more for a larger bird. Parts will thaw in 4 to 9 hours.

## Microwave Method

For more rapid defrosting, chicken or turkey, whole or parts, can be placed in a microwave oven set on Defrost or Low. The following suggestions make it easy.

### Whole Chicken:
● Remove any metal twist tie from plastic bag-wrapped chicken. Place in the oven.
● Microwave on Defrost or Low for 9 to 11 minutes.
● Remove the chicken from the bag and place it in a glass baking dish.
● Cover wing tips, ends of legs and any other areas that feel warm with small pieces of aluminum foil.
● Microwave on Defrost or Low for 9 to 11 minutes or until the chicken is cool to the touch and has a moist surface.
● Run cold water inside the chicken until the giblets can be removed.

### Cut-Up Chicken:
● Place plastic- or paper-wrapped chicken pieces in the oven.
● Microwave on Defrost or Low for 7 to 8 minutes.
● Unwrap the chicken pieces and turn over onto a glass baking dish.
● Microwave on Defrost or Low for 7 to 8 minutes or until the pieces can be separated.
● Separate the chicken pieces in the baking dish and let stand for 2 to 5 minutes or until soft to the touch.

### Turkey:
● Place the turkey in wrappings, breast-side down, in the oven.
● Microwave on Defrost or Low for 2 to 3 minutes per pound. Rotate the turkey one-half turn.
● Microwave on Defrost or Low for 2 to 3 minutes per pound.
● Remove the wrappings and place the turkey, breast-side up, in microwave-safe roasting pan. Cover the wing tips, ends of legs and any warm or brown areas with small pieces of aluminum foil, securing them with wooden toothpicks.
● Microwave on Defrost or Low for 2 to 3 minutes per pound.
● Rotate the pan one-half turn and check the breast for warm spots and cover with aluminum foil, if found.
● Microwave on Defrost or Low for 2 to 3 minutes per pound.

- Remove the metal clamp from the legs; run cold water into the neck and body cavities to loosen the giblets. The turkey should feel soft and cool and interior should feel cold and slightly icy.

After the poultry is thawed, it should be prepared and cooked immediately.

Ready-to-cook chilled poultry from the store requires little preparation before cooking. Giblets and neck should be removed from whole birds. All parts should be washed carefully in cold water with special attention paid to the inside of the bird. Everything should be dried well, using paper toweling, before cooking.

# 1

---

# Roasts

N othing makes a dinner table more festive than a chicken or turkey, roasted golden brown and surrounded by all the trimmings. Roast turkey is still America's number one favorite for Thanksgiving and Christmas, and a stuffed roast chicken, perhaps because of the little extra time it takes to fix, still signifies a special occasion.

Turkeys for roasting can weigh anywhere from 8 to over 24 pounds; a plump roasting chicken will weigh 5 to 6 pounds, and a broiler/fryer, suitable for a smaller family, should weigh about 4 to 5 pounds.

One of the most enjoyable decisions is choosing the stuffing to be served with the bird. Recipes vary from country to country and region to region. Some families have favorites, such as the Old-Fashioned Bread Stuffing (page 24), handed down from generation to generation, never to be varied. Others like to experiment and try new versions—sometimes two at a time, one at each end of a larger bird (Potato Stuffing and Cornbread-Sausage Stuffing would make a good pair).

Stuffing can be sweet, savory, crunchy or smooth, but all of them add subtle flavor to the poultry's flesh and complement its texture. When preparing the stuffing, ¾ cup should be allowed for each pound of ready-to-cook poultry (any extra can always be baked separately in an ovenproof dish or casserole), and most recipes allow ½ cup stuffing for each serving.

It's easy to produce perfectly cooked picture-book roast poultry by following the suggestions given in the following Turkey Facts and directions of individual recipes for Roast Turkey and Roast Chicken with Herbs. There is a good assortment of stuffings to choose from on the following pages as well as appropriate relishes guaranteed to dress up the festive bird.

To make sure the cooked bird slices perfectly, let it stand at least 20 minutes before slicing, to allow the juices to settle back into the meat. Then follow the carving directions on page 19.

## TURKEY FACTS

- Thaw the turkey, if frozen, following the directions on the wrapper.
- Allow ¾ cup stuffing per pound of turkey for birds over 10 pounds, ½ cup stuffing per pound of turkey for birds under 10 pounds.
- Place the turkey on a rack in a shallow roasting pan.
- Do not cover the pan or add water. Insert a meat thermometer, if used, into the thickest part of the thigh, but not touching the bone.
- Roast in a slow oven (325°), following the chart.

| Weight | Unstuffed | Stuffed |
| --- | --- | --- |
| 8 to 12 pounds | 3–4 hours | 4–5 hours |
| 12 to 16 pounds | 3½–5 hours | 4½–6 hours |
| 16 to 20 pounds | 4½–6 hours | 5½–7 hours |
| 20 to 24 pounds | 5½–6½ hours | 6½–7½ hours |

- If the turkey starts to brown too fast, protect it with a tent of aluminum foil.

### Turkey is done when
- Meat thermometer registers 180° to 185°.
- Drumstick moves up and down easily.
- Juices of bird run clear yellow, not pink, when meat is pierced with a two-tined fork.

### After the feast
Always remove the stuffing from the turkey before refrigerating both the bird and stuffing separately.

# HOW TO CARVE A ROAST TURKEY

**Step 1. Removing the legs** Press the leg away from the body. The joint connecting the leg may snap free; if not, sever it with a knife. Cut the dark meat completely from the body contour carefully with a knife.

**Step 2. Slicing the dark meat** Separate the drumstick from the thigh by cuttting through the connecting joint. Tilt the drumstick and cut off even slices.

**Step 3. Slicing the thigh** Hold the thigh firmly with a fork. Cut off even slices parallel to the bone.

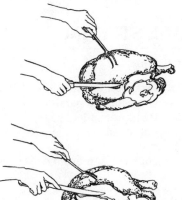

**Step 4. Preparing the breast** In preparing the breast for easy slicing, place the knife parallel and as close to the wing as possible. Make a deep cut into the breast, cutting right to the bone to create your base cut. All the breast slices will stop at this vertical cut.

**Step 5. Carving the breasts** After the base cut, begin to slice the breast. Carve downward, ending at the base cut. Start each new slice slightly up on the breast. Keep the slices thin and even.

# ROAST TURKEY

*Roast at 325° for about 4 hours.*
*Makes 8 servings.*

| | |
|---|---|
| 1 turkey (about 12 pounds) | 1 cup (2 sticks) butter, melted |
| Traditional Sage Stuffing | Salt and pepper |
| (recipe follows) | Giblet Gravy (recipe follows) |

**1.** Thaw the turkey if frozen; remove the giblets and neck. Preheat the oven to slow (325°).
**2.** Stuff body cavity loosely with Traditional Sage Stuffing; close with skewers and string. Stuff neck cavity with Sausage Stuffing variation (or use Traditional Stuffing in neck cavity also, if you wish.) Close cavity. Tie legs together; fold wings under bird. Place bird, breast-side up, on rack in roasting pan. Brush with melted butter; sprinkle with salt and pepper. Insert meat thermometer into thickest part of thigh without touching bone. A "tent" of aluminum foil may be placed loosely over turkey to delay browning. Remove foil for last half hour of roasting.
**3.** Roast in a slow oven (325°) for about 4½ hours, or until the meat thermometer registers 185° or the drumstick and thigh move easily. Brush the turkey occasionally with butter during roasting. When the turkey is done, remove from oven to carving board and let stand 20 minutes at room temperature to make carving easier.
**4.** After dinner is over, remove all the stuffing from the turkey cavity before refrigerating both the leftover turkey and stuffing separately.

# TRADITIONAL SAGE STUFFING

*Makes about 10 cups.*

| | |
|---|---|
| 35 to 40 slices of bread, cubed | ½ teaspoon pepper |
| 1 cup (2 sticks) butter | ½ cup chopped parsley |
| 3 medium-size onions, chopped (1½ cups) | 3 tablespoons leaf sage, crumbled |
| 3 cups chopped celery with tops | 2 eggs |
| 1 teaspoon salt | 1½ cups chicken broth |

**1.** Dry bread overnight or in a very slow oven (250°) to make cubes; place in a large bowl. (You should have 10 cups.)
**2.** Melt butter in large skillet. Sauté onion and celery until tender, about 15 minutes. Add to bread with salt, pepper, parsley and sage.

**3.** Beat eggs lightly in a small bowl; stir into stuffing. Add enough of the chicken broth to make a moist mixture.

**4.** Stuff turkey cavity lightly. Spoon any extra stuffing into a buttered casserole. Spoon a little extra chicken broth over top and bake, covered or uncovered, with turkey during last half hour of roasting.

**Sausage Stuffing:** Brown ¼ pound pork sausage in skillet, breaking into small pieces with a fork. Drain on paper toweling. Add to one quarter of the Traditional Sage Stuffing mixture; mix well. Use to stuff neck cavity. Makes about 3 cups.

# GIBLET GRAVY

*Makes about 5 cups.*

| | | | |
|---|---|---|---|
| | Turkey neck and giblets | | Pinch of pepper |
| 1 | medium-size onion, | 1 | bay leaf |
| | chopped (½ cup) | 4 | cups water |
| | Few celery tops | ½ | cup all-purpose flour |
| 1 | teaspoon salt | 1 | cup water |

**1.** Combine turkey neck, giblets (except liver), onion, celery tops, salt, pepper, bay leaf and the 4 cups water in a medium-size saucepan.

**2.** Heat to boiling; lower the heat and cover. Simmer for 1 hour and 40 minutes; add the liver. Simmer 20 minutes longer or until tender.

**3.** Strain the broth and measure; add more water if necessary to make 4 cups. Chop the giblets; reserve.

**4.** After turkey is removed from roasting pan, remove rack. Tilt pan and pour off all but ½ cup of fat. Add flour; stir over low heat until bubbly, about 1 minute.

**5.** Add the 4 cups giblet broth and the remaining 1 cup water to the pan; stir and scrape over low heat until all the browned bits are dissolved. Cook, stirring constantly, until gravy thickens and bubbles. Lower the heat; simmer for 5 minutes. Stir in the chopped giblets. Taste; add more salt and pepper, if needed.

---
**TIPS FOR TURKEY LEFTOVERS**

• Wrap and freeze slices and pieces in recipe-size portions and label carefully.

• Plan to make broth with the carcass within two days. Freeze broth in ice cube trays if not used within three days. Remove from trays and store cubes in plastic bag in freezer. Use cubes, as needed, for stock.

---

# ROAST CHICKENS WITH HERBS

Try chicken instead of turkey for Thanksgiving; it's quicker.
*Roast at 375° for 2½ to 3 hours.*
*Makes 12 servings.*

| | | | |
|---|---|---|---|
| 2 | roasting chickens (5 to 6 pounds each) | 2 | cloves garlic, finely chopped |
| 2 | teaspoons salt | 1 | tablespoon chopped parsley |
| ½ | teaspoon pepper | 1 | teaspoon leaf rosemary, crumbled |
| | Mushroom-Herb Stuffing OR: Fruited Brown Rice Stuffing (recipes follow) | 1 | teaspoon paprika |
| | | ½ | teaspoon leaf thyme, crumbled |
| ½ | cup (1 stick) butter or margarine | | Chicken Pan Gravy (recipe follows) |
| 1 | tablespoon Dijon-style mustard | | Grapes (optional) |
| | | | Watercress (optional) |

**1.** Preheat the oven to moderate (375°).

**2.** Sprinkle chicken cavities with salt and pepper. Reserve the livers for the Mushroom-Herb Stuffing, if you wish.

**3.** Stuff the neck and body cavities lightly with either Mushroom-Herb Stuffing or Fruited Brown Rice Stuffing. Skewer neck skin to back; close body cavity and tie legs to tail. Place chickens breast-side up on a rack in a large roasting pan.

**4.** Blend the butter, mustard, garlic, parsley, rosemary, paprika and thyme in a small bowl. Rub part of butter over birds.

**5.** Roast in the preheated moderate oven (375°) for 2½ to 3 hours or until tender, basting and brushing with the remaining herb butter every 30 minutes. Remove the strings and skewers. Transfer the chickens to a heated serving platter; keep warm. Let stand for 15 to 20 minutes before carving. Reserve roasting pan with drippings.

**6.** Meanwhile make the Chicken Pan Gravy.

**7.** Garnish the platter with grapes and watercress, if you wish. Serve with gravy, buttered cubed sweet potatoes and Brussels sprouts.

**Chicken Pan Gravy:** Measure 4 tablespoons drippings from the roasting pan into a large saucepan. Pour off remaining excess drippings from the roasting pan. Add 1 cup boiling water to the pan; stir to loosen the browned bits. Pour into 4-cup glass measure. Add chicken broth or water to measure 2½ cups. Set aside. Stir ⅓ cup all-purpose flour into the drippings in the saucepan to make a smooth paste. Cook, stirring constantly, for 1 minute. Gradually stir in reserved broth and ½ cup dry white wine or dry vermouth. Cook, stirring constantly until the sauce thickens and bubbles, 3 minutes. Taste for seasoning; add more, if you wish. Makes 12 servings.

## MUSHROOM-HERB STUFFING

*Makes 6 servings (enough to stuff one 5- to 6-pound roasting chicken).*

| | | | |
|---|---|---|---|
| 2 | chicken livers (optional) | ¼ | cup chopped parsley |
| 5 | tablespoons butter or margarine | 1 | package (8 ounces) herb-seasoned stuffing mix |
| 1 | medium-size onion, chopped (½ cup) | ½ | teaspoon leaf marjoram, crumbled |
| 2 | cups coarsely chopped mushrooms | ¾ | cup boiling water |

**1.** Sauté the livers, if using, in the butter in a skillet for 5 minutes or until they lose their pink color. Remove to a board and chop.
**2.** Sauté the onions and mushrooms in the butter in the same skillet until the onions start to brown very slightly. Remove the skillet from the heat; stir in the parsley, stuffing mix, marjoram and chicken livers, if you wish. Add the water; toss lightly to moisten evenly.

## FRUITED BROWN RICE STUFFING

*Makes 6 servings (enough to stuff one 5- to 6-pound roasting chicken).*

| | | | |
|---|---|---|---|
| 1 | small onion, chopped (¼ cup) | ½ | teaspoon leaf sage, crumbled |
| 4 | tablespoons butter or margarine | 1 | cup sliced celery |
| 1 | cup brown rice | 1 | cup diced dried apricots |
| 2 | cups chicken broth or water | 1 | cup pecan halves, coarsely chopped |
| ¼ | cup chopped parsley | ½ | cup raisins |
| ½ | to 1 teaspoon salt | | |

**1.** Sauté the onion in the butter in a large saucepan until soft, 5 minutes. Stir in the rice. Add the broth; bring to boiling. Lower the heat; cover. Simmer, covered, until the rice has absorbed all liquid, about 40 minutes. Remove from the heat.
**2.** Stir in the parsley, salt, sage, celery, apricots, pecans and raisins.

# CORN-SAUSAGE STUFFING

*Makes 20 servings (10 cups).*

1   pound sausage meat
3   medium-size onions,
     chopped (1½ cups)
8   cups day-old bread cubes
     (16 slices)
1   tablespoon dried parsley
     flakes

1½   teaspoons poultry seasoning
1   teaspoon salt
¼   teaspoon pepper
1   can (about 17 ounces)
     cream-style corn

**1.** Cook the sausage in a large skillet, stirring to break it up, until browned. Remove from the skillet. Pour off all but ¼ cup of the sausage fat. Cook the onion in the fat until soft.
**2.** Combine the bread cubes with the parsley, poultry seasoning, salt and pepper. Add the onion mixture, sausage and corn; toss well. Stuff the turkey.

*Note:* Refrigerate any leftover stuffing. Form into 2-inch balls. Bake in the pan around the turkey for the last 30 minutes of roasting.

# OLD-FASHIONED BREAD STUFFING

*Makes about 16 servings.*

1   large onion, chopped
     (1 cup)
1   cup (2 sticks) butter or
     margarine
1   cup finely chopped celery
2   teaspoons poultry seasoning
½   teaspoon salt

¼   teaspoon pepper
1   can (13¾ ounces) chicken
     broth (1¾ cups)
14   cups cubed white bread
     (28 slices)
½   cup chopped parsley

Sauté the onion in the butter in a large skillet until soft but not brown. Stir in the celery, poultry seasoning, salt, pepper and chicken broth. Bring to boiling; then pour over the bread and parsley in a large bowl. Toss lightly until evenly moist. Stuff the turkey.

# ORANGE-PECAN STUFFING

*Makes 12 servings (6 cups).*

| | | | |
|---|---|---|---|
| 2 | large navel oranges | 1 | cup chopped pecans |
| 1 | large onion, diced (1 cup) | ¼ | cup chopped parsley |
| 1 | cup chopped celery | 1 | teaspoon salt |
| ½ | cup (1 stick) butter or margarine | ¼ | teaspoon pepper |
| 4 | cups cubed white bread (8 slices) | ¼ | teaspoon leaf thyme, crumbled |

**1.** Grate 1 tablespoon rind from one orange; reserve. Cut the skin from the oranges. Section over a large bowl. (You should have 1 cup orange sections.) Reserve.

**2.** Sauté the onion and celery in the butter in a skillet until soft. Add the oranges, rind, bread, pecans, parsley, salt, pepper and thyme. Toss.

**3.** Stuff the turkey or spoon the stuffing into a buttered 2-quart baking dish and cover.

**4.** Bake in a preheated slow oven (325°) during the last 30 minutes the turkey roasts.


# POTATO STUFFING

*Makes 4 generous servings.*

| | | | |
|---|---|---|---|
| 1 | pound potatoes (about 3 medium size) | 6 | tablespoons margarine |
| 1 | medium-size onion, chopped (½ cup) | 3 | slices white bread, cubed |
| | | 1 | teaspoon poultry seasoning |
| 2 | large celery stalks, chopped (1 cup) | ½ | teaspoon salt |
| | | ⅛ | teaspoon pepper |
| | | ¼ | cup hot water |

**1.** Pare and quarter the potatoes. Cook in a small amount of boiling salted water until just tender, about 15 minutes. Drain and reserve.

**2.** Sauté the onion and celery in the margarine in a large skillet until tender. Add the bread cubes; sauté, stirring often, until lightly browned.

**3.** Dice the potatoes; add to the skillet. Cook for 5 minutes. Stir in the poultry seasoning, salt, pepper and water. Transfer to a medium-size bowl; cover; refrigerate until ready to use.

# EASY HERB-CELERY STUFFING

If you bake this quick-fix stuffing in the turkey rather than in a casserole, add only ¾ cup water.

*Bake at 325° for 1 hour.*
*Makes 12 cups, or enough to stuff a 12-pound turkey.*

2    **cups finely chopped celery**
1    **medium-size onion,**
     **chopped (½ cup)**
½    **cup (1 stick) butter or**
     **margarine**
1    **package (14 ounces) herb-**
     **seasoned stuffing mix**

1    **teaspoon leaf sage,**
     **crumbled**
1    **can (10¾ ounces)**
     **condensed chicken broth**
1¼ **cups water**

**1.** Cook the celery and onion in the butter in a large skillet until tender but not brown, about 15 minutes. Combine the stuffing mix and sage in a large bowl. Add the celery mixture, chicken broth and water and toss until well mixed.
**2.** Place in a greased 13½ x 8½ x 2-inch baking dish. Cover with aluminum foil.
**3.** Bake in a slow oven (325°) for 1 hour.


# CORNBREAD-SAUSAGE STUFFING

*Enough for 1 broiler/fryer. Double for 2. Each chicken serves 4.*

¼    **pound sausage meat**
½    **cup chopped green onions**
¼    **cup chopped celery**
¼    **teaspoon salt**

⅛    **teaspoon pepper**
¼    **teaspoon leaf thyme,**
     **crumbled**
3    **cups crumbled cornbread**

**1.** Brown the sausage in a small skillet, breaking up the pieces with a wooden spoon until no traces of pink remain. Remove to paper toweling with a slotted spoon. Sauté the onion and celery in the fat remaining in the skillet. (If there are more than 2 tablespoons fat, remove and reserve.)
**2.** When the onions are soft, stir in the salt, pepper, thyme and sausage. Refrigerate if you are not using immediately. Toss with the cornbread crumbs just before stuffing and roasting the chicken.

# SAUSAGE AND CARROT STUFFING

Be sure the sausage is cooked very well before stuffing the bird.
*Makes enough for a 10-pound turkey.*

¼ **pound sausage meat or link**    ½   **cup water**
     **sausage with casings removed**   6   **cups cubed white bread**
½ **cup grated carrot**                   **(12 slices)**
1   **sweet green pepper, halved,**
     **seeded and chopped**

**1.** Sauté the sausage in a large skillet, breaking it up with a fork, until lightly browned. Add the carrot and green pepper; continue cooking over low heat until the pepper is tender and the sausage is cooked.
**2.** Add the water to the sausage-vegetable mixture and bring to boiling. Pour over the bread cubes in a large bowl. Toss to mix well.

# APPLE AND SAUSAGE STUFFING

Enough savory stuffing for a 10- to 12-pound festive turkey.
*Makes 10 cups.*

8   **cups cubed white bread**     ½   **cup water**
     **(16 slices)**                     2   **large apples, pared,**
1   **pound sausage meat**             **quartered, cored and**
1   **large onion, chopped**          **chopped**
     **(1 cup)**                       1   **teaspoon salt**

**1.** Spread the bread cubes on large cookie sheets; let stand at room temperature overnight; spoon into a large bowl.
**2.** Sauté the sausage in a medium-size skillet, breaking it up with a fork, until lightly browned. With a slotted spoon, transfer the sausage to the bowl with the bread cubes.
**3.** Pour off all but 2 tablespoons of the drippings from the skillet. Add the onion; sauté until tender. Stir in the water and apples; bring to boiling. Pour over the sausage and bread mixture; add salt; toss lightly until the entire mixture is evenly moist throughout.

# FRUITED STUFFING

Apples and raisins add the perfect touch to your holiday roast goose.

*Bake at 325° for 1 hour.*
*Makes 8 servings.*

| | | | |
|---|---|---|---|
| 1 | can (1 pound) sliced apples | 1 | package (8 ounces) |
| | Water | | prepared bread stuffing mix |
| ½ | cup (1 stick) butter or | 1 | cup chopped pecans |
| | margarine | ½ | cup seedless raisins |

**1.** Drain the apple liquid into a 1-cup glass measure and add water to make 1 cup. Bring to boiling in a large saucepan. Stir in the butter until melted.

**2.** Add the prepared stuffing, apples, pecans and raisins; toss lightly to mix the fruits with the stuffing mix. Spoon into a 6-cup casserole; cover.

**3.** Bake in a slow oven (325°) during the last hour of roasting the turkey.

# TROPICAL STUFFING

Try coconut and pineapple for a truly tangy stuffing for
Rock Cornish hens.

*Makes about 2½ cups.*

| | | | |
|---|---|---|---|
| 1½ | cups soft white bread (3 slices) | 1 | tablespoon grated orange rind |
| ⅓ | cup flaked coconut | 2 | tablespoons butter or |
| ¼ | cup finely chopped celery | | margarine, melted |
| ¼ | cup drained crushed pineapple | | |

**1.** Combine the bread crumbs, coconut, celery, pineapple, orange rind and butter in a medium-size bowl; toss lightly to blend.

**2.** Stuff into a 3½-pound broiler/fryer just before roasting.

# ROAST TURKEY BREAST WITH BARBECUE SAUCE

This easy-to-carve, all white meat roast keeps warm for hours.
*Roast at 325° for 3 to 3½ hours.*
*Makes about 8 servings.*

| | |
|---|---|
| 1 turkey breast (8 to 9 pounds), defrosted | Barbecue Sauce (recipe follows) |
| 3 tablespoons butter or margarine, softened | |

**1.** Place the turkey breast, skin-side up, on a rack in a shallow open roasting pan. Rub the skin well with the butter. Insert a meat thermometer in the thick part of the breast, not touching the bone.
**2.** Roast in a moderate oven (325°) for 2½ hours, basting frequently with the pan drippings.
**3.** Brush with Barbecue Sauce and continue to roast, brushing occasionally with the sauce, 1 to 1½ hours longer or until juices run yellow when breast is pierced with a fork. Meat thermometer should register 180°.

*Note:* The turkey can be removed from the oven when done and covered with aluminum foil to keep it warm while the potatoes and dressing bake.

# BARBECUE SAUCE

*Makes about 2 cups.*

| | |
|---|---|
| ⅓ cup chopped onion | ¼ cup chili sauce |
| 2 cloves garlic, minced | ⅓ cup red wine vinegar |
| 2 tablespoons vegetable oil | 1 teaspoon hickory salt |
| 1 jar (12 ounces) apricot preserves | |

Sauté the onion and garlic in the oil in a small saucepan until soft. Stir in the preserves, chili sauce, vinegar and salt. Simmer for approximately 20 minutes.

# CAPE COD RELISH

Cranberries and orange team in this spicy fresh relish.

*Makes 8 servings (4 cups).*

1   package (12 ounces) fresh
    or frozen cranberries
1   large orange, quartered
    and seeded
1   lemon, quartered and
    seeded

1   cup sugar
1   teaspoon ground cinnamon
½   teaspoon ground cloves

**1.** Wash the cranberries; drain and remove any stems. Put the cranberries, orange and lemon quarters into the container of an electric food processor fitted with a chopping blade; cover. Process until coarsely chopped.

**2.** Add the sugar, cinnamon and cloves to the cranberry mixture in a large bowl; mix thoroughly. Cover. Refrigerate.

# APPLE AND PEAR SLAW

Two of winter's best fruits team with shredded cabbage and a tangy orange dressing.

*Makes 6 servings.*

2   large apples
2   ripe pears
½   cup mayonnaise or salad
    dressing

⅓   cup orange juice
4   cups shredded cabbage
½   cup chopped walnuts
½   cup raisins

**1.** Quarter and core the apples and pears; dice and place them in a medium-size bowl.

**2.** Combine the mayonnaise and orange juice in a cup. Drizzle a few tablespoons of dressing over the fruit and toss to coat well. Cover the bowl with plastic wrap and refrigerate at least 1 hour.

**3.** At serving time, layer the shredded cabbage in the bottom of a salad bowl; toss the walnuts with the apples and pears. Spoon the fruit mixture over the cabbage; top with the raisins. Pour the remaining orange dressing over the salad; toss well.

# RAISINBERRY RELISH

Try this savory relish in place of just-plain cranberry jelly with your next roast turkey or chicken.

*Makes 10 servings (5 cups).*

| | | | |
|---|---|---|---|
| 2 | cups golden raisins | 2 | tablespoons lemon juice |
| 3 | cups water | 1 | package (12 ounces) fresh |
| 1 | large apple, cored, | | or frozen cranberries |
| | quartered and chopped | 1 | teaspoon poultry seasoning |
| 1 | medium-size onion, | ½ | teaspoon celery seeds |
| | chopped (½ cup) | ½ | teaspoon salt |
| ½ | cup sugar | ½ | cup chopped walnuts |

**1.** Combine the raisins, water, apple, onion, sugar and lemon juice in a large saucepan.

**2.** Bring to boiling over high heat, stirring often until the sugar dissolves. Lower the heat; simmer for 10 minutes.

**3.** Add the cranberries, poultry seasoning, celery seeds and salt. Return to boiling; then simmer for 10 minutes or until the liquid is about the same level as the raisins and cranberries.

**4.** Remove from the heat; stir in the walnuts. Cool; spoon into a 6-cup glass or ceramic container with a tight-fitting lid. Refrigerate for up to 1 month.

# CRANBERRY RELISH MOLD

*Makes 8 servings.*

| | | | |
|---|---|---|---|
| 1 | package (6 ounces) cherry | 2 | cups cranberry juice |
| | flavored gelatin | 2 | cups sliced celery |
| 2 | cups boiling water | | |

**1.** Dissolve the gelatin in the boiling water in a large bowl; stir in the cranberry juice until blended.

**2.** Freeze, stirring several times, for 30 minutes or until the gelatin is as thick as unbeaten egg white.

**3.** Fold in the celery until it is evenly distributed. Pour into a 6-cup mold or bowl. Refrigerate for 4 hours or overnight.

**4.** To unmold, run a thin-bladed knife around the edge of the mold; dip the mold into a saucepan of hot water for 30 seconds or until the mold loosens. Invert the mold onto a moistened serving plate. Refrigerate until serving time.

# 2

## Fried and Sautéed Chicken

Two chicken dishes for which this country is internationally famous are Maryland Fried Chicken and Chicken in a Basket. As there are with many of the great regional dishes of the world, there can be slight variations in the recipes. Our versions are given on the following pages.

### *FRYING*

Generally, *frying* is the term used for cooking foods in a plentiful amount of fat.

*Deep-frying* is the method used to produce chicken that is very crispy on the outside and tender and juicy inside. The recipe for Double Crunchy Fried Chicken is a good example. Chicken pieces are given a thick coating of batter, bread crumbs or seasoned flour, which helps to seal the outside of the chicken as soon as it comes into contact with the hot fat. Among the factors contributing to successful frying are the type and purity of the fat used, its temperature and the depth and amount in the pan. Best results are obtained with a heavy

Dutch oven or specially designed deep-fat fryer large enough to allow plenty of room for the food to submerge and cook quickly and evenly. Chicken should be cooked, a few pieces at a time for about 10 minutes, in fat heated to 375°F.

*Shallow-frying (pan-frying)* is usually done in a large heavy, deep skillet that easily holds up to 1 inch of fat. The chicken should be coated, as for deep-frying, the fat should be very hot (375°F) and plenty of room should be left in the skillet so a few pieces at a time can be cooked quickly and evenly.

*Sautéing* uses very little fat, which can be vegetable oil or melted butter or margarine. It is the method used for quick-cooking chicken, usually small or thin pieces. Boned chicken breasts and thighs lend themselves especially well to sautéing, and when the breasts are pounded thin, they are the basis of many delicious, quick and easy-to-cook chicken scaloppine dishes. At the end of this chapter is a basic recipe for scaloppine, using boned chicken breasts, with six unusually appealing variations.

## Smoke-free Frying

Vegetable shortening is ideal for deep-fat frying because of its high smoking point. Heat shortening to depth and temperature indicated in the recipe for proper frying.

The new butter-flavored vegetable shortening is excellent for sautéing as well as for deep-fat frying. Use it in place of vegetable oil and butter to provide the frying performance of oil and impart a buttery flavor.

# CHICKEN IN A BASKET

Cold fried chicken is always a favorite, and this one is especially delicious.

*Makes 8 servings.*

| | |
|---|---|
| 1½ cups *unsifted* all-purpose flour | 2 eggs beaten with ¼ cup water |
| 1 teaspoon salt | 2 broiler/fryers (2½ to 3 pounds each), quartered |
| 1 teaspoon sugar | Vegetable oil for frying |
| 1 teaspoon paprika | |
| ½ teaspoon pepper | |

**1.** Combine the flour, salt, sugar, paprika and pepper in a shallow baking dish. Pour the egg mixture into another shallow dish.

**2.** Dip the chicken pieces, one at a time, into the flour mixture to coat them lightly. Then dip each piece in the egg mixture. Roll again in the flour, turning to coat completely.

**3.** Pour enough vegetable oil into a large saucepan or Dutch oven to make a 2-inch depth. Heat to 375° on a deep-fat frying thermometer.

**4.** Fry the leg and thigh quarters for about 18 minutes and the breast and wing quarters for 12 minutes. Cool; cover and refrigerate.

## MARYLAND FRIED CHICKEN WITH CREAM GRAVY AND BISCUITS

Fried chicken served Southern style is a favorite all around the country.

*Makes 4 servings.*

| | |
|---|---|
| 1 broiler/fryer (3 pounds), cut up | Vegetable oil |
| ½ cup all-purpose flour | 1 cup half-and-half |
| 2 teaspoons salt | 1 package (4½ ounces) |
| ½ teaspoon pepper | buttermilk baking mix |
| ½ teaspoon leaf marjoram, crumbled | |

**1.** Shake the chicken in a plastic bag with the flour, salt, pepper and marjoram until thoroughly coated. Reserve 2 tablespoons of the flour mixture.

**2.** Pour enough vegetable oil into a large skillet to make a 1-inch depth. Heat to 375° on a deep-fat frying thermometer or until a cube of bread turns golden in 60 seconds.

**3.** Fry the chicken pieces, a few at a time, until brown. Remove and drain on paper toweling. Pour off the oil from the skillet into a measuring cup. Return 2 tablespoons to the skillet.

**4.** Return the chicken, skin-side up, to the skillet. Cover; cook over low heat for 30 minutes or until the chicken is tender. Uncover and cook 10 minutes longer to crisp the skin. Remove to a serving platter.

**5.** Sprinkle the reserved 2 tablespoons of flour into the fat in the skillet; cook for 1 minute. Add the half-and-half, stirring and scraping up the browned bits. Cook, stirring constantly, until thickened and bubbly. Pour into a gravy boat.

**6.** Bake biscuits following baking-mix label directions; serve with the chicken. Pass the gravy to spoon over the biscuits and chicken.

# DOUBLE CRUNCHY FRIED CHICKEN

Tender and moist, with a crunchy crust.

*Makes 8 servings.*

| | | | |
|---|---|---|---|
| 2 | broiler/fryers (about 3 pounds each), cut up | 1 | teaspoon paprika |
| 1 | cup light cream | 1 | teaspoon poultry seasoning |
| 2 | cups all-purpose flour | | Vegetable oil or shortening |
| 1 | teaspoon salt | | Carrot curls (optional) |
| ½ | teaspoon pepper | | Radish roses (optional) |
| | | | Parsley (optional) |

**1.** Place the chicken pieces in a large shallow dish; pour the cream over the top; turn the chicken to coat it. Cover; refrigerate for several hours.

**2.** Combine the flour, salt, pepper, paprika and poultry seasoning in a plastic bag. Add the chicken pieces, a few at a time, and shake to coat them well. Dip each again in the remaining cream; shake again in the flour mixture.

**3.** Pour enough vegetable oil or melt enough vegetable shortening in a large heavy saucepan or Dutch oven to make a depth of 2 inches; heat to 375° on a deep-fat frying thermometer.

**4.** Fry the chicken pieces, a few at a time, turning once. Fry the breast, legs and thighs for about 18 to 20 minutes and wings for about 12 minutes or until crisp and tender. Remove to paper toweling to drain. Serve at room temperature or cold. Garnish with carrot curls, radish roses and parsley, if you wish.

## CRISPY FRIED CHICKEN

*Makes 4 servings.*

| | | | |
|---|---|---|---|
| 1 | 3½-pound frying chicken, cut up | 1 | egg |
| ⅓ | cup all-purpose flour | ⅛ | cup milk |
| ⅓ | cup pancake flour | | Salt and pepper to taste |
| | | 1 | cup vegetable oil |

**1.** Pull or cut off the chicken skin. Mix both flours in a plastic bag. Beat the egg, milk and seasonings together; add to the chicken; mix well. Shake the chicken a few pieces at a time in the flour mixture until completely coated. Set aside.

**2.** Heat the oil in a heavy skillet or Dutch oven. Add the chicken to the pan in a single layer and fry over medium heat until golden brown on all sides. It usually takes about 15 to 25 minutes for chicken parts to cook, depending on how large and thick each piece is. Legs and thighs take the longest to cook. Always raise the heat when adding a new batch to the oil; then lower the heat after a few minutes.

**3.** Place the cooked chicken on paper toweling to absorb excess oil. Keep warm on a large platter, loosely covered with a piece of aluminum foil, until served.

## BEER BATTER FRIED CHICKEN

Crispy chicken prepared with a light coating of beer batter.

*Makes 8 servings.*

| | |
|---|---|
| 1¾ cups *sifted* all-purpose flour | 2 broiler/fryers (2½ pounds each), cut up |
| 1½ teaspoons salt | Parsley (optional) |
| ½ teaspoon pepper | Onion rings (optional) |
| 1 can (12 ounces) beer | |
| Vegetable oil | |

**1.** Combine the flour, salt and pepper in a medium-size bowl. Beat in beer with a wire whisk or rotary beater until smooth. Let stand for 30 minutes.

**2.** Pour enough vegetable oil in a large skillet or saucepan to make a 1-inch depth. Heat to 375° on a deep-fat frying thermometer or until a cube of bread turns golden in about 60 seconds.

**3.** Dip the chicken pieces into the beer batter a few at a time, allowing excess to drain back into the bowl.

**4.** Fry the chicken pieces, turning once, for 30 minutes or until the chicken tests done. Place on paper toweling to drain. Keep warm in a 250° oven until all the chicken is browned. Garnish the platter with parsley and serve with onion rings, if you wish.

---

### TASTY OVEN-FRIED CHICKEN

For quick and tasty oven-fried chicken, use instant coatings. Packaged bread crumbs, corn flake crumbs and instant potato flakes are three of the many on your pantry shelf right now. Season each coating with your favorite herbs and spices; then roll moistened drumsticks in the mixture. Drizzle with melted butter or margarine and bake in a hot oven (400°) for 40 minutes.

---

# CHICKEN CROQUETTES KIEV STYLE

*Makes 4 servings.*

| | | | |
|---|---|---|---|
| 1 | broiler/fryer (about 3 pounds) | 1 | tablespoon minced parsley |
| 3 | tablespoons butter or margarine | 1 | teaspoon lemon juice |
| ⅓ | cup *un*sifted all-purpose flour | ¼ | cup all-purpose flour |
| 1 | cup milk | ½ | cup packaged unseasoned bread crumbs |
| 1 | teaspoon salt | 1 | egg |
| | Pinch of pepper | 1 | tablespoon water |
| ⅓ | cup butter, softened | | Vegetable oil for frying |
| 2 | tablespoons minced chives | | Hot buttered noodles (optional) |
| | | | Dairy sour cream (optional) |

**1.** Simmer the chicken in salted water to cover in a kettle or Dutch oven for about 45 minutes or until tender. Drain. Cool; skin and bone. Grind in a food grinder using the finest disk. (You should have 2½ to 3 cups ground chicken.)

**2.** Melt the 3 tablespoons butter in a medium-size saucepan. Stir in the flour and cook for 1 minute; gradually stir in the milk. Cook, stirring constantly, until the sauce is smooth and very thick. Remove from the heat. Stir in the chicken, salt and pepper. For easier shaping, chill the mixture until cold, at least 2 hours, or freeze about 1 hour.

**3.** Combine the ⅓ cup butter with the chives, parsley and lemon juice in a small bowl. Spread the mixture onto wax paper to a 2½-inch square. Freeze or chill until firm. (Chicken and herb butter may be prepared the day before.)

**4.** Divide the chicken croquette mixture into 8 equal portions. Place ¼ cup flour and crumbs on separate pieces of wax paper. Beat the egg and water in a small bowl. Drop one portion into the flour; pat with floured hands into a 4-inch square. Repeat with the other portions.

**5.** Cut the herb butter into eight equally wide sticks. Place a stick in the center of a patty; bring the chicken over the butter to enclose it; seal the ends. Shape into a 3-inch log about 1½ inches thick.

**6.** Roll in flour; dip in beaten egg; then roll in crumbs to coat evenly. Place on a cookie sheet; chill for 30 minutes or several hours.

**7.** To cook the croquettes, heat 1 inch of oil in a large saucepan to 375°. Fry the croquettes, 2 or 3 at a time, for about 3 minutes or until golden brown, turning carefully with a slotted spoon. Drain on paper toweling; keep warm while cooking the rest. Serve with hot buttered noodles and sour cream, if you wish.

# TURKEY CROQUETTES

*Makes 4 servings.*

¼ cup (½ stick) butter or margarine
¼ cup all-purpose flour
½ teaspoon salt
¼ teaspoon pepper
¼ teaspoon ground nutmeg
1 teaspoon instant onion
1 cup milk
2 teaspoons Worcestershire sauce
1 cup soft bread crumbs (2 slices)

2 cups finely chopped cooked turkey
½ cup all-purpose flour
1 egg, slightly beaten
¾ cup packaged unseasoned bread crumbs
  Vegetable oil
1 jar (8 ounces) processed cheese spread, heated

**1.** Melt the butter in a large saucepan; stir in the flour, salt, pepper, nutmeg and instant onion.

**2.** Slowly add the milk and Worcestershire sauce. Cook over medium heat, stirring constantly, until thickened and bubbly. Remove from the heat.

**3.** Blend in the soft bread crumbs and turkey. Shape into 8 croquettes. Roll each lightly in flour. Dip in beaten egg and roll in packaged bread crumbs.

**4.** Pour enough oil into a skillet to make a 1- to 1½-inch depth; heat to 375°. Fry the croquettes until golden, about 2 minutes, turning once. Drain on paper toweling. OR: Shape the turkey mixture into 8 patties; dip in flour and then in beaten egg and bread crumbs. Heat ¼ cup vegetable oil in a large skillet. Brown the patties, 4 at a time, adding more oil for the second batch if necessary.

**5.** Meanwhile, heat the cheese spread following label directions. Spoon over the hot croquettes.

# LINGUINE WITH CHICKEN IN GARLIC SAUCE

A chicken version of the favorite seafood dish, with lots of pasta to soak up the delicious garlic-scented sauce.

*Makes 4 servings.*

| | |
|---|---|
| 1 pound boneless chicken breasts, skinned | ½ cup (1 stick) butter |
| 1 egg, beaten | 3 cloves garlic, minced |
| 1 cup packaged unseasoned bread crumbs | 1 tablespoon lemon juice |
| ½ teaspoon salt | ½ teaspoon salt |
| ¼ teaspoon pepper | ¼ teaspoon pepper |
| ½ cup vegetable oil | ¼ cup chopped parsley |
| 1 package (1 pound) linguine | 2 tablespoons butter, softened |
| | Lemon wedges |

**1.** Cut the chicken into ½-inch pieces. Dip the chicken, a few pieces at a time, first in beaten egg and then in bread crumbs that have been mixed with the salt and pepper. Spread the coated pieces on a platter; repeat with the remainder. This can be done several hours ahead and refrigerated.

**2.** Heat the oil in a large skillet. Add one third of the chicken, sauté for 30 seconds or just until the crumbs are golden brown. Remove the chicken with a slotted spoon; repeat with the remaining pieces. Discard the oil in the skillet; wipe it out.

**3.** Cook the linguine following label directions. While it is cooking, melt ½ cup of the butter in the skillet. Add the garlic; cook for 1 minute. Add the chicken, lemon juice, salt and pepper; toss to coat the chicken with the sauce. Do not allow the chicken to cook further.

**4.** Drain the pasta; toss with the remaining 2 tablespoons butter; spoon onto a heated platter. Spoon the chicken and sauce over. Sprinkle with the parsley; serve with lemon wedges.

## CHICKEN CUTLETS PARMESAN

*Makes 6 servings.*

| | |
|---|---|
| 1½ cups cracker crumbs* | 1½ pounds cooked chicken breast slices and pieces |
| ½ cup grated Parmesan cheese | |
| ¼ cup minced parsley | 3 eggs, slightly beaten |
| ½ teaspoon salt | 3 tablespoons vegetable oil |
| ¼ teaspoon pepper | 2 lemons, cut into wedges |

**1.** Combine the cracker crumbs with the cheese, parsley, salt and pepper. Dip the chicken slices and pieces first in the eggs and then in the cracker crumb mixture, coating well.

**2.** Heat the oil in a large skillet; add the chicken pieces gradually and sauté until golden. (Do not let the pieces touch or they will steam and not brown.) Serve with lemon wedges.

\* Crush about 30 saltine crackers with a rolling pin between 2 pieces of wax paper or in a sealed plastic bag to yield 1½ cups cracker crumbs, or use packaged cracker crumbs.

## SAUTÉED CHICKEN CUTLETS

*Makes 6 servings.*

| | | | |
|---|---|---|---|
| 3 | whole chicken breasts (about 10 ounces each), skinned, boned and halved | ¾ | cup packaged unseasoned bread crumbs |
| ½ | teaspoon salt | ½ | cup (1 stick) butter or margarine |
| ¼ | teaspoon pepper | | Lemon wedges (optional) |
| 2 | eggs | | Thinly sliced tomatoes |
| 2 | tablespoons lemon juice | | (optional) |
| ½ | cup all-purpose flour | | Tartar Sauce (recipe follows) |

**1.** Place each chicken breast between two pieces of wax paper. Pound gently with a wooden mallet until the meat is as thin and even as possible. Remove the paper; sprinkle each cutlet with salt and pepper.

**2.** Beat the eggs with the lemon juice in a shallow plate; place the flour and bread crumbs each on a separate piece of wax paper.

**3.** Dip the cutlets first in the egg mixture, then in the flour, back into the eggs and then into the bread crumbs. Place on a rack to dry.

**4.** Melt the butter in one or two large skillets. When the butter has begun to brown slightly, add cutlets and sauté until golden brown, turning once. Remove to a serving platter. Garnish with lemon wedges and thinly sliced tomatoes, if you wish. Serve with Tartar Sauce.

**Tartar Sauce:** Combine 1 cup mayonnaise, 2 tablespoons minced green onion, 2 tablespoons finely chopped celery, 2 tablespoons sweet pickle relish, 2 tablespoons drained capers and 1 tablespoon lemon juice in a small bowl; mix well; cover and refrigerate.

# CHICKEN ATHENA

A takeoff on the popular Steak Diane.

*Makes 8 servings.*

| | | | |
|---|---|---|---|
| 8 | chicken breasts fillets (about 3 pounds) | 1 | teaspoon Dijon-style mustard |
| ¼ | cup (½ stick) butter or margarine | ½ | teaspoon salt |
| 3 | tablespoons lemon juice | 2 | tablespoons chopped chives |
| 3 | tablespoons Worcestershire sauce | 2 | tablespoons chopped parsley |
| | | | Lemon wedges (optional) |

**1.** Sauté the chicken breasts, 4 at a time, in the butter in a large skillet a few minutes on each side, until they feel springy to the touch. Transfer to a serving platter; keep warm.

**2.** Pour off the fat from the skillet. Pour any juices that accumulate in the serving platter back into the skillet. Add the lemon juice, Worcestershire, mustard and salt; bring to boiling. Stir in the chives and parsley. Pour over the chicken breasts. Garnish with lemon wedges, if you wish.

# TURKEY SCHNITZEL

*Makes 4 servings.*

| | | | |
|---|---|---|---|
| 1 | egg | ¼ | teaspoon pepper |
| ¾ | cup packaged seasoned bread crumbs | 1 | cup dry red wine |
| 1 | pound boneless turkey cutlets, pounded thin | 1 | tablespoon Worcestershire sauce |
| ¼ | cup olive oil | 4 | fried eggs |
| ½ | teaspoon salt | 4 | anchovy fillets |
| | | 1 | tablespoon drained capers |

**1.** Beat the egg slightly in a shallow dish. Spread the crumbs on wax paper. Dip the cutlets into the beaten egg; then coat with the crumbs. Let stand for 5 minutes to set the crumbs.

**2.** Sauté the cutlets in the oil in a large skillet for about 5 minutes on each side or until browned. Sprinkle with salt and pepper. Remove from the skillet to a warm platter.

**3.** Add the wine and Worcestershire to the skillet. Cook rapidly until the liquid is reduced to half.

**4.** Top the cutlets with fried eggs, anchovy fillets and capers. Spoon the sauce over.

# TURKEY SCALOPPINE

*Makes 4 servings.*

1 package (1¾ pounds) fresh turkey thighs
2 cloves garlic, quartered
¼ cup vegetable oil
1 teaspoon salt
Pinch of pepper
2 tablespoons all-purpose flour
1 teaspoon paprika

Pinch of nutmeg
1 medium-size onion, thinly sliced
½ cup dry white wine
2 cans (4 ounces each) sliced mushrooms, undrained
¼ cup chopped parsley
Hot buttered noodles (optional)

**1.** Cut the meat from the bone in thin slices.
**2.** Sauté the garlic in the oil in a large skillet for 2 minutes; discard the garlic.
**3.** Sprinkle the turkey with salt and pepper; sauté in the garlic-flavored oil in the skillet for about 5 minutes. Combine the flour, paprika and nutmeg; sprinkle over the slices.
**4.** Stir in the onion, wine and mushroom liquid. Cover; cook for 20 minutes, stirring occasionally until the turkey is tender.
**5.** Stir in the mushrooms and heat until thoroughly hot; sprinkle with parsley. Serve over hot buttered noodles, if you wish.


## *SCALOPPINE VARIATIONS*

# BASIC RECIPE

*Makes 4 servings.*

2 whole chicken breasts (about 14 ounces each), skinned, boned and halved*

½ teaspoon salt
¼ teaspoon pepper
All-purpose flour

Place the chicken breast halves between sheets of wax paper and pound firmly with a meat mallet or rolling pin until they are ¼ inch thick or thinner. Sprinkle with salt and pepper; dip in flour and pat briskly to remove the excess.

* See diagrams on page 12.

# SCALOPPINE WITH PEPPERS

*Start with the Basic Recipe (page 43).*

| | | | |
|---|---|---|---|
| 1 | large sweet green pepper | 1 | clove garlic, minced |
| 1 | large sweet red pepper | ¼ | cup dry red wine |
| 3 | tablespoons olive or vegetable oil | 1 | tablespoon red wine vinegar |

**1.** Halve the peppers; seed; cut lengthwise into ½-inch strips.

**2.** Heat 2 tablespoons of the oil in a large skillet. Add the scaloppine and sauté until golden brown on both sides, about 5 minutes.

**3.** When the meat is done, remove to a platter; keep warm. Add the remaining tablespoon of oil to the skillet. Add the pepper strips; sauté until tender. Add the garlic and sauté for 1 minute.

**4.** Stir in the wine and vinegar, stirring to coat the peppers with the pan juices. Spoon the peppers and juices over the scaloppine.


# SCALOPPINE WITH LEMON PEEL

*Start with the Basic Recipe (page 43).*

| | | | |
|---|---|---|---|
| 1 | lemon | 1 | large clove garlic, minced |
| 1 | tablespoon vegetable oil | ¼ | cup dry white wine |
| 1 | tablespoon butter or margarine | ½ | cup chicken broth |
| ½ | teaspoon leaf rosemary, crumbled | ½ | cup dairy sour cream |

**1.** Remove the peel from the lemon (yellow part only) with a potato peeler. Stack the strips on a chopping board and cut crosswise into fine julienne strips.

**2.** Heat the oil and butter in a large skillet. Sauté the scaloppine until golden brown on both sides, about 5 minutes.

**3.** Sprinkle the rosemary and garlic over the scaloppine and shake the pan to distribute evenly for about 30 seconds. Add the wine and chicken broth. Cook, uncovered, until the pan liquid has reduced a little.

**4.** Remove the scaloppine to a warm platter. Stir the sour cream and half of the lemon peel into the liquid in the skillet. Heat over low heat, but do not boil. Pour the sauce over the scaloppine and sprinkle with the remaining lemon peel.

# SCALOPPINE IN MUSTARD SAUCE

*Start with the Basic Recipe (page 43).*

| | | | |
|---|---|---|---|
| 1 | tablespoon vegetable oil | ¼ | cup dry sherry |
| 1 | tablespoon butter or margarine | 1 | to 2 tablespoons Dijon-style mustard |
| ½ | cup chicken broth | ¼ | cup light cream |

**1.** Heat the oil and butter in a large skillet. Add the scaloppine and sauté until the meat is golden brown on both sides, about 5 minutes. Remove to a warm platter; keep warm.

**2.** Drain any fat remaining in the skillet. Add the chicken broth, sherry and mustard to taste. Simmer, stirring to loosen the browned bits from the bottom of the pan, until the mixture is slightly reduced.

**3.** Add the light cream and continue to simmer until the sauce has thickened, about 2 to 3 minutes. Pour the sauce over the scaloppine.


# SCALOPPINE WITH ORANGE SAUCE

*Start with the Basic Recipe (page 43).*

| | | | |
|---|---|---|---|
| 2 | large navel oranges | 2 | teaspoons tomato paste |
| 1 | tablespoon olive oil | 1 | cup chicken broth |
| 1 | tablespoon butter or margarine | 2 | tablespoons minced parsley |
| 1 | small onion, minced (¼ cup) | | |

**1.** Grate the rind of 1 orange; reserve. Cut off all remaining rind and white from both oranges. Cut each orange in half lengthwise, then cut crosswise into ½-inch-thick slices.

**2.** Heat the oil and butter in a large skillet. Add the scaloppine and sauté until golden on both sides, about 5 minutes. Remove to a platter; keep warm.

**3.** Add the onion to the skillet; sauté until soft but not brown, about 3 minutes. Stir in the tomato paste, chicken broth and rind. Return the scaloppine to the pan; cover; simmer until tender, about 5 minutes.

**4.** When the scaloppine is tender, remove to a warm platter. Add the orange slices to the sauce in the skillet and heat through. Spoon over the scaloppine. Sprinkle with parsley.

# SCALOPPINE NORMANDY

*Start with the Basic Recipe (page 43).*

| | | | |
|---|---|---|---|
| 2 | tart cooking apples, quartered, cored and sliced | 1 | small onion, minced (¼ cup) |
| 2 | tablespoons butter or margarine | ½ | cup chicken broth |
| 1 | tablespoon vegetable oil | ½ | cup light cream |
| | | 2 | tablespoons brandy |

**1.** Sauté the apple slices in the butter in a large skillet just until tender. Remove the apples to a warmed platter; keep warm.

**2.** Heat the oil with the butter remaining in the skillet. Add the scaloppine and sauté until golden brown on both sides, about 5 minutes. Remove the scaloppine to the platter with the apples.

**3.** Add the onion to the skillet and sauté until tender. Drain any fat remaining in the pan. Add the chicken broth and cook briskly until reduced by half. Add the cream and brandy and continue to cook until the sauce has thickened slightly. Pour over the meat and apples.


# SCALOPPINE AND ZUCCHINI AVGOLEMONO

*Start with the Basic Recipe (page 43).*

| | | | |
|---|---|---|---|
| 1 | egg beaten with 2 tablespoons water | 1 | pound zucchini, cut into ½-inch-thick slices |
| ⅔ | cup packaged unseasoned bread crumbs | 1 | cup chicken broth |
| 3 | tablespoons olive oil | 3 | egg yolks |
| 1 | tablespoon butter or margarine | 2 | tablespoons lemon juice |
| | | ¼ | cup grated Parmesan cheese |

**1.** Dip the scaloppine in the egg mixture; then coat evenly with the bread crumbs.

**2.** Heat 2 tablespoons of the oil and the butter in a large skillet. Add the scaloppine and sauté until golden brown on both sides, about 5 minutes. Remove to a platter; keep warm.

**3.** Heat the remaining tablespoon of oil in the skillet. Add the zucchini slices in 1 layer; sauté, turning once, until tender. Remove and arrange evenly over the scaloppine; keep warm in a slow oven.

**4.** Drain all the fat from the skillet. Add the broth; heat to boiling. Beat the egg yolks and lemon juice in small bowl. Add the hot broth, a little at a time; then return the mixture to the skillet; cook over very low heat, stirring constantly, until the sauce thickens slightly. (Do not boil.) Pour over the scaloppine and zucchini. Sprinkle with the cheese.

# SICILIAN SCALOPPINE

*Bake at 400° for 10 minutes.*
*Makes 6 servings.*

| | | | |
|---|---|---|---|
| 1 | eggplant (about 1 pound) | ⅓ | cup olive or vegetable oil |
| 1 | tablespoon salt | 1 | egg beaten with |
| 3 | whole chicken breasts | | 2 tablespoons water |
| | (about 14 ounces each), | 1 | jar (about 16 ounces) |
| | skinned, boned and halved | | spaghetti sauce |
| ½ | teaspoon salt | ½ | pound mozzarella cheese, |
| ¼ | teaspoon pepper | | cut into 6 slices |
| | All-purpose flour | | |
| 1 | tablespoon butter or | | |
| | margarine | | |

**1.** Pare the eggplant and cut off the ends; cut into 6 slices. Sprinkle the slices with salt and set aside for 30 minutes to drain. Rinse with water; pat dry with paper toweling.
**2.** Place the chicken breast halves between sheets of wax paper and pound firmly with a meat mallet or rolling pin until they are ¼ inch thick or thinner. Sprinkle with salt and pepper; dip in flour and pat briskly to remove the excess.
**3.** Heat the butter and 1 tablespoon of the oil in a large skillet. Sauté the scaloppine until golden brown on both sides, about 5 minutes. Remove the meat to paper toweling as it browns.
**4.** Coat the eggplant slices with flour; dip in the egg mixture. Heat the remaining oil in the skillet. Add the eggplant; sauté until golden brown on both sides. Drain on paper toweling as the slices are browned.
**5.** Pour half the spaghetti sauce into a shallow baking dish. Alternate slices of scaloppine, eggplant and mozzarella cheese, slightly overlapping, until the bottom of the dish is covered with 1 layer. Drizzle the top with the remaining sauce.
**6.** Bake in a hot oven (400°) for 10 minutes or until sauce is bubbly.

# HERBED SCALOPPINE WITH WHITE BEANS

*Makes 4 servings.*

| | | | |
|---|---|---|---|
| 2 | whole chicken breasts (about 14 ounces each), skinned, boned and halved | 4 | tablespoons olive oil |
| ½ | teaspoon leaf oregano, crumbled | 1 | tablespoon red wine vinegar |
| | | 1 | clove garlic, halved |
| | | 1 | bay leaf |
| ½ | teaspoon leaf basil, crumbled | ½ | cup chicken broth |
| ½ | teaspoon salt | ½ | cup dry white wine |
| ¼ | teaspoon pepper | 1 | tablespoon tomato paste |
| 1 | can (20 ounces) cannellini (white kidney beans) | 2 | green onions, thinly sliced |
| | | 2 | tablespoons chopped parsley |

**1.** Place the chicken breast halves between sheets of wax paper and pound firmly with a meat mallet or rolling pin until they are ¼ inch thick or thinner.

**2.** Combine the oregano, basil, salt and pepper in a small bowl. Sprinkle the mixture evenly on both sides of the scaloppine.

**3.** Place the cannellini in a sieve and rinse briefly with warm water. Drain and place in small saucepan with 2 tablespoons of the olive oil and the wine vinegar.

**4.** Heat the remaining 2 tablespoons of oil in a large skillet. Add the garlic and bay leaf. Sauté until both begin to turn brown; discard. Add the meat and sauté until golden on both sides, about 5 minutes.

**5.** Combine the broth, wine and tomato paste in a small bowl. Pour over the scaloppine. Simmer, stirring up the browned bits on the bottom of the pan. Turn the scaloppine to coat with the sauce. Simmer until the liquid is reduced to about ½ cup.

**6.** Heat the beans over moderate heat until hot; stir in the green onions. Pour into a shallow dish. Arrange the scaloppine over the beans and cover with the sauce. Sprinkle with parsley.

# 3

## Barbecued and Broiled Chicken

**B**arbecuing and broiling are two of the quickest ways to cook, because the food is placed on an open rack directly under or over the source of heat—usually a gas grill or charcoal fire.

Over the last ten years, commercial barbecue grills have been designed to incorporate a wider range of features than earlier models and easier, more reliable cooking. One of the most popular additions to the cookout repertoire is a rotisserie broiler—the modern-day version of cooking over an open-pit fire. A whole bird is threaded onto a spit, which rotates slowly over the heat, producing wonderfully flavorful and tender, moist meat. Roasting chickens and small turkeys are a particularly good choice for this kind of barbecuing, since they are large enough to cook through slowly without drying out. Wine-Basted Barbecued Turkey and Teriyaki Turkey are good examples.

To increase the flavor and succulence of broiled and barbecued poultry, the pieces of chicken or turkey are often marinated before cooking or brushed with a basting sauce. Three marinades and three glazes are given at the end of this chapter.

Tips for successful barbecuing are also included on the following pages, as well as directions for preparing whole birds for cooking on the rotisserie.

## BARBECUE SAFETY TIPS

Accidents can ruin an otherwise pleasurable barbecue. The following advice can ensure that your barbecue is safe and enjoyable.

### The Right Location

● Never use a charcoal grill in your home or garage; indoors, use only equipment especially designed for indoor use.
● Set the grill in an open area on level ground. Check for stability before lighting the fire. Be extra cautious on windy days.

### Proper Dress

● Roll up sleeves, tuck in shirttails and make sure scarves and apron strings won't hang over the grill.
● Wear a large apron of denim or other heavy material and potholder-type gloves as protection against sparks and grease spatters.

### Start the Fire

● The safest way to start a fire is to spread charcoal over lighted wood shavings or kindling. There are also commercially available products that are quite safe, used as directed—electric starters with the UL label and "treated" solid starters.

### Intensifying the Fire

● To freshen a fire, place more charcoal briquettes around those already smoldering.
● We don't recommend liquid starters; however, if you prefer them, never use them once the fire has been started, even if it appears to be out.

# BROILING OUTDOORS

## How to Build a Good Bed of Coals

● Start the fire for the barbecue about 45 minutes to 1 hour prior to cooking. For easy cleanup, first line the firebox with heavy-duty aluminum foil.

● Whether you use charcoal briquettes or loose charcoal, a good starter is needed. Use a combustible liquid product, newspaper and kindling wood or one of the new electric starters.

● If you use liquid starter (which we do not recommend), pile the coals in a pyramid; saturate with starter; then let stand for a few minutes before carefully igniting. Again, never add starter to an already burning fire.

● For paper and kindling, wad pieces of newspaper into small balls and add thin pieces of wood. Make a pyramid in the center of the firebox. When it's briskly burning, add the charcoal bit by bit.

● When the coals are ignited and burning, spread them out just over the area you will be using.

● The fire is ready when the coals are covered with a gray ash.

## How to Have Perfectly Barbecued Poultry

● Trim the excess fat from poultry to prevent fire flare-ups.

● Cook poultry at the distance from the heat and for the length of time specified in each recipe.

● Control the heat. If a vigorous flame flares up, use water in a sprinkler bottle to extinguish the flames without diminishing the intensity of the heat.

● Learn to be the judge of when the food is done to your family's taste.

## THE DRUGSTORE WRAP

This is the only way to wrap and seal packets of food for the barbecue. It is essential that the seal be tight, so that the juices of the cooking food won't spill over into the fire.

Start by placing the item to be wrapped in the center of a piece of heavy-duty aluminum foil that is large enough to go around the food and allow for folding at the top and sides. Bring the two long sides up and over the food and fold them over about 1 inch (Fig. 1). Make a crease the entire length; make one more tight fold to bring the wrapping down to the level of the food surface. Press out the air toward the ends (Fig. 2). Fold the ends up and over, pressing out the air and shaping to the contours of the food (Fig. 3).

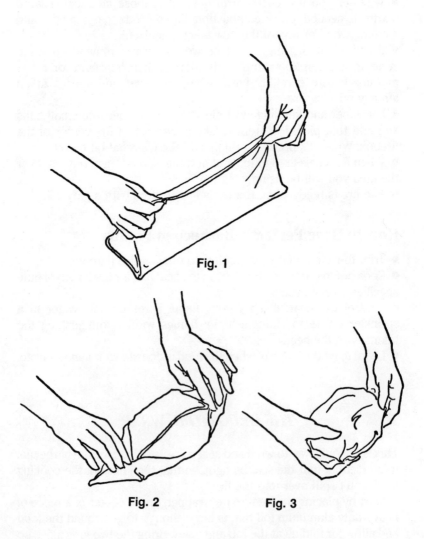

Fig. 1

Fig. 2          Fig. 3

# BARBECUED CHICKEN

Cooking chicken before brushing it with sauce keeps it
from charring too much.

*Makes 8 servings.*

| | | | |
|---|---|---|---|
| 2 | broiler/fryers (about 3 pounds each), cut up | ½ | teaspoon pepper |
| 1 | teaspoon salt | ½ | recipe Piquant Barbecue Sauce (recipe follows) |

**1.** Sprinkle the chicken pieces with salt and pepper. Place the chicken on an aluminum foil-lined grill over gray coals. Cook slowly, turning occasionally, for about 45 minutes or until almost fork-tender.
**2.** Remove the aluminum foil from the grill. Place the chicken directly on the grill; brush generously with Piquant Barbecue Sauce. Continue to grill, turning often and brushing with sauce, until the chicken is fork-tender and well glazed. Heat any leftover sauce to serve with the chicken.

# PIQUANT BARBECUE SAUCE

Tangy and delicious, it's an all-around sauce for almost any meat.

*Makes about 3¼ cups.*

| | | | |
|---|---|---|---|
| 1 | large onion, finely chopped (1 cup) | ½ | cup firmly packed brown sugar |
| 1 | clove garlic, finely chopped | ½ | cup lemon juice |
| 3 | tablespoons butter or margarine | ½ | cup bottled steak sauce |
| 1 | can (1 pound) tomato purée | 1 | tablespoon salt |

**1.** Sauté the onion and garlic in the butter in a large saucepan until golden and tender, about 5 minutes.
**2.** Stir in the purée, sugar, lemon juice, steak sauce and salt. Bring to boiling; lower the heat. Simmer, partially covered, stirring occasionally, for 20 minutes.

# ORANGE-GINGER-SOY CHICKEN

A zingy combination of sweet and tangy makes the marinade
for this chicken.

*Makes 8 servings.*

2   broiler/fryers (about 3
    pounds each), quartered
1   can (6 ounces) frozen
    orange juice concentrate,
    undiluted and thawed
⅓   cup dry sherry

⅓   cup soy sauce
1   teaspoon ground ginger
1   clove garlic, mashed
¼   teaspoon pepper
    Hot cooked rice

**1.** Arrange the chicken in a shallow glass or enamel dish. Combine
the orange juice, sherry, soy sauce, ginger, garlic and pepper in a
4-cup glass measure. Pour the orange mixture evenly over the chick-
en. Marinate for at least 2 hours at room temperature or in the
refrigerator overnight, turning the chicken occasionally.
**2.** Drain the chicken, reserving the marinade. Place the chicken on
the grill, bone-side down. Grill for 40 minutes, turning often and
brushing generously with the reserved marinade until the chicken is
fork-tender. Heat any remaining marinade to serve with the chicken.
Serve with hot rice.

# LEMONY CHICKEN WINGS
# AND SHRIMP KABOBS

Here's an unsusual kabob combination with a wonderful
lemon-herb flavor.

*Makes 6 servings.*

9   chicken wings
    (about 1½ pounds)
1   pound frozen shelled and
    deveined shrimp, thawed

    Lemon-Herb Marinade
    (recipe follows)
¼   cup (½ stick) butter or
    margarine, melted

**1.** Divide the chicken wings by cutting through the joints. Remove the
wing tips and save for soup. Combine the wings and shrimp with the
Lemon-Herb Marinade in a bowl. Marinate for 2 hours at room
temperature, or in refrigerator overnight.
**2.** Drain the wings and shrimp, reserving the marinade. Place the
wings on an aluminum foil-lined grill. Grill for 15 minutes over gray

coals, turning once or twice or until golden brown and almost tender. Spear the chicken and shrimp alternately on 6 skewers.

**3.** Grill directly over the coals, brushing with the butter and marinade and turning often until shrimp and chicken are tender, about 5 minutes.

**Lemon-Herb Marinade:** Combine ⅔ cup lemon juice, ⅓ cup olive oil, 1 teaspoon salt, 1 teaspoon sugar and 1½ teaspoons crumbled leaf tarragon in a small bowl. Stir well. Makes 1 cup.

## SOUTHERN BARBECUED CHICKEN

The South has always been famous for its fried chicken, and now it has come up with a winner for the outdoor grill. The sauce recipe makes 2¾ cups and will keep for days in the refrigerator in a tightly sealed container.

*Makes 4 servings.*

| | | | |
|---|---|---|---|
| 2 | broiler/fryers (2½ pounds each) | ¼ | teaspoon liquid red-pepper seasoning |
| 1 | tablespoon vegetable oil | 2 | cloves garlic, finely chopped |
| | Salt and pepper | 3 | tablespoons vegetable oil |
| | | | Salt and pepper to taste |
| ***Southern Barbecue Sauce*** | | ¼ | teaspoon red pepper flakes |
| 2 | tablespoons butter | ½ | bay leaf |
| 6 | tablespoons vinegar | 2 | tablespoons sugar |
| ¼ | cup water | 1 | teaspoon paprika |
| 1½ | cups catsup | 2 | tablespoons lemon juice |
| 2 | tablespoons Worcestershire sauce | | |

**1.** Split the chicken and place skin-side up on a flat surface and flatten with heel of your hand or a mallet to help it lie flat on the grill. Rub it with a little oil and sprinkle with salt and pepper.

**2.** To make Southern Barbecue Sauce, combine the ingredients in a saucepan. Heat on the side of the grill; do not allow it to boil.

**3.** Grill the chicken skin-side up 6 inches from the hot coals for about 10 minutes or until browned. Brush with the sauce, turn and brush the bone side with sauce. Continue grilling, brushing often with the sauce, until the chicken is tender but not dry, about 30 minutes in all.

**4.** Remove the chicken to a serving platter and give it a final brushing with the sauce.

# POLLO DI ANNA

This grilled chicken is delicious served with grilled zucchini and sweet red peppers.

*Makes 4 servings.*

½  cup olive or peanut oil
1  large clove garlic, chopped
1  tablespoon dark brown
   sugar
1  teaspoon fresh lemon juice
1  tablespoon chopped fresh
   basil OR: ½ teaspoon leaf
   basil, crumbled

1  broiler/fryer (about 2½
   pounds), quartered
½  teaspoon salt
⅛  teaspoon pepper
   Grilled Zucchini
   (recipe follows)
   Grilled Peppers
   (recipe follows)

**1.** Heat the oil, garlic and sugar in a small saucepan, stirring until the sugar is dissolved. Remove from the heat and stir in the lemon juice and basil.
**2.** Brush over the chicken and let marinate for 5 to 10 minutes.
**3.** Grill, skin-side up, 6 inches from hot coals, for 15 minutes; turn and brush with the marinade; grill 15 minutes longer or until tender but not dry.
**4.** Before serving sprinkle with salt and pepper. While the chicken is grilling, cook the zucchini and peppers.

**Grilled Zucchini:** Split 4 medium-size zucchini lengthwise and brush both sides with oil. Sprinkle the cut side with garlic salt and pepper. Place on the grill and turn frequently to prevent burning. Baste with additional oil if the zucchini appears to be drying out. When fork-tender, remove from the grill and roll in grated Parmesan cheese.

**Grilled Peppers:** Place whole sweet peppers, preferably red, on the grill and cook until their skins blister and bubble. Remove from the grill and peel off the charred skin and remove the seeds. If the skin doesn't come off easily, return the peppers to the grill. Slice into sections.

# GINGER CHICKEN

*Makes 4 servings.*

| | | | |
|---|---|---|---|
| 2 | chicken breasts (about 10 ounces each), halved | ¼ | teaspoon salt |
| | | | Pinch of pepper |
| 2 | tablespoons sesame seeds | ½ | cup vegetable oil |
| 1 | teaspoon ground ginger | | |

**1.** Wash the chicken and pat it dry on paper toweling. Put the chicken in a large shallow dish.

**2.** Crush 1 tablespoon of the sesame seeds and mix with the ginger, salt, pepper and oil. Pour over the chicken; turn the chicken over to coat with the mixture. Cover; marinate in the refrigerator for 1 hour or longer.

**3.** Remove the chicken from the marinade; add the remaining sesame seeds to the marinade.

**4.** Grill the chicken 6 inches from the hot coals, skin-side up, for 15 minutes; turn and brush the cooked side with the reserved marinade. Grill for 10 minutes longer; turn again, brush with the marinade and grill for 5 minutes. Turn again and cook another 4 to 5 minutes or just long enough to toast the sesame seeds.

# BARBECUED TURKEY LEGS

*Makes 6 servings.*

| | | | |
|---|---|---|---|
| 2 | packages (2½ pounds each) fresh or frozen turkey legs | 1 | envelope garlic-flavored salad-dressing mix |
| 1 | container (8 ounces) plain yogurt | 1 | tablespoon lemon juice |

**1.** Thaw the turkey legs if frozen; dry with paper toweling. Combine the yogurt, salad-dressing mix and lemon juice in a shallow dish large enough to hold the legs in one layer. Brush the legs with the yogurt mixture; cover; refrigerate overnight.

**2.** Wrap the legs in individual aluminum foil packets, reserving the yogurt. Place on the grill 5 to 6 inches from grayed coals for 1 hour.

**3.** Unwrap and place the legs on the grill to brown. Brush with the reserved yogurt, turning often. Grill for 45 minutes or until the juices run clear when pierced with a fork. Heat any remaining marinade to serve with the turkey.

# JOHNNY APPLESEED CHICKEN

A crusty barbecued chicken flavored with orange, apple,
honey and lemon.

*Makes 8 servings.*

| | | | |
|---|---|---|---|
| 2 | broiler/fryers (about 3 pounds each), quartered | 1 | cup bottled steak sauce |
| ½ | teaspoon garlic powder | ½ | cup apple juice |
| 1 | teaspoon salt | ⅓ | cup honey |
| ½ | teaspoon pepper | ¼ | cup lemon juice |
| 1 | can (6 ounces) frozen orange juice concentrate, thawed | | |

**1.** Sprinkle the chicken with garlic powder, salt and pepper. Place on the grill, skin-side up, about 8 inches from grayed coals. Grill for 15 minutes. Turn over; grill for 15 minutes.

**2.** Combine the juice concentrate, steak sauce, apple juice, honey and lemon juice in medium-size bowl; mix until well blended. Pour into a shallow 13 x 9 x 2-inch baking pan. Place the hot chicken in the marinade. Turn to coat all sides; let for stand 10 minutes.

**3.** Remove the chicken, draining well. Place on the grill, skin-side up. Grill for 5 minutes on each side, brushing with the marinade, or until browned and crusty. Reheat any leftover marinade. Pass separately.

---

**SAFETY TIP**

Always be sure to place the grill on a nonconductive surface—never on damp concrete or grass. When a three-prong plug is provided, extension cords should be the same three-wire type.

# WINE-BASTED BARBECUED TURKEY

There's no drying out when the meat is barbecued on a spit.

*Makes 8 to 10 servings.*

| | | | |
|---|---|---|---|
| 1 | small turkey (9 to 11 pounds), preferably self-basting | 1 | teaspoon leaf rosemary, crumbled |
| ½ | cup dry white wine | 1 | teaspoon salt |
| ½ | cup vegetable oil | | Pinch of pepper |

**1.** Truss and balance the turkey in the center of the spit, securing it with the prongs at the ends.

**2.** Combine the wine, oil, rosemary, salt and pepper in a bowl.

**3.** Roast over hot coals, basting every 15 minutes or so with the wine mixture for about 4 to 4½ hours or until the juices run clear when the thigh area of the turkey is pierced with a fork.

---

## HOW TO MAKE A DRIP PAN

Fat flare-ups will be a problem of the past when you place a custom-size drip pan under the meat you are kettle-grilling or roasting on the rotisserie.

**1.** Tear off three 24-inch pieces of 18-inch-wide heavy-duty aluminum foil. Fold in half to make a double thickness (Fig. 1).

**2.** Turn up the edges 2 inches on each side and press edges firmly together to form mitered corners (Fig 2).

**3.** Press mitered corners inward, toward pan sides, to make a firm pan (Fig. 3).

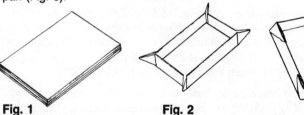

**Fig. 1**        **Fig. 2**        **Fig. 3**

**Note:** This will give you an 8 x 14-inch drip pan. If this is not the right size for your needs, begin with the size pan you will need; add 4 inches to both the length and the width; then double the measurement of the width.

# BARBECUE TIPS

## Rotisserie Cooking over Charcoal

• Keep your grill in a sheltered spot, away from the wind as much as possible.

• First be sure to build and start your charcoal fire properly. (See page 51.) An 8- to 10-pound turkey will take at least 5 pounds of charcoal briquettes in a pyramid in the center of the grill bottom (or coal pan, if your unit has one).

• Try the electric or chimney-type starter or solid fibrous cubes.

• Let the briquettes burn to just the right stage before putting the roast on the spit. They'll generally require between 20 and 40 minutes. Always use a drip pan when rotissing. The pan is important, as it will catch fatty drippings, control fat flare-ups and eliminate excessive smoke.

• For a quick temperature test, hold your hand at cooking height, palm side down. If you can keep it in position for only 2 seconds, the temperature is high (or hot).

• Remove all excess fat from turkey and prepare, following recipe. Let stand at room temperature at least 1 hour before cooking.

• Be sure turkey is well tied into a uniform shape to prevent uneven cooking and to allow it to rotate evenly. Push rotisserie spit, lengthwise, through the center of turkey and fasten ends in place with holding forks. (See diagram on page 61.) If it is off balance, remount.

• Place rotisserie rod into rotor and watch the turning of the bird to be sure it rotates evenly.

• Use a meat thermometer when rotissing. (The cooking times are only guides, as wind and weather can affect actual cooking time.)

• Push the meat thermometer into the thickest part of the thigh, not touching the bone or the rod.

• If any part of your turkey overbrowns, cover the spot with aluminum foil.

• It is not necessary to keep the grill rack on during rotissing, but you can cook other food during the rotisserie process. Just arrange it on the grill away from where the roast drips into the pan. This is best for long-cooking foods, like potatoes or acorn squash.

• Remove the roast when the thermometer registers 175°.

**Note:** If recipe has a baste, baste every 30 minutes during cooking. Add glaze, if any, during the last 20 minutes of cooking.

## HOW TO TRUSS POULTRY

Secure neck skin with a metal skewer; push tail into cavity and secure with a metal skewer. Press wings against side of breast and wrap a long piece of cotton twine twice around the bird and tie securely; loop a second long piece of twine several times around drumsticks and tie. If poultry is stuffed, be sure to secure opening with small metal skewers and lace closed with twine.

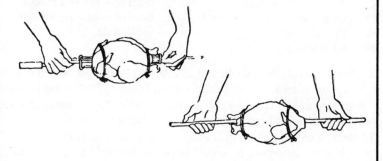

Fig. 1                              Fig. 2

## POINTS ON ROTISSERIE COOKING

Roast chickens and turkeys are more moist and flavorful when cooked over the coals, turning slowly on a rotisserie. In Fig. 1 you see how the roast or poultry should balance evenly on the rotisserie rod for even cooking. Fig. 2 shows how the holding forks should be inserted securely to prevent the meat from slipping while roasting. Fig. 3 illustrates how the gray coals should be piled to the back of the grill with the drip pan directly under the grilling poultry to prevent flare-ups that give a burned flavor, rather than a charcoal taste, to foods.

Fig. 3

# TERIYAKI TURKEY

Soy sauce and wine add an Oriental flavor to chicken and other poultry.

*Rotiss for 3 hours.*
*Makes 8 servings.*

| | |
|---|---|
| 1 fresh or frozen turkey, thawed (about 8 pounds) | 1 clove garlic, minced |
| 2 cups dry white wine | 1 teaspoon salt |
| ½ cup peanut or vegetable oil | ½ teaspoon ground ginger |
| ½ cup soy sauce | Bottled cranberry chutney (optional) |
| ¼ cup lemon juice | |

**1.** Truss the turkey and place it in a large plastic bag. Add the wine, oil, soy sauce, lemon juice, garlic, salt and ginger. Tie the bag and turn the turkey in the bag to coat it evenly. Allow to marinate at room temperature for 1 hour, turning once or twice.

**2.** Build a slow fire in a grill with a rotisserie, positioning the coals around a foil drip pan, or set a gas or electric grill to low, following manufacturer's directions.

**3.** Insert the spit through the center of the turkey, lengthwise, and test for balance by rotating spit on hands. Fasten the turkey with holding pins; place the rotisserie rod into position. Add 1 cup water to the foil drip pan; cover the grill.

**4.** Rotiss, basting often with the marinade, for 3 hours or until a meat thermometer inserted in the thickest part of the thigh registers 175° or until juices run clear yellow. Serve with cranberry chutney, if you wish.

**Variations:** Substitute 2 cups dry vermouth and ½ cup bottled steak sauce for the white wine and soy sauce in this recipe.

# FAVORITE HERB-GRILLED CHICKEN

This sauce is best made a few hours in advance of using. If refrigerated, whip it for a few seconds. It can be used on chicken parts or on a whole spit-roasted chicken.

*Makes 6 servings.*

| | | | | |
|---|---|---|---|---|
| ½ | cup vegetable oil | ⅛ | teaspoon leaf thyme, crumbled | |
| ¼ | cup cider vinegar | | | |
| 1 | egg | | Pinch of garlic powder | |
| 1 | teaspoon salt | | Pinch of paprika | |
| ¼ | teaspoon pepper | 6 | broiler/fryer chicken | |
| 1 | teaspoon poultry seasoning | | portions OR: one 4- to | |
| ¼ | teaspoon leaf oregano, crumbled | | 5-pound roasting chicken | |

**1.** Combine the oil, vinegar, egg, salt, pepper, poultry seasoning, oregano, thyme, garlic powder and paprika in a small bowl; beat with a fork to blend. Brush over the chicken.

**2.** Grill the chicken, skin-side up, 6 inches from hot coals, for 15 minutes. Turn and baste with the sauce. Continue turning and basting for about 30 minutes longer or until the chicken is tender but not dry.

**3.** For a whole chicken, adjust and secure the chicken on the barbecue spit so it will turn freely. Brush all over with the sauce. Place the spit about 6 inches from hot coals. Start the spit rotating and roast the chicken, brushing it frequently with sauce, for about 1½ hours or until the juices run clear when the thigh area is pierced with a fork.

## *BROILING INDOORS*

## Broiler Tips

To broil chicken successfully:

● Preheat the broiler for 10 minutes, or follow manufacturer's directions.

*Note:* If you have an electric broiler, be sure to keep the oven open a crack while broiling, or the broiler element will go off and the chicken will cook, but not broil.

● Season the chicken with salt and pepper, your favorite herbs and melted butter, margarine, vegetable oil or bottled salad dressing.

• Place the chicken on the rack of the broiler pan and broil, 4 to 7 inches from the heat, turning and frequently basting with the fat, until the chicken is tender, about 40 minutes. You may also wish to brush the chicken with a glaze (see page 69) during the last 20 minutes.

# CHICKEN KABOBS

A fun dish to serve with rice pilaf and coleslaw.

*Makes 4 servings.*

| | | | |
|---|---|---|---|
| 1 | medium-size sweet green pepper, cut into sixteen 1-inch chunks | 12 | medium-size mushrooms |
| | | ⅓ | cup vegetable oil |
| | | 1 | clove garlic, minced |
| 2 | medium-size onions, each cut into 6 wedges and separated at natural layers | ⅔ | cup dry white wine |
| | | 1 | small onion, minced (¼ cup) |
| 1 | pound boned chicken, cubed | 1 | teaspoon salt |
| 1 | medium-size zucchini, cut into 1-inch-thick slices | ¼ | teaspoon pepper |
| | | ½ | teaspoon leaf tarragon, crumbled |
| 2 | medium-size tomatoes, each cut into 6 wedges | | |

**1.** Blanch the pepper and onion pieces in boiling water in a small saucepan for 2 minutes.
**2.** Thread the chicken pieces on skewers alternately with the blanched pepper and onion and the zucchini, tomatoes and mushrooms. Put the filled skewers in a shallow glass or ceramic dish.
**3.** Combine the oil, garlic, wine, onion, salt, pepper and tarragon in a screw-top jar. Shake well to blend; pour over the kabobs. Refrigerate for about 1 hour or until ready to cook, turning the kabobs several times in the marinade.
**4.** Broil about 6 inches from the heat, basting with the marinade and turning several times, for about 10 minutes or until the chicken is tender and cooked through.

# LEMON-BUTTER BROILED CHICKEN

Chicken quarters broiled with herbs and dry wine have
outdoor grilled flavor.

*Makes 4 servings.*

| | |
|---|---|
| 1 broiler/fryer (3 pounds), quartered | 2 tablespoons lemon juice |
| ½ teaspoon seasoned salt | ½ teaspoon leaf tarragon, crumbled |
| ¼ teaspoon pepper | ½ teaspoon leaf chervil, crumbled |
| ¼ cup (½ stick) butter or margarine | 2 tablespoons dry vermouth |

**1.** Sprinkle the chicken quarters with salt and pepper.
**2.** Melt the butter in small saucepan; add the lemon juice, tarragon, chervil and vermouth; brush lightly over the quarters.
**3.** Place the chicken, skin-side down, on the rack of the broiler.
**4.** Broil, 6 inches from the heat, for 20 minutes, basting frequently. Turn; broil for 15 to 20 minutes longer or until nicely browned, brushing with the remaining lemon-butter.

# ORANGE-BROILED CHICKEN

*Makes 8 servings.*

| | |
|---|---|
| 2 broiler/fryers, quartered (about 5 pounds) | ½ cup honey |
| 1 teaspoon salt | ½ cup orange juice |
| ½ teaspoon pepper | 4 tablespoons soy sauce |

**1.** Arrange the chicken on an aluminum foil-lined broiling pan. Sprinkle with salt and pepper. Broil 5 inches from the heat. Turn over several times with tongs until browned and tender, about 25 minutes.
**2.** Combine the honey, orange juice and soy sauce in a small saucepan and heat until bubbly. Baste the chicken pieces liberally with the honey mixture during the last 10 minutes of cooking.

# BROILED CHICKEN WITH HONEY-MUSTARD GLAZE

*Makes 4 servings.*

| | |
|---|---|
| 1 broiler/fryer (2½ to 3 pounds), cut up | 1 clove garlic, minced |
| ⅓ cup honey | ½ teaspoon pepper |
| 2 teaspoons soy sauce | 3 tablespoons Dijon-style mustard |
| 1 tablespoon orange juice | |

**1.** Adjust the broiler pan so the rack is about 6 inches from the heat; preheat the broiler. Trim the excess skin and fat from the chicken; pat the chicken pieces dry; arrange on an aluminum foil-lined cookie sheet. (This saves cleanup.)
**2.** Stir the honey, soy sauce, orange juice, garlic and pepper together in a small bowl until smooth; brush over the chicken.
**3.** Broil the chicken, skin-side down, until golden, about 15 minutes, basting once or twice. Turn; baste again. Broil, skin-side up, until golden, about 15 minutes, basting occasionally with the honey mixture.
**4.** Brush the mustard over the skin side of the chicken. Continue broiling just until the mustard begins to bubble, less than 1 minute. Serve hot or cold.

# DEVILED CHICKEN LEGS

You can substitute halved chicken breasts for the chicken legs: Simply reduce broiling time by 10 minutes.
*Makes 4 servings.*

| | |
|---|---|
| 4 chicken legs with thighs (2½ to 3 pounds) | ½ cup white wine |
| Salt and pepper | Pinch of cayenne pepper |
| 4 tablespoons (½ stick) butter or margarine | 1 teaspoon finely minced shallots or onion |
| 2 tablespoons prepared hot mustard | ¾ cup packaged unseasoned bread crumbs |
| | ¼ cup finely chopped parsley |

**1.** Preheat the broiler. Cut the legs about halfway through at the joint but do not sever completely. Sprinkle with salt and pepper.

**2.** Melt the butter in a shallow metal baking dish big enough to hold legs in single layer. Add the chicken and turn to coat on both sides with butter. Arrange the pieces skin-side up.

**3.** Broil about 4 inches from the heat for 5 minutes; turn and broil for another 5 minutes. Baste with the butter from the dish.

**4.** Mix the mustard, ¼ cup of the wine, cayenne pepper and shallots together; spoon about half the mixture over the chicken pieces. Sprinkle the chicken with about one third of the crumbs. Broil for another 15 minutes.

**5.** Turn the chicken pieces, brush with the remaining mustard mixture and sprinkle with the remaining crumbs. Broil for about 15 minutes.

**6.** Lift the pieces out of the pan and keep warm. Add the remaining wine to the baking dish and scrape the sides and bottom of the pan; add the parsley. Spoon the sauce over the chicken.

## TANDOORI TURKEY BREASTS

*Makes 3 to 4 servings.*

| | |
|---|---|
| ½ cup plain yogurt | 1 teaspoon ground ginger |
| ½ teaspoon ground coriander | 1 tablespoon lemon juice |
| ¼ teaspoon turmeric | ¼ teaspoon ground cumin |
| ¼ teaspoon ground allspice | 1 package (1 pound) fresh |
| 1 tablespoon vegetable oil | boneless turkey breast |
| ½ teaspoon salt | Hot cooked rice |
| ½ teaspoon paprika | Lemon wedges |
| 1 clove garlic, chopped | |

**1.** Combine all the ingredients, except the turkey, rice and lemon wedges, in the container of an electric blender; whirl at high speed until smooth.

**2.** Make 3 diagonal slashes in each turkey piece. Place in a shallow dish; pour the yogurt mixture over. Cover; marinate in a cool place for 4 to 5 hours or refrigerate overnight.

**3.** Broil 5 inches from the heat for 20 minutes, turning once. Brush on more marinade if the meat appears dry. Move closer to the heat for the last 5 minutes if more browning is desired.

**4.** Stir the remaining marinade into the hot cooked rice; arrange the turkey over the rice and serve with lemon wedges.

# TEXAS-STYLE BARBECUED CHICKEN

*Makes 12 servings.*

| | | | |
|---|---|---|---|
| 4 | tablespoons salt | 3 | broiler/fryers (2½ pounds |
| 3 | tablespoons pepper | | each), quartered |
| 2 | tablespoons garlic powder | 1 | cup (2 sticks) butter, |
| 2 | tablespoons ground bay leaf | | softened |
| 1 | tablespoon paprika | ¼ | cup lemon juice |
| 2 | tablespoons dry mustard | | |

**1.** Combine the salt, pepper, garlic powder, bay leaf, paprika and mustard in a small bowl; mix well.

**2.** Rub the seasoning mix on both sides of the chicken quarters. Stir the butter and lemon juice in a bowl until blended; brush part over the chicken.

**3.** Grill the chicken, skin-side down, 6 inches from grayed coals for 20 minutes. Turn, brush again; continue grilling for about 20 minutes longer or until the juices no longer run pink when the chicken is pierced with a 2-tined fork. OR: Broil, 6 inches from heat, skin-side up, for 20 minutes. Turn and brush again; broil 20 minutes longer.

# KANSAS BARBECUED CHICKEN

Lots of good flavor in this easy-to-do, crispy-brown chicken.

*Makes 6 servings.*

| | | | |
|---|---|---|---|
| 3 | broiler/fryers (about | 1 | cup dry white wine |
| | 3 pounds each), halved | ½ | cup tarragon vinegar |
| ½ | teaspoon salt | 1 | teaspoon leaf thyme, |
| ¼ | teaspoon pepper | | crumbled |
| 1½ | cups olive oil | | |

**1.** Rinse the chicken; pat dry and rub with salt and pepper; place in a large shallow baking dish.

**2.** Combine the olive oil, wine, vinegar and thyme in a medium-size bowl. Pour over the chicken; turn the chicken to coat it well with the marinade; cover with plastic wrap. Refrigerate several hours or overnight, turning the chicken in the marinade several times.

**3.** Place the chicken halves on a lightly oiled grill or preheated broiler pan, bony side toward heat. Grill over grayed coals or broil 6 to 8 inches from the heat, for 15 minutes. Brush with the marinade; turn; grill for 15 minutes. Brush again with the marinade. Continue grilling, turning occasionally and brushing with the marinade, for 15 minutes or until tender and golden.

## MARINADES AND GLAZES

Place raw poultry parts in one of these marinades. Cover and refrigerate overnight. Drain before broiling.

**Wine Marinade:** Makes about 1½ cups. Combine 1 cup dry red wine and ½ cup olive or vegetable oil in a screw-top jar. Crush and chop 3 cloves garlic with 1 teaspoon salt on cutting board until almost paste-like; add to wine and oil. Add 1 teaspoon coarsely ground black pepper. Cover; shake.

**Sweet and Sour Marinade:** Makes about 3 cups. Cook ½ pound dried apricots in 1½ cups water for 30 minutes; stir in ½ cup sugar; let cool; purée. Sauté 3 large onions, sliced, in 2 tablespoons vegetable oil; add purée, ½ teaspoon salt and ⅓ cup vinegar. Bring to boiling; cool.

**Yogurt Marinade:** Makes about 3 cups. Combine 2 cups plain yogurt, 1 cup dry white wine, 2 tablespoons freshly squeezed lemon juice, 1 medium-size onion, chopped (½ cup), 2 teaspoons salt and 2 teaspoons sugar in large screw-top jar. Cover and shake to blend. Refrigerate for at least 1 hour.

Brush poultry with one of these glazes while broiling.

**Tomato-Soy Glaze:** Makes about 2 cups. Combine 1 can (15 ounces) tomato sauce, 1 medium-size onion, chopped (½ cup), 1 large clove garlic, minced, ¼ cup soy sauce, ¼ cup red wine vinegar and 1 tablespoon cornstarch in a medium-size saucepan. Stir over moderate heat until mixture thickens. Cool and chill.

**Orange-Mustard Glaze:** Makes about 1½ cups. Combine 1 can (6 ounces) frozen orange juice concentrate, 1¼ cups water, 1 cup packed light brown sugar, ¼ cup cider vinegar and 2 tablespoons prepared mustard in a medium-size saucepan. Heat to boiling, stirring often; simmer for 20 minutes.

**Fruit-Wine Glaze:** Makes about 2 cups. Purée 1 can (about 1 pound) pitted Bing cherries with 2 tablespoons cornstarch in blender or processor; pour into saucepan. Stir in 1 cup red wine and ¼ cup light corn syrup. Bring to boiling, stirring constantly; then simmer until thick and clear.

# 4

## Stews, Ragouts and Braised Dishes

In the old days, long, slow simmering in a pot was the only way to soften the tough meat of hens that were past the egg-laying stage. To improve the taste, innovative cooks would toss in a delightful mixture of vegetables and seasonings to create stews that were worthy of any rich man's table.

Today, you can go traditional one better by using readily available roasting chickens or broiler/fryers that are much more tender and flavorful than stewing fowls. Slow simmering on top of the stove produces the rich, savory taste of old-fashioned stew—but in a fraction of the time it took in grandmother's day.

All of the stews, ragouts and braised dishes featured in this chapter combine whole or cut-up chicken with a plentiful assortment of vegetables, herbs, seasonings and fruit. Chicken Paprika with Spätzle and Boiled Turkey Dinner are two of the traditional favorites included, while Chicken and Grapes and Black Olives or Caribbean Chicken and Squash Stew offer a more exotic blend of flavors.

# CARIBBEAN CHICKEN AND SQUASH STEW

*Makes 8 servings.*

1 broiler/fryer (3 pounds), cut up
2 tablespoons vegetable oil
2 medium-size onions, sliced
½ to 1 teaspoon red pepper flakes
½ teaspoon leaf thyme, crumbled
1 can (10¾ ounces) condensed chicken broth
1 can (1 pound) stewed tomatoes
1 teaspoon salt
1 pound smoked pork butt, cut into ½-inch cubes
¼ cup shredded coconut
2 large sweet potatoes (1 pound), pared and cut into cubes
1 medium-size butternut squash (1½ pounds), pared, seeded and cut into wedges
1 package (10 ounces) frozen peas
Hot cooked rice

**1.** Brown the chicken a few pieces at a time in the oil in a large Dutch oven or heavy kettle; remove the pieces as they brown. Add the onion to the drippings in the pan and sauté until golden. Stir in the red pepper flakes and thyme. Return the chicken pieces to the pan.

**2.** Add the chicken broth, tomatoes, salt, pork and coconut. Bring to boiling; lower the heat and cover. Simmer for 15 minutes. Add the sweet potatoes and squash. Simmer for 35 to 40 minutes longer or until the chicken and vegetables are tender. Stir in the peas; cook for 5 minutes. Serve over hot cooked rice.

# CASSEROLE BRAISED CHICKEN

This bacon-and-herb flavored chicken with fresh vegetables makes an easy one-pot company or family dinner.

*Makes 4 servings.*

| | |
|---|---|
| 4 slices bacon | 12 small white onions |
| 1 whole broiler/fryer (3 pounds) | (1 pound), peeled but left whole |
| 1½ teaspoons salt | 3 carrots, cut into 3-inch sticks |
| ¼ teaspoon pepper | |
| ½ cup chopped carrot | ¾ cup chicken broth |
| ½ cup chopped celery with leaves | ¾ cup dry white wine |
| 1 medium-size onion, chopped (½ cup) | 3 large celery stalks, cut into 1½-inch-long pieces |
| 1 clove garlic, minced | ½ pound mushrooms, halved |
| ¼ teaspoon leaf thyme, crumbled | 2 tablespoons butter |
| ¼ teaspoon leaf marjoram, crumbled | 3 tablespoons all-purpose flour |

**1.** Cook the bacon slices until crisp in a flameproof casserole or Dutch oven. Remove to paper toweling to drain. Pour off the drippings into a glass measure. Return 4 tablespoons to the casserole. (Add butter if you do not have enough bacon drippings.)

**2.** Rub chicken inside and out with 1 teaspoon salt and pepper. Brown on all sides in the fat. Remove from the casserole.

**3.** Add the chopped carrot, celery, onion and garlic; cook until vegetables are soft, 5 minutes. Stir in the remaining ½ teaspoon salt with the thyme and marjoram. Return the chicken and add the white onions and carrots, chicken broth and wine. Cover and lower the heat; simmer for 30 minutes. Add the celery and mushrooms; cook for 15 minutes longer or until the chicken and vegetables are tender.

**4.** Remove the chicken to a heated serving platter. Remove the vegetables with a slotted spoon and arrange them around the chicken. Pour the pan juices through a large strainer over a bowl; press any remaining vegetables through the strainer.

**5.** Melt the butter; stir in the flour and cook for 1 minute. Add the strained pan juices and cook, stirring constantly, until the gravy is thickened and bubbly. Serve with the chicken.

# MARINATED CHICKEN RAGOUT

*Makes 4 servings.*

| | | | |
|---|---|---|---|
| 1 | broiler/fryer (about 2½ pounds) | 4 | potatoes (1½ pounds) |
| 1 | clove garlic | ½ | teaspoon leaf oregano, crumbled |
| 1 | teaspoon salt | 1 | package (10 ounces) frozen peas |
| ¼ | teaspoon pepper | | |
| | Celery leaves | | |

**1.** Day before serving: Cut the chicken into 8 pieces, reserving the neck and backbones for step 3.

**2.** Mince the garlic on a chopping board; sprinkle with ½ teaspoon of the salt and the pepper; mince again until it is almost a paste. Spread a little on each chicken piece, rubbing in well. Place in a bowl, cover and refrigerate overnight.

**3.** Combine the neck and backbones with water to cover in a medium-size saucepan; add some celery leaves. Cover and simmer for 45 minutes. Remove from the heat, strain and cool; refrigerate overnight.

**4.** On the day of serving: Pat the chicken dry without removing the seasonings. Remove 2 tablespoons of fat from the chilled broth. Heat in a Dutch oven. Brown the chicken on all sides (about 15 minutes); remove to a plate.

**5.** While the chicken is browning, pare and cut the potatoes into ½-inch cubes. Sauté the potatoes in the chicken fat in the Dutch oven for about 5 minutes. Sprinkle with the remaining ½ teaspoon salt and oregano. Return the chicken to pan.

**6.** Heat 1 cup of the broth just to boiling; add to the chicken. Cover tightly, lower the heat and simmer for 20 minutes, basting frequently with the pan juices.

**7.** Stir in the frozen peas; cook for 5 more minutes.

# CHICKEN RAGOUT WITH PEAS AND MUSHROOMS

The delicate flavor of tarragon makes this French stew extra special.

*Makes 4 to 6 servings.*

¼ cup plus 3 tablespoons all-purpose flour
1 broiler/fryer (about 3 pounds), cut up
⅓ cup olive or vegetable oil
2 medium-size onions, sliced
2 cloves garlic, chopped
1 pound mushrooms, sliced
1 teaspoon leaf tarragon, crumbled
1 teaspoon salt
¼ teaspoon pepper
2 bay leaves
1 can (13¾ ounces) chicken broth
1 cup dry white wine
1 package (10 ounces) frozen peas

**1.** Place ¼ cup of the flour and the chicken in a plastic bag; shake to coat the chicken thoroughly.

**2.** Heat the oil in a large skillet; brown the chicken on both sides; remove to a heavy kettle or Dutch oven. Drain the oil, and return 3 tablespoons to the kettle.

**3.** Add the onions, garlic and mushrooms to the skillet; sauté, stirring occasionally, until the onions are tender. Add the tarragon, salt, pepper, bay leaves, chicken broth and wine; heat; pour over the chicken. Simmer, covered, for 1 hour or until the chicken is tender.

**4.** Blend the remaining 3 tablespoons flour with a small amount of cold water in a cup; stir into the stew. Add the peas; bring to boiling. Cook and stir until the sauce thickens and the peas are tender.

# TURKEY RAGOUT IN PUFF PASTRY

Delicate golden pastry tops this creamy turkey-vegetable mixture.
*Makes enough for two meals (6 servings each).*

| | | | |
|---|---|---|---|
| 1 | frozen turkey breast (about 5 pounds) | 1 | cup dry white wine or chicken broth |
| 4 | tablespoons butter or margarine | | Flaky Pastry Top (recipe follows) |
| 2 | large onions, sliced | 2 | cans (10¾ ounces each) condensed golden mushroom soup |
| 1 | carrot, diced | | |
| 2 | cloves garlic, crushed | | |
| 1 | teaspoon salt | 1 | can (16 ounces) Italian plum tomatoes |
| 1 | teaspoon leaf thyme, crumbled | | |
| ½ | teaspoon leaf marjoram, crumbled | 24 | small white onions, peeled and parboiled for 15 minutes |
| ¼ | teaspoon pepper | 1 | pound carrots, sliced and parboiled for 15 minutes |
| 1 | bay leaf | 2 | cups frozen green peas |

**1.** Partially thaw the turkey breast in the refrigerator overnight. Brown on all sides in butter in a Dutch oven. Stir in the onions, carrot and garlic. Sauté for 10 minutes; add the salt, thyme, marjoram, pepper, bay leaf and wine. Bring to boiling; cover. Braise for 2 to 2½ hours or until the turkey breast is tender.

**2.** Prepare the Flaky Pastry Top.

**3.** Remove the turkey breast to a shallow pan; let cool for 30 minutes. Then remove the turkey meat from the bones. Pull or cut into generous-size pieces. Strain the cooking liquid into 4-cup glass measure; skim off the fat. There should be about 2½ cups liquid; pour into the Dutch oven. Add the mushroom soup; cook and stir until smooth. Add the tomatoes, turkey, onion and carrots to the sauce; simmer for 15 minutes. Stir in the peas; heat for 5 minutes longer. Spoon half of the turkey mixture into a heated 6- or 7-cup low soufflé or other straight-sided dish about 8 inches in diameter; fit the baked pastry round on top. Serve immediately.

**4.** Cool the remaining turkey mixture; spoon into 1 or 2 boilable freezer bags. Seal, label and freeze.

**5.** To reheat, boil the bags in a large kettle of boiling water for 30 to 40 minutes or until heated through. Transfer to a serving dish; fit the baked pastry round over the filling.

**Flaky Pastry Top:** Remove one sheet of pastry from a 17¼-ounce package frozen puff pastry. Return the remaining pastry to the freezer. Let the pastry sheet thaw on the counter for 20 minutes. Unfold the pastry onto a lightly floured surface. Cut a round from the pastry 1 inch larger than the top rim of your serving dish. Transfer to a cookie sheet; brush the top with beaten egg. Cut fancy shapes from trimmings; arrange them on top of the pastry round in a decorative pattern; brush the decorations with egg. Bake in a moderate oven (350°) for 25 minutes or until puffed and golden. Prepare the remaining pastry in the same manner when ready to heat and serve the second half of the Turkey Ragout.

# BOILED TURKEY DINNER

*Makes 4 large servings.*

| | | | |
|---|---|---|---|
| 4 | medium-size turkey legs (2½ pounds), fresh or frozen, thawed | 2 | celery stalks, halved |
| | | 4 | medium-size carrots, scraped and quartered |
| 3 | quarts water | 5 | medium-size potatoes, pared and halved (1¾ pounds) |
| 1 | tablespoon salt | | |
| 1 | teaspoon pepper | 2 | tablespoons chopped parsley |
| 2 | large onions, quartered | | |

**1.** Combine the turkey legs with the water, salt and pepper in a kettle or Dutch oven. Bring to boiling and skim off the foam. Lower the heat and cover; simmer for 30 minutes.

**2.** Add the onions, celery and carrots; cover; simmer for another 20 minutes. Add the potatoes and a little more water if needed. Cover; simmer for 30 minutes longer or until the potatoes are tender.

**3.** Remove and discard the skin from the legs and transfer to a warm platter. Spoon vegetables around the turkey; spoon a little broth over all, and sprinkle with parsley.

**4.** Cool the remaining broth; refrigerate or freeze for soup or gravy.

# CAROLINA BRUNSWICK STEW

While purists may prepare this stew with native rabbit or squirrel, we've substituted popular chicken.

*Makes 6 servings.*

1 broiler/fryer (about 3 pounds), quartered
4 cans (13¾ ounces each) chicken broth
1 can (1 pound, 12 ounces) tomatoes, undrained
6 medium-size potatoes, pared and diced (2 cups)
1 large onion, chopped (1 cup)
¼ pound fully cooked smoked ham, chopped
½ teaspoon pepper
1 package (10 ounces) frozen lima beans
1 package (10 ounces) frozen whole-kernel corn

**1.** Bring the chicken and broth to boiling in a large kettle or Dutch oven. Lower the heat, simmer for 45 minutes or until the chicken is very tender. Skim the fat from the surface.
**2.** Remove the chicken from the broth, allowing the broth to continue simmering for another 10 minutes.
**3.** Cool the chicken slightly; then remove the meat from the bones. Return the meat to the broth along with the tomatoes, potatoes, onion, ham and pepper. Simmer for 1 hour.
**4.** Add the beans and corn to the stew; simmer for 15 minutes.

# CHICKEN AND RICE DELUXE

A tempting meal in a pot.

*Makes 4 servings.*

1 broiler/fryer (2½ pounds), cut up
¼ cup (½ stick) margarine
1 large onion, chopped (1 cup)
1 medium-size sweet green pepper, chopped (1 cup)
2 celery stalks, chopped
1 cup long-grain white rice
2 cups water
1 can (10¾ ounces) condensed cream of mushroom soup
1 envelope onion soup mix
¼ teaspoon pepper

1. Brown the chicken on both sides in the hot margarine in a Dutch oven. Remove with tongs to a plate. Stir in the onions, green pepper and celery. Cook until the vegetables are soft.

2. Add the rice, water, mushroom soup, onion soup mix and pepper. Bring to boiling. Return the chicken to the pan. Lower the heat; cover and simmer for 1 hour or until the rice is tender.

## CURRIED CORN AND CHICKEN

This dish goes well with hot cooked rice.

*Makes 4 servings.*

| | | | |
|---|---|---|---|
| 1 | broiler/fryer (about 3 pounds), quartered | 1 | clove garlic, crushed |
| ⅓ | cup all-purpose flour | ½ | teaspoon leaf thyme, crumbled |
| 1 | teaspoon salt | 1 | cup dry white wine |
| ½ | teaspoon pepper | 4 | ears corn, shucked and cut into 1-inch-long pieces |
| 10 | tablespoons (1¼ sticks) butter | 1 | cup heavy cream |
| 1 | tablespoon curry powder | ½ | cup toasted blanched almonds |
| ½ | pound mushrooms, sliced | | |
| 2 | medium-size onions, sliced | ½ | cup raisins |

1. Coat the chicken with flour, salt and pepper. Melt 6 tablespoons of the butter in a large skillet. Sauté the chicken on both sides until golden brown. Remove the chicken with a slotted spoon to a plate; keep warm.

2. Add the curry powder and remaining 4 tablespoons of butter to the skillet. Sauté the mushrooms, onions and garlic until tender, about 3 minutes. Stir in the thyme and wine. Return the chicken to the skillet; lower the heat; cover and simmer for 35 minutes.

3. Add the corn; simmer for 10 minutes. Add the heavy cream, stirring until blended. Cook until thoroughly heated but do not allow to boil. Sprinkle with the almonds and raisins.

# CHICKEN FRICASSEE

Make this old-fashioned Sunday dinner chicken dish with a roasting chicken or broiler/fryers instead of a stewing chicken.

*Makes 8 servings.*

1 roasting chicken (5 pounds), or 2 broiler/fryers (2½ pounds each), cut up
1 medium-size onion
1 celery stalk, halved
1 carrot
4 whole cloves
4 whole black peppercorns
2 teaspoons salt
1 bay leaf
12 small white onions (1 pound), peeled but left whole
1 pound carrots, pared and cut into 1½-inch-long pieces
1 package (10 ounces) frozen lima beans
3 tablespoons butter
3 tablespoons all-purpose flour
¼ teaspoon pepper
½ teaspoon leaf thyme, crumbled
3 egg yolks
1 cup light cream
1 tablespoon lemon juice
Chopped parsley (optional)

**1.** Place the chicken in a large kettle or Dutch oven with water to cover. Bring to boiling, skim off the foam. Add the onion, celery, carrot, cloves, peppercorns, 1 teaspoon of the salt and bay leaf. Lower the heat; cover and simmer roaster for 45 minutes, broiler/fryers for 30 minutes, or until chicken is tender, but does not fall away from bones. Remove to a large serving bowl; keep warm.

**2.** Strain the stock; return to the kettle; add the white onions and carrots; cover and cook for 20 minutes or until firm-tender; add lima beans and cook for 5 minutes longer. Remove the vegetables with a slotted spoon; add to the serving bowl; measure out 2 cups chicken stock. (Use remainder for soups and gravies.)

**3.** Melt the butter in a large skillet; add the flour, remaining salt, pepper and thyme; cook for 1 minute; carefully stir in the 2 cups of stock; cook stirring constantly, until thick and bubbly. Beat the eggs with the cream; add slowly to the stock in the skillet, stirring constantly. Cook until bubbly, about 2 minutes, over medium-low heat; add the lemon juice. Spoon over the chicken and vegetables. Sprinkle with chopped parsley, if you wish.

# CHICKEN WITH GRAPES AND BLACK OLIVES

A mellow wine sauce and tender green grapes enhance this juicy chicken.

*Makes 4 servings.*

| | |
|---|---|
| 1 teaspoon salt | 1 can (13¾ ounces) chicken broth |
| ½ teaspoon pepper | |
| 1 broiler/fryer (3 pounds), quartered | 1 teaspoon leaf chervil, crumbled |
| 2 tablespoons butter or margarine | 2 tablespoons cornstarch |
| | ¼ cup cold water |
| 2 tablespoons vegetable oil | 2 cups seedless green grapes |
| 1 medium-size onion, sliced | 2 cans (6 ounces each) pitted black olives, drained |
| 1 clove garlic, crushed | |
| 1 cup dry white wine | |

**1.** Sprinkle salt and pepper on both sides of the chicken pieces. Heat the butter and oil in a large skillet; cook the chicken on both sides until browned. Remove the chicken to a platter as it browns.
**2.** Sauté the onion and garlic in the oil remaining in the skillet, about 3 minutes or until tender. Add the wine, chicken broth and chervil. Return the chicken to the skillet; cover; simmer over medium heat until the chicken is tender, about 35 minutes.
**3.** Stir the cornstarch into the cold water and pour the mixture into the skillet; cook, stirring constantly, until sauce thickens and clears.
**4.** Add the grapes and olives. Cook just until thoroughly heated.

# JAMBALAYA

An economical version of the famous Southern specialty.

*Makes 6 servings.*

| | | | |
|---|---|---|---|
| 1 | large onion, chopped (1 cup) | 1 | cup chopped cooked chicken |
| 1 | sweet green pepper, cut into strips | ¾ | cup long-grain white rice |
| ¾ | cup sliced celery | 2 | tablespoons chopped parsley |
| 1 | clove garlic, crushed | 1 | bay leaf |
| 2 | tablespoons vegetable oil | ¼ | teaspoon leaf thyme, crumbled |
| 1 | can (10¾ ounces) condensed chicken broth | ¼ | teaspoon Worchestershire sauce |
| ¾ | cup water | ⅛ | teaspoon cayenne pepper |
| 1 | can (15 ounces) tomato sauce | 5 | frankfurters (½ pound), sliced |

**1.** Sauté the onion, pepper, celery and garlic in the oil in a large skillet until soft. Stir in the remaining ingredients.

**2.** Bring to boiling; lower the heat. Cover and simmer for 30 to 40 minutes, or until the rice is tender. Stir once or twice. Remove the bay leaf before serving.

# BREAST OF CHICKEN NEAPOLITAN-STYLE

*Makes 4 servings.*

| | | | |
|---|---|---|---|
| 2 | whole chicken breasts (about 12 ounces each) | 1 | can (10¾ ounces) condensed tomato bisque |
| 1 | teaspoon salt | ½ | cup dry red wine |
| ½ | teaspoon pepper | ½ | teaspoon leaf oregano, crumbled |
| 3 | tablespoons olive oil | | |
| 8 | small white onions, peeled but left whole | ½ | teaspoon leaf basil, crumbled |
| ½ | pound mushrooms, quartered | 3 | tablespoons minced parsley |
| 1 | clove garlic, minced | 6 | pitted ripe olives, sliced |

**1.** Cut the chicken breasts in half through the breast bones; sprinkle with salt and pepper; let stand for 5 minutes.

**2.** Sauté the chicken, skin-side down, in the hot oil in a large skillet for 5 minutes; turn. Add the onions, mushrooms and garlic; cook for 5 minutes.

**3.** Combine the soup, wine, oregano and basil in a 2-cup glass measure; pour over the chicken. Bring to boiling; lower the heat; cover. Cook for 15 minutes or until the chicken is tender. Stir in the parsley and olives.

## CHICKEN ROSEMARY WITH ORZO

*Makes 4 servings.*

| | | | |
|---|---|---|---|
| 1 | broiler/fryer (2½ pounds) | 1 | clove garlic, minced |
| 1 | teaspoon salt | 1 | cup tomato juice |
| ¼ | teaspoon pepper | 1 | cup orzo (rice-shaped pasta) |
| ¾ | teaspoon leaf rosemary, crumbled | 2 | tablepoons grated Romano cheese |
| 1 | medium-size onion, chopped (½ cup) | 2 | tablespoons chopped parsley |

**1.** Cut the chicken into serving pieces. Combine the salt, pepper and rosemary in a small cup; rub into the chicken on all sides. Place skin-side down in a large skillet; brown slowly, for about 10 minutes. (The chicken will brown in its own melting fat.)

**2.** Add the onion and garlic; cover and cook until soft. Stir in the tomato juice; cook, covered, for 20 minutes; remove the lid; cook for 10 minutes longer.

**3.** While the chicken cooks, prepare the orzo following label directions; drain; toss with the cheese. Place on a serving platter; arrange the chicken on top. Pour the sauce over and sprinkle with parsley.

# PLANTATION SKILLET

A colorful mixture of traditional Southern foods is presented in this quick and easy dish. It goes nicely with rice and a salad-dessert combination of fresh pineapple and papaya.

*Makes 6 servings.*

¼ cup vegetable oil
½ pound broccoli (about one-third bunch), trimmed, stems pared, and cut into diagonal slices (⅛ inch thick)
2 chicken breast halves, skinned, boned and cut into strips about ½ inch wide (1¼ pounds)
4 chicken thighs, skinned, boned and cut into strips about ½ inch wide (1 pound)

2 medium-size sweet potatoes, pared and cut into ⅛-inch-thick slices (½ pound)
1 cup fresh or frozen whole-kernel corn
⅔ cup orange juice
1 tablespoon cornstarch
¼ teaspoon salt
⅛ teaspoon ground allspice
1 tablespoon honey
1 tablespoon soy sauce
1 tablespoon dry white wine

**1.** Heat the oil in a large skillet. Add the broccoli, chicken breasts and thighs. Cook and stir over high heat about 1 minute. Add the sweet potatoes and cook another several minutes. Finally, add the corn; stir and cook about 1 minute.
**2.** Stir the orange juice into the cornstarch in a small bowl. Add the salt, allspice, honey, soy sauce and wine.
**3.** Pour the sauce over the mixture in the skillet. Cook and stir until the sauce thickens slightly and the vegetables reach the desired degree of doneness.

# CHICKEN-TOMATO STEW

*Makes 5 servings.*

1 broiler/fryer (3½ pounds), cut up
1 teaspoon salt
½ teaspoon pepper
1 tablespoon vegetable oil
1 large onion, finely chopped

1 large carrot, shredded
1 clove garlic, finely chopped
1 can (28 ounces) Italian-style tomatoes, broken up
1½ teaspoon leaf basil, crumbled

1. Sprinkle the chicken with ½ teaspoon of the salt and ¼ teaspoon of the pepper. Brown the chicken on all sides in the oil in a large skillet. Remove the chicken from the pan; pour off all but 1 tablespoon of the drippings.

2. Add the onion, carrot and garlic to the skillet; sauté over medium heat until the onion is tender. Add the tomatoes, basil, remaining salt and pepper; bring to boiling. Return the chicken to the skillet; lower the heat; cover and simmer for 30 minutes, or until the chicken is tender.

## THRIFTY CHICKEN AND VEGETABLES

Even children who won't eat their vegetables will love this popular recipe.

*Makes 6 servings.*

| | |
|---|---|
| ½ cup all-purpose flour | 1½ cups sliced carrots |
| 2 teaspoons salt | ½ cup water |
| ¼ teaspoon pepper | 3 cups sliced celery |
| 1 broiler/fryer (3 pounds), cut up | 1 medium-size sweet green pepper, chopped (1 cup) |
| 3 tablespoons vegetable oil | Celery leaves (optional) |
| 1 large onion, chopped (1 cup) | |

1. Combine the flour, 1 teaspoon of the salt and pepper in a paper or plastic bag. Add the chicken, a few pieces at a time; shake to coat evenly. Heat the oil in large skillet. Add the chicken and brown slowly on both sides, about 20 minutes.

2. Push the chicken to one side of the pan; add the onion and carrots. Sauté until the onion is soft. Add the water and remaining teaspoon of salt. Cover. Simmer for 30 minutes or until the chicken is almost tender.

3. Add the celery and green pepper. Continue to cook until the chicken is tender, about 15 minutes. Spoon onto a serving platter; garnish with the celery leaves, if you wish.

# CHICKEN PAPRIKA WITH SPÄTZLE

Quick-cooking paprika-flavored chicken in sour cream sauce,
served with tender homemade dumplings.

*Makes 6 servings.*

| | | | |
|---|---|---|---|
| 1 | broiler/fryer (3 to 3½ pounds), cut up | 1 | large onion, chopped (1 cup) |
| ½ | cup all-purpose flour | 2 | tablespoons paprika |
| 1 | teaspoon salt | 1 | cup chicken broth |
| ¼ | teaspoon pepper | 1 | cup light cream |
| ½ | cup (1 stick) butter or margarine | ½ | cup dairy sour cream |
| | | | Spätzle (recipe follows) |
| | | | Chopped parsley (optional) |

**1.** Shake the chicken in a plastic bag with the flour, ½ teaspoon of salt and pepper until coated. Reserve 2 tablespoons of the flour mixture.
**2.** Brown the chicken in the butter in a large skillet. Pour the pan fat into a measuring cup. Measure and return 3 tablespoons to the skillet.
**3.** Sauté the onion in the fat until light golden brown, about 10 minutes. Add the paprika, remaining ½ teaspoon salt and chicken broth. Bring to boiling; lower the heat; return the chicken, turn to coat. Cook, covered, for 30 minutes or until the chicken is tender. Remove the chicken; keep warm.
**4.** Stir in the light cream. Make a paste of the reserved 2 tablespoons flour mixture and sour cream; slowly stir into the skillet. Cook, stirring constantly, over low heat until thickened. (Do not boil.) Return the chicken. Serve over Spätzle. Sprinkle with chopped parsley, if you wish.

# SPÄTZLE

*Makes 6 servings.*

| | | | |
|---|---|---|---|
| 3 | cups *sifted* all-purpose flour | 1 | cup water |
| 1 | teaspoon salt | ¼ | cup (½ stick) butter or margarine, melted |
| ⅛ | teaspoon white pepper | | |
| 3 | eggs, slightly beaten | | |

**1.** Combine the flour, salt and pepper in a medium-size bowl; make a well in center. Add the eggs and water to the well and mix thoroughly.
**2.** Scoop up dough on a spatula and cut off small pieces with a knife into boiling salted water. As the Spätzle rise to the top, scoop out with a slotted spoon and put in a covered bowl until all are made. Toss with melted butter; keep warm.

# 5

## Casseroles, Baked Dishes and Pies

asseroles and pies can be practically a meal in themselves, needing little but a tossed salad and French bread or muffins to round them out. They are a boon to hostesses, particularly apartment dwellers with tiny kitchens, for they save time in cooking, serving and dishwashing.

Today, a wide assortment of attractive casseroles and baking dishes are available, which do double-duty for cooking and serving. Some new Pyroceram containers even go straight from the freezer to the oven to the dining table.

Casseroles provide the perfect ending for leftovers, and many superb recipes have been created from scraps of turkey or chicken plus bits of this and that. Turkey Vegetable Pie Amandine and Chicken Casserole with Apples and Cheese are just two of the delicious examples included in this chapter.

# HOW TO FREEZE AND HEAT CASSEROLES

A few casseroles in the freezer and a microwave oven in the kitchen can mean the difference between supper on the table in minutes and early evening madness. Here are some tips on how to get the most efficient use out of both your freezer and your oven.

• *Plastic Wrap:* Layer or spoon casserole mixture into a serving-size microwave-safe casserole; cover with plastic wrap and freeze until firm. Remove frozen casserole from its dish and wrap in additional plastic wrap; label, date and return the parcel to the freezer.

• *Aluminum Foil:* Line a serving-size microwave-safe casserole with heavy-duty aluminum foil, leaving enough foil over the edge to make a tight seal over the food. Layer or spoon casserole mixture into the container. Fold edges of aluminum foil up and over, pressing to make a tight seal. Freeze until the mixture is firm. Remove aluminum foil-covered casserole from its container; label, date and return it to the freezer.

• *To Heat:* Layered casseroles must be heated without stirring, while other combinations, such as bean dishes can be stirred.

• *Layered Casseroles:* Remove plastic wrap or aluminum foil and return food to its original casserole. Microwave on High for 4 minutes; cover food loosely with wax paper; microwave on Medium for 18 to 28 minutes, or until the center is heated, rotating the dish a half turn twice. Cover with the casserole lid or aluminum foil and allow to stand for 3 to 5 minutes.

• *Stirrable Casseroles:* Remove the plastic wrap or aluminum foil and return the food to its original casserole. Cover loosely with plastic wrap. Microwave on Defrost or Low for 3 to 4 minutes for every 2 cups of food or until defrosted. Stir food and cover. Microwave on Medium for 2 to 4 minutes for every 2 cups of food or until heated through, stirring once. Allow to stand for 2 to 5 minutes.

# POLENTA WITH CHICKEN LIVERS

*Bake at 350° for 10 minutes.*
*Makes 6 servings.*

| | | | |
|---|---|---|---|
| 1 | quart water | 1½ | pounds chicken livers |
| 1 | teaspoon salt | 1 | cup plus 2 tablespoons |
| 1 | cup yellow cornmeal | | water |
| 2 | sweet green peppers, | 2 | chicken bouillon cubes |
| | halved, seeded and | 1 | tablespoon tomato paste |
| | cut into strips | ¼ | teaspoon pepper |
| 2 | medium-size onions, sliced | 2 | teaspoons cornstarch |
| 4 | tablespoons margarine | | |

**1.** Bring 1 quart of water and the salt to boiling in a medium-size saucepan; sprinkle in the cornmeal, stirring constantly to prevent lumping. Lower the heat; cook, stirring often, until thickened, about 30 minutes. Spread the mixture (polenta) in a lightly greased 13 x 9 x 2-inch baking dish to cool and set.

**2.** Sauté the peppers and onions in 2 tablespoons of the margarine in a large skillet until crisp-tender. Remove the vegetables with a slotted spoon; reserve.

**3.** Add the remaining 2 tablespoons of margarine to the skillet. Sauté the chicken livers until browned. Add 1 cup of water, bouillon cubes, tomato paste and pepper; bring to boiling, stirring to dissolve the cubes. Blend the cornstarch and remaining 2 tablespoons of water in a cup until smooth; stir into the skillet mixture. Cook, stirring often, until thickened. Return the sautéed vegetables to the skillet.

**4.** Cut the polenta into 6 portions. Place each portion in an individual baking dish. Top with the chicken liver mixture; cover.

**5.** Bake in a moderate oven (350°) until bubbly-hot, about 10 minutes.

# CURRIED TURKEY AND BROCCOLI

*Bake at 350° for 20 minutes.*
*Makes 6 servings.*

| | | | |
|---|---|---|---|
| 3 | tablespoons butter or margarine | 1 | cup light cream |
| 1 | small onion, chopped (¼ cup) | 1 | teaspoon tomato paste |
| 3 | tablespoons all-purpose flour | 2 | packages (10 ounces each) frozen broccoli spears, thawed |
| ½ | teaspoon salt | 12 | slices cooked turkey (1 pound) |
| ⅛ | teaspoon pepper | ¼ | cup sliced unblanched almonds |
| 2 | teaspoons curry powder | | Chutney |
| 1 | cup Turkey Broth (page 129) or canned chicken broth | | Sliced unblanched almonds |

**1.** Melt the butter in a medium-size saucepan. Sauté the onion just until soft. Stir in the flour, salt, pepper and curry powder. Heat for 1 minute. Stir in the broth and cream. Cook, stirring constantly, for 5 minutes. Add the tomato paste and cook for 3 minutes longer.
**2.** Pour half the sauce into an 8-cup shallow baking dish. Arrange the broccoli along the sides; overlap the turkey slices in the middle. Pour the remaining sauce over the turkey. Sprinkle with the almonds.
**3.** Bake in a moderate oven (350°) for 20 minutes or until the sauce is bubbly. Serve with chutney and additional almonds.


# SOUFFLÉ-TOPPED TURKEY CASSEROLE

*Bake at 375° for 35 minutes.*
*Makes 6 servings.*

| | | | |
|---|---|---|---|
| ¼ | cup (½ stick) butter or margarine | 1 | tablespoon butter or margarine |
| ¼ | cup all-purpose flour | 1 | small onion, chopped (¼ cup) |
| ¾ | teaspoon salt | ½ | cup sliced celery |
| ⅛ | teaspoon pepper | ¼ | pound mushrooms, sliced |
| | Pinch of cayenne pepper | ½ | cup grated Parmesan cheese |
| 2½ | cups milk | 2 | eggs, separated |
| 2 | cups cubed cooked turkey | | |

**1.** Melt the ¼ cup butter in a medium-size saucepan; stir in the flour, salt, pepper and cayenne. Cook for 1 minute. Pour in 2 cups of the milk; heat, stirring constantly, until the sauce thickens and bubbles. Continue cooking and stirring 3 minutes longer. Remove from the heat.

**2.** Measure ½ cup sauce into a medium-size bowl; reserve. Add the turkey and remaining ½ cup of milk to the sauce in the pan.

**3.** Melt the 1 tablespoon of butter in a skillet; sauté the onion, celery and mushrooms just until soft, about 5 minutes. Combine with the turkey. Spoon into the bottom of 6- to 8-cup shallow baking dish.

**4.** Bake in a moderate oven (375°) for 5 minutes or until bubbly around the edges.

**5.** Stir the Parmesan cheese into the reserved sauce. Beat in the egg yolks, one at a time. Beat the egg whites in a small bowl with an electric mixer until stiff but not dry; fold into the yolk mixture.

**6.** Remove the baking dish from the oven; spread the soufflé mixture over the turkey. Return to the oven and bake for 30 minutes longer or until puffed and brown. Serve at once.

## CHICKEN AND STUFFING STRATA

A great way to use that leftover chicken.
*Bake at 375° for 45 minutes.*
*Makes 4 servings.*

| | |
|---|---|
| ½ package (8 ounces) herb-seasoned stuffing mix (2 cups) | 3 eggs |
| | 2½ cups milk |
| | 1 teaspoon salt |
| 1½ cups chopped cooked chicken | 2 ounces Swiss cheese, shredded (½ cup) |
| ¼ cup minced celery | |
| 1 medium-size onion, chopped (½ cup) | |

**1.** Sprinkle 1 cup of the stuffing mix in the bottom of a buttered 8x8x2-inch pan. Sprinkle the chicken, celery and onion over. Top with remaining stuffing mix.

**2.** Beat the eggs slightly in medium-size bowl; stir in the milk and salt. Pour over the stuffing; sprinkle with the cheese. Cover and refrigerate for 1 hour or overnight.

**3.** Bake in a moderate oven (375°) for 45 minutes or until puffed and golden. Remove to wire rack. Let stand for 10 minutes before serving.

# BAKED CHICKEN FRICASSEE

Get the old-time flavor of chicken baked in cream with this new-fashioned version. It's better than Grandma used to make.

*Bake at 350° for 2 hours.*
*Makes 4 servings.*

| | | | |
|---|---|---|---|
| 1 | broiler/fryer (about 3½ pounds), cut up | 1 | bay leaf |
| 1 | can (10¾ ounces) condensed chicken broth | ¼ | cup (½ stick) butter or margarine, softened |
| 12 | small white onions, peeled but left whole | ¼ | cup all-purpose flour |
| | | ¾ | cup heavy cream |
| 1 | small onion, stuck with 4 cloves | ½ | pound fresh mushrooms, sliced OR: 2 cans (4 ounces each) sliced mushrooms, drained |
| 1 | small carrot, diced | | |
| 3 | tablespoons chopped parsley | ¼ | teaspoon leaf thyme, crumbled |
| 1 | teaspoon salt | ½ | teaspoon paprika |
| 3 | whole black peppercorns | | |

**1.** Arrange the chicken pieces in a 10-cup casserole. Add the soup, white onions, onion stuck with cloves, carrot, parsley, salt, peppercorns and bay leaf. Cover.

**2.** Bake in a moderate oven (350°) for 1 hour and 45 minutes. Carefully remove the cover. With tongs or a slotted spoon, remove the onion stuck with cloves and bay leaf. Mix the butter with the flour and drop, bit by bit, into the liquid, stirring well as you do. Then add the heavy cream, mushrooms and thyme, stirring well again. Re-cover.

**3.** Continue baking for 15 minutes longer or until the sauce is thickened and the chicken is tender. Sprinkle with paprika before serving.

# CHICKEN-TORTILLA CASSEROLE

*Bake at 375° for 30 minutes.*
*Makes 6 to 8 servings.*

1  package (1 dozen) frozen corn tortillas, refrigerated or thawed
   Vegetable oil
2  cans (10¾ ounces each) condensed cream of chicken or mushroom soup
½  soup-can water
1  can (4 ounces) diced mild green chilies, drained

3  cans (5 ounces each) chunk chicken, drained
2  packages (4 ounces each) shredded Cheddar cheese (2 cups)
1  jar (4 ounces) pimientos, drained and cut into slivers
1  small head iceberg lettuce, shredded
1  large onion, diced

**1.** Cook the tortillas, 1 at a time, in ¼ inch hot oil in a small skillet until just softened; drain on paper toweling.

**2.** Combine the soup, water and chilies in a medium-size bowl.

**3.** Layer the ingredients in a 2-quart baking dish this way: Place 3 tortillas in the bottom, overlapping to fit. Add 1 can of chicken, ½ cup cheese and some slivered pimiento, then top with one quarter of the soup mixture. Repeat layering 2 more times, ending with tortillas, soup mixture, then cheese. Cover with aluminum foil.

**4.** Bake in a moderate oven (375°) for 30 minutes or until hot and bubbly. Cut into wedges. Serve with lettuce and onion.

# CHICKEN-NOODLE SPANISH DINNER

*Bake at 375° for 30 minutes.*
*Makes 8 servings.*

1 package (8 ounces) brown-and-serve sausages, each halved crosswise
2 teaspoons curry powder
¼ teaspoon saffron threads, crumbled
1½ cups water
1 can (1 pound) stewed tomatoes
4 packages (3 ounces each) chicken-flavored instant ramen noodles
1 package (2 pounds) frozen fried chicken (10 pieces)
1 package (10 ounces) frozen peas
1 package (8 ounces) frozen cooked shrimp

**1.** Cook the sausage halves in a large skillet until well browned. Stir in the curry and saffron; add the water and tomatoes; bring to boiling. Stir in 2 of the seasoning packets from the noodles.
**2.** Place the noodles in a greased paella pan or shallow baking pan. Pour the sausage mixture over the noodles. Arrange the chicken on top.
**3.** Bake in a moderate oven (375°) for 15 minutes. Add the peas and shrimp; gently toss with a fork to mix with the noodles. Bake for 15 minutes more or until the chicken is heated through and the peas are tender.

# QUICK CHICKEN-NOODLE CASSEROLE

Nice with a fresh spinach salad.
*Bake at 425° for 25 minutes.*
*Makes 4 servings.*

1 can (10¾ ounces) condensed cream of celery soup
¾ cup milk
1 cup grated Parmesan cheese
2 tablespoons minced onion
1 clove garlic, minced
1 can (6 ounces) sliced mushrooms, drained
1 teaspoon salt
¼ teaspoon pepper
3½ cups cooked medium-size noodles (6 ounces, uncooked)
2 cups cubed cooked chicken

**1.** Blend the soup, milk and ¾ cup of the cheese in a large bowl. Stir in the onion, garlic, mushrooms, salt and pepper; mix well; add the noodles and chicken; mix thoroughly.

**2.** Spoon into a 2-quart baking dish. Sprinkle with the remaining ¼ cup of cheese.

**3.** Bake in a hot oven (425°) for 25 minutes or until bubbly and the top is golden.

*Note:* This casserole can be frozen after step 2. When ready to serve, defrost at room temperature for 2 hours; then proceed to step 3.

## EASY OVEN CHICKEN AND VEGETABLES

Golden brown chicken with leeks and mushrooms is an easy main dish.

*Bake at 375° for 1½ hours.*

*Makes 6 servings.*

| | |
|---|---|
| 2 cups sliced leeks (white part only) | 6 chicken thighs (1½ pounds) |
| 1 pound mushrooms | ¼ cup dry vermouth or dry white wine |
| 2 tablespoons butter or margarine | 1 can (10¾ ounces) condensed cream of mushroom soup |
| 6 chicken legs (1½ pounds) | ¼ teaspoon pepper |

**1.** Sauté the leeks and mushrooms in the butter in a large skillet, stirring frequently until tender, about 5 minutes. Transfer to a 13 x 9 x 2-inch baking dish.

**2.** Arrange the chicken pieces, skin-side up, on the vegetable mixture.

**3.** Mix the wine, soup and pepper in a 2-cup glass measure. Pour over the chicken, covering it completely.

**4.** Bake in a moderate oven (375°) for 1½ hours, basting occasionally, or until the chicken is tender.

# BAKED CHICKEN AND
# STUFFING CASSEROLE

*Bake at 350° for 1 hour.*
*Makes 6 servings.*

| | | | |
|---|---|---|---|
| 1 | small onion, chopped (¼ cup) | ¾ | cup water |
| 1 | cup chopped celery | 6 | cups bread cubes, toasted |
| ½ | cup plus 3 tablespoons butter or margarine | ½ | cup coarsely chopped pecans |
| 1 | teaspoon or envelope instant chicken broth | ¼ | cup chopped parsley |
| ¼ | teaspoon pepper | 3 | whole chicken breasts, split |
| | | 3 | tablespoons all-purpose flour |
| | | ½ | teaspoon salt |

**1.** Sauté the onion and celery in the ½ cup butter in a small skillet until tender, about 8 minutes; add instant chicken broth, ⅛ teaspoon of the pepper and the water. Remove from the heat.

**2.** Combine the bread cubes, pecans and parsley in a large bowl; add the butter mixture; toss gently to moisten evenly. Spread stuffing in shallow 2-quart casserole.

**3.** Heat the remaining butter in a large skillet. Shake the chicken with the flour, salt and remaining ⅛ teaspoon pepper in a plastic bag. Place the chicken in the skillet; brown slowly on all sides over medium heat. Arrange over the stuffing. Cover.

**4.** Bake in a moderate oven (350°) for 50 minutes. Uncover and bake for 10 to 15 minutes longer or until the chicken is crisp and tender.

# CHICKEN CASSEROLE WITH APPLES AND CHEESE

A make-ahead casserole for buffet entertaining—chicken, apples, onion and Swiss and Parmesan cheeses in one tasty dish.

*Bake at 350° for 35 minutes.*
*Makes 6 servings.*

| | | | |
|---|---|---|---|
| 5 | tablespoons butter or margarine, softened | ¼ | teaspoon pepper |
| 3 | medium-size red cooking apples (1 pound), halved, cored and sliced (3 cups) | 1 | cup shredded Swiss cheese |
| | | ½ | cup grated Parmesan cheese |
| | | ¼ | cup unseasoned bread crumbs |
| 2 | large onions, thinly sliced (2 cups) | ½ | teaspoon leaf thyme, crumbled |
| 3 | boneless chicken breasts (1¾ pounds), halved | 2 | tablespoons brandy, Applejack, or apple cider |
| 1 | teaspoon salt | | |

**1.** Preheat the oven to moderate (350°). Coat a 6-cup oval or rectangular baking dish with 1 tablespoon of the butter.

**2.** Sauté the apples and onions in the remaining butter in a large skillet until very tender, about 10 minutes. Do not brown. Spoon evenly into the prepared baking dish.

**3.** Rub the chicken breasts with salt and pepper. Arrange them down the center of the apple mixture, overlapping them slightly.

**4.** Combine the Swiss cheese, Parmesan cheese, bread crumbs and thyme in a medium-size bowl; sprinkle evenly over the chicken and apple mixture. Drizzle the brandy over all.

**5.** Bake in the preheated moderate oven (350°) for 35 minutes or until the cheese mixture is golden brown and the chicken is tender.

# CHICKEN AND BROCCOLI AU GRATIN

Attractive slices of chicken and bright green broccoli are topped with a velvety wine-laced cheese sauce.

*Bake at 350° for 25 minutes.*
*Makes 6 servings.*

| | | | |
|---|---|---|---|
| 2 | packages (10 ounces each) frozen broccoli spears | ½ | teaspoon dry mustard |
| 2 | whole cooked chicken breasts* | 1 | cup chicken broth (reserved from chicken) |
| ¼ | cup (½ stick) butter or margarine | ½ | cup light cream |
| ¼ | cup all-purpose flour | 1 | cup shredded Cheddar cheese |
| ½ | teaspoon salt Pinch of white pepper | 2 | tablespoons dry white wine Grated Parmesan cheese |

**1.** Cook the broccoli following label directions; drain. Cut the spears into smaller pieces. Remove the skin and bone from the chicken breasts; slice the meat.

**2.** Melt the butter in a medium-size saucepan; blend in the flour, salt, pepper and mustard. Stir in chicken broth and cream; cook over medium heat, stirring constantly, until sauce thickens and bubbles for 1 minute. Add the Cheddar cheese and stir until melted. Stir in the wine. Remove from the heat.

**3.** Arrange the broccoli spears in the bottom of a greased 8- or 9-inch-square baking dish. Overlap the chicken slices on the broccoli. Pour the sauce over the chicken. Sprinkle lightly with Parmesan cheese.

**4.** Bake in a moderate oven (350°) for 25 minutes or until heated through and the top starts to brown.

* To cook the chicken: Split 2 chicken breasts; place in a medium-size saucepan; add just enough water to cover (about 1½ cups), ½ teaspoon salt, ⅛ teaspoon pepper, ½ small onion and ⅛ teaspoon leaf thyme. Bring to boiling; cover. Simmer over low heat until the chicken is tender, about 30 minutes. Remove the chicken from the broth. Boil the broth, uncovered, until reduced to 1 cup; strain. Reserve the broth for the sauce.

# CURRIED LIMAS AND CHICKEN WINGS

A hearty, mildly seasoned casserole with peas and carrots.

*Bake at 350° for 30 minutes.*
*Makes about 8 servings.*

| | | | |
|---|---|---|---|
| 1 | pound dried lima beans | 3 | carrots, sliced (1½ cups) |
| 3 | cups water | 2 | teaspoons curry powder |
| 8 | chicken wings (about 1¼ | ¼ | teaspoon ground cinnamon |
| | pounds) | 2 | tablespoons all-purpose flour |
| ¼ | cup (½ stick) butter or | 2 | teaspoons salt |
| | margarine | 1 | cup milk |
| 1 | large onion, chopped | 1 | package (10 ounces) frozen |
| | (1 cup) | | peas |

**1.** Pick over the beans and rinse under cool running water. Combine the beans and water in a large kettle; cover, let soak overnight. Or, to quick-soak, bring to boiling, boil for 2 minutes, remove from the heat; let stand for 1 hour.

**2.** Bring the soaked beans to boiling; lower the heat; partially cover and simmer for 35 minutes or until the beans are almost tender.

**3.** Cut each chicken wing at the joint to separate the 2 large sections. Melt the butter in a large skillet; add the wings and cook slowly until brown on all sides. Remove each wing to paper toweling when it has browned.

**4.** Add the onion, carrots, curry powder and cinnamon to the fat remaining in the skillet. Sauté until the onion is tender. Stir in the flour and salt. Drain the beans, reserving the liquid. There should be 2 cups liquid; if not, add water to make that amount.

**5.** Add the reserved liquid to the flour mixture; cook, stirring constantly, until thickened and boiling. Add the milk and peas; bring to boiling. Combine the beans, chicken wings and curry sauce in a 3- to 4-quart baking dish; cover.

**6.** Bake in a moderate oven (350°) for 30 minutes or until the beans are tender, stirring once halfway through baking.

# TURKEY VEGETABLE PIE AMANDINE

A great way to use leftover turkey and stuffing from the holidays.

*Bake at 350° for 50 minutes.*
*Makes 6 servings.*

½ cup diced carrot
½ cup diced celery
1 medium-size onion, diced (½ cup)
3 tablespoons butter or margarine
3 tablespoons all-purpose flour
1 teaspoon leaf rosemary, crumbled
½ teaspoon salt
⅛ teaspoon pepper
1 cup heavy cream
1 cup chicken broth
1 tablespoon dry Marsala
2 cups cooked turkey cut into ½-inch pieces (about 1 pound)
½ cup turkey stuffing (homemade or packaged)
½ cup cooked peas (fresh or frozen)
¼ cup slivered almonds
1 package (about 11 ounces) piecrust mix

**1.** Sauté the carrot, celery and onion in the butter in a large skillet until soft, about 5 minutes.

**2.** Stir in the flour, rosemary, salt and pepper; cook for 1 minute. Stir in the cream, chicken broth and Marsala; cook until mixture thickens, about 5 minutes. Remove from heat; stir in turkey, turkey stuffing, peas and almonds. Set aside.

**3.** Preheat the oven to moderate (350°).

**4.** Prepare the piecrust following label directions. Roll out half the pastry on lightly floured surface with lightly floured rolling pin to a 12-inch round. Fit in deep-dish 9-inch pie plate. Trim overhang to ½ inch. Spoon turkey mixture into plate.

**5.** Roll out remaining pastry to a 12-inch round. Fit over the filling. Trim the overhang even with bottom crust. Pinch to seal edges. Turn sealed edge under. Pinch again to make stand-up edge; flute. Cut steam vents in top. Place on cookie sheet or aluminum foil.

**6.** Bake in preheated moderate oven (350°) for 50 minutes, or until filling is bubbly and pastry is golden.

**Individual Pies:** Spoon turkey mixture into six (4½ x 1¼-inch) aluminum tart pans. Prepare 1 package piecrust mix following label directions. Divide pastry into 6 equal pieces. Roll each out on a lightly floured surface to a 6-inch round. Cover pies; trim overhang to ½ inch; fold edges under flush with rim. Pinch to make stand-up edge;

pressing lightly to inside of pan to seal; flute. Cut steam vents in tops. Place on large cookie sheet. Bake in preheated moderate oven (350°) for 35 minutes, or until pastry is golden.

**To Freeze Pies:** Place *unbaked* pies on a large cookie sheet; freeze until firm. Wrap individually in aluminum foil; label and date.

**To Bake Frozen Pies:** Remove aluminum foil from pies. Place frozen pies on a large cookie sheet. Bake in a preheated hot oven (400°) for 35 minutes or until filling is bubbly and pastry is golden.

## OLD-FASHIONED CHICKEN POT PIE

An up-to-date version that keeps in all the good flavor of this family favorite.
*Bake at 400° for 30 minutes.*
*Makes 6 servings.*

| | | | |
|---|---|---|---|
| 1 | broiler/fryer (3 pounds), cut up | ¼ | cup (½ stick) butter or margarine |
| 1 | teaspoon salt | 4 | tablespoons all-purpose flour |
| ¼ | teaspoon pepper | ½ | teaspoon salt |
| 12 | small white onions. (1 pound), peeled but left whole | ¼ | teaspoon pepper |
| | | 1 | cup milk |
| 1 | pound carrots, pared and cut into 1½-inch-long pieces | 1 | package (about 11 ounces) piecrust mix |
| 1 | package (10 ounces) frozen peas | 1 | egg yolk |
| | | 2 | teaspoons water |

**1.** Place the chicken in a large kettle or Dutch oven with water to cover. Bring to boiling; skim off foam. Add salt and pepper. Cover the kettle, lower the heat; simmer for 30 minutes or until the chicken is tender. Remove chicken from broth and let cool until easy to handle.
**2.** Add the onions and carrots to broth; bring to boiling; lower the heat; simmer for 20 minutes or until vegetables are just tender; add peas. Drain the vegetables; reserve the stock. Measure out 1 cup of the stock. (Use remainder for soups and gravies.)
**3.** Meanwhile, skin and bone the chicken. Cut into bite-size pieces. Combine with the vegetables in a large bowl.

**4.** Melt the butter in a medium-size saucepan. Add the flour, salt and pepper. Cook, stirring, for 1 minute. Stir in the reserved 1 cup chicken stock and the milk. Cook, stirring constantly, until thickened and bubbly. Pour over the chicken and vegetables; stir to coat thoroughly.
**5.** Spoon the chicken filling into a 10-inch deep pie plate.
**6.** Prepare the piecrust mix following label directions. Roll out to fit the top of the pie plate. Cut several vents for steam to escape. Fit over filling; trim overhang to 1-inch. Turn edge under and flute. Beat the egg yolk with the water; brush over the top.
**7.** Bake in a hot oven (400°) for 30 minutes or until the piecrust is golden brown and the chicken mixture is bubbly-hot.

## BISTRO CHICKEN POT PIES

This mouth-watering chicken pot pie is like a chicken stew—large chunks of chicken, onion, and mushroom, all melded together with just the slightest flavor of bacon.

*Bake at 400° for 35 minutes.*
*Makes 6 servings.*

| | | | |
|---|---|---|---|
| 3 | ounces slab bacon, diced | 2 | tablespoons all-purpose flour |
| 1 | cup water | | |
| 6 | tablespoons butter or margarine | ¼ | teaspoon leaf thyme, crumbled |
| 2 | whole chicken breasts (14 ounces each), skinned, boned, halved and cut into 1¼-inch pieces | ¼ | teaspoon leaf basil, crumbled |
| | | 1 | cup chicken broth |
| | | 1 | cup dry red wine |
| | | 2 | teaspoons tomato paste or catsup |
| 12 | small white onions (1 pound), halved | 1 | clove garlic, minced |
| 12 | mushrooms (¾ pound), quartered | 1 | package (about 11 ounces) piecrust mix |

**1.** Simmer the bacon for 10 minutes in the water in a small saucepan; drain; pat dry on paper toweling.
**2.** Sauté the bacon in 1 tablespoon of the butter in a large skillet until lightly browned and fat is rendered. Remove the bacon with a slotted spoon; place on paper toweling to drain. Add 1 tablespoon of the butter to the drippings in the skillet.

**3.** Brown the chicken pieces a few at a time, in the skillet. Remove with a slotted spoon to a bowl. Add 2 tablespoons of the butter to the skillet.

**4.** Brown the onions in the skillet; cover. Simmer for 10 minutes, shaking the pan occasionally. Place the onions in the bowl with the chicken. Add the remaining 2 tablespoons of butter to the skillet.

**5.** Sauté the mushrooms in the skillet just until golden. Remove to a small bowl.

**6.** Return the chicken and onions to the skillet. Sprinkle the flour, thyme and basil over; toss lightly to coat. Gradually stir in the chicken broth, wine, tomato paste and garlic. Cook slowly over a medium heat, stirring constantly, until the mixture thickens, about 2 minutes. Lower the heat; cover. Simmer for 15 minutes. Stir in the bacon and mushrooms.

**7.** Preheat the oven to hot (400°).

**8.** Spoon the chicken mixture into six (4½ x 1¼-inch) aluminum foil tart pans. Prepare the piecrust mix following label directions. Divide it into 6 equal pieces. Roll each out on a lightly floured surface to a 6-inch round. Cover the pies; trim the overhang; fold the edges under flush with the rim. Pinch to make a stand-up edge, pressing lightly to the inside of the pan to seal; flute. Cut steam vents in the tops. Place on a large cookie sheet. Bake in a preheated hot oven (400°) for 35 minutes, or until the filling is bubbly and the pastry is golden.

*To Freeze:* Place *unbaked* individual pies on a large cookie sheet; freeze until firm. Wrap individually in aluminum foil; label and date.

*To Bake Frozen Pies:* Remove aluminum foil from pies. Place frozen pies on a large cookie sheet. Bake in a preheated hot oven (400°) for 35 minutes or until filling is bubbly and pastry is golden.

# ORIENTAL SWEET AND SOUR CHICKEN PIE

A perky blend of chicken, pineapple, soy sauce and water chestnuts.

*Bake at 375° for 35 minutes.*
*Makes 6 servings.*

| | | | |
|---|---|---|---|
| 1 | cup chicken broth | ½ | teaspoon salt |
| 2 | whole chicken breasts (14 ounces each), skinned, boned and halved | ⅛ | teaspoon pepper |
| | | 2 | tablespoons soy sauce |
| | | ¼ | cup rice wine vinegar or cider vinegar |
| 1 | cup sliced celery | | |
| 1 | cup sliced green onion | 1 | can (8 ounces) water chestnuts, drained and thinly sliced |
| 1 | teaspoon minced fresh ginger OR: ¼ teaspoon ground ginger | | |
| | | ½ | package (about 11 ounces) piecrust mix |
| 2 | tablespoons cornstarch | | |
| 1½ | teaspoon sugar (optional) | | |

**1.** Bring the chicken broth to boiling in a large skillet; lower the heat; add the chicken; cover. Simmer for 15 minutes or until the chicken is tender. Remove the chicken from the broth; cool slightly.

**2.** Add the celery, onion and ginger to the broth; simmer, uncovered for 5 minutes.

**3.** While the vegetables are cooking, combine the cornstarch, sugar, if used, salt, pepper, soy sauce and vinegar in a small cup; mix until smooth. Cut the chicken into bite-size pieces; set aside.

**4.** Gradually stir the cornstarch mixture into the vegetable broth, stirring constantly, until the mixture thickens. Add the chicken pieces, pineapple and water chestnuts; mix to coat thoroughly. Spoon into a 1½-quart baking dish.

**5.** Preheat the oven to moderate (375°).

**6.** Prepare the pastry following label directions. Roll out on a lightly floured surface with a lightly floured rolling pin to a piece slightly larger than the top of the casserole. Fit over the filling. Trim the overhang to ½ inch; fold the edge under, flush with the side of the baking dish (pastry should be inside dish). Pinch to make a stand-up edge; flute. Cut steam vents in the top. Place on a cookie sheet or aluminum foil.

**7.** Bake in a preheated moderate oven (375°) for 35 minutes or until the filling is bubbly and the pastry is golden.

# SCOTTISH LAMB AND CHICKEN LIVER PIE

A creamy, wine-spiked combination of chicken livers and lamb cubes
under a puffy golden crust.

*Bake at 425° for 15 minutes; then at 350° for 20 minutes.*
*Makes 6 servings.*

| | | | |
|---|---|---|---|
| 7 | tablespoons butter | ½ | teaspoon salt |
| ⅓ | cup chopped small white onions | ¼ | teaspoon pepper |
| 1½ | pound lean lamb, cut into 1-inch cubes | ⅛ | teaspoon leaf thyme, crumbled |
| | All-purpose flour for dredging | ⅛ | teaspoon leaf rosemary, crumbled |
| 1 | pound chicken livers, cut into ½-inch cubes | 1 | package (10 ounces) tiny frozen peas, thawed |
| 1 | can (13¾ ounces) beef broth | ¼ | cup heavy cream |
| ¼ | cup dry Madeira wine | 1 | sheet (half of a 17¼-ounce package) prerolled frozen puff pastry, thawed |

**1.** Melt 2 tablespoons of the butter in a large heavy kettle; add the white onion and cook over low heat until soft, about 5 minutes. Remove the onion; reserve.

**2.** Dredge the lamb cubes in the flour. Add 3 tablespoons of the butter to the kettle; sauté the lamb a few cubes at a time (if kettle is crowded) over medium heat until brown all over. Remove the lamb; reserve. Dredge the chicken livers in flour. Add the remaining 2 tablespoons of butter to the kettle. Sauté the livers until evenly browned. Remove the livers; reserve separately.

**3.** Pour ½ can beef broth into the kettle. Cook over medium heat, loosening any browned particles on the bottom of the kettle. Add the remaining broth, Madeira, salt, pepper, thyme and rosemary. Add the lamb cubes and onion; cover and simmer for 45 minutes, stirring occasionally. Taste; add salt and pepper, if needed.

**4.** Preheat the oven to hot (425°).

**5.** Add the livers, peas and cream to the lamb mixture. Spoon the mixture into a shallow 1½-quart baking dish.

**6.** Fit the puff pastry slightly larger than dish, rolling it out slightly if necessary. Moisten the edges of the dish and place the pastry on top. Press the edges down lightly. Cut a vent hole in the center.

**7.** Bake in a preheated hot oven (425°) for 15 minutes; lower the oven temperature to moderate (350°) and bake for 20 minutes or until golden and puffed.

# CHICKEN, SAUSAGE AND LEEK PIE BASQUE STYLE

An inspired combination of favorite foods laced with a touch of herbs makes this pleasing filling.

*Bake at 425° for 25 minutes.*
*Makes 6 servings.*

Flaky Pastry (recipe follows)
8 tablespoons butter
6 medium-size leeks (white part only), washed and cut into 1-inch pieces
2 whole chicken breasts (about 2 pounds), skinned, boned and cut into 1-inch pieces
3 chicken thighs (about 1 pound), skinned, boned and cut into 1-inch pieces
1 package (8 ounces) precooked sausages
6 tablespoons all-purpose flour
3 cups chicken broth (from 2 cans, each 13¾ ounces)
¼ cup light cream
1 teaspoon minced parsley
1 teaspoon minced chives
½ teaspoon salt
¼ teaspoon pepper
Pinch of leaf tarragon, crumbled
1 egg yolk beaten with 3 tablespoons light cream

**1.** Prepare the Flaky Pastry; reserve.
**2.** Melt 2 tablespoons of the butter in a medium-size saucepan. Add the leeks; cook, covered until soft, about 10 minutes.
**3.** Sauté the chicken and sausage in 3 tablespoons of the butter in a large skillet over medium heat until golden. Remove the chicken and sausage with a slotted spoon; reserve.
**4.** Melt the remaining 3 tablespoons of butter in the same skillet. Blend in the flour, stirring constantly; cook for 1 minute. Gradually add the chicken broth, stirring constantly, until smooth and thickened. Blend in the cream, parsley, chives, salt, pepper and tarragon. Taste; add additional seasoning, if necessary.
**5.** Remove 1 cup of sauce and set aside to serve later. Add the chicken, sausage and leeks to the remaining sauce.
**6.** Preheat the oven to hot (425°).
**7.** Roll out two thirds of the pastry on a floured surface to a 14-inch round; fit into a 10-inch pie plate. Spoon in chicken-sausage mixture.
**8.** Roll out the remaining pastry to a 13-inch round; cut several slits for steam vents. Cover the pie; seal the edge; flute. Beat the egg yolk with the cream; brush over the pastry.

**9.** Bake in a preheated hot oven (425°) for 25 minutes or until golden. Heat the remaining sauce to serve with the pie.

# FLAKY PASTRY

*Makes enough for a 2-crust 10-inch pie.*

Combine 3 cups *sifted* all-purpose flour and 1 teaspoon salt in a medium-size bowl. Cut in 1 cup vegetable shortening with a pastry blender or two knives until mixture is crumbly and texture is size of peas. Sprinkle ½ cup ice water over mixture, stirring with a fork just until it holds together and leaves side of bowl clean. Gather into a ball.

# TURKEY SUPPER PIES

*Preheat oven to 450°. Bake at 400° for 20 minutes.*
*Makes 8 pies.*

| | | | |
|---|---|---|---|
| 1 | package (10 ounces) frozen chopped broccoli | ½ | pound cooked turkey, coarsely chopped |
| 1 | egg yolk | 1 | package (17¼ ounces) prerolled frozen puff pastry |
| 2 | tablespoons dairy sour cream | | |
| 1 | teaspoon lemon juice | 1 | egg white, lightly beaten |
| ¼ | teaspoon salt | | Mock Hollandaise Sauce |
| ⅛ | teaspoon pepper | | (recipe follows) |
| 4 | ounces Monterey Jack cheese, shredded | | |

**1.** Cook the frozen broccoli following label directions; drain, pressing out as much liquid as possible; cool to room temperature. Beat the egg yolk with the sour cream, lemon juice, salt and pepper in a bowl. Stir in the cheese, turkey and broccoli. Refrigerate until cold.
**2.** Thaw the frozen pastry sheets for 20 minutes at room temperature or until pliable but still very cold. Roll out each sheet on a lightly floured surface to a 13-inch square; divide into 4 equal quarters; repeat with second sheet.
**3.** Divide the filling equally among the 8 pastry squares, leaving a 1-inch border of uncovered pastry on all sides. Brush the borders

generously with some of the beaten egg white. Fold the squares diagonally in half to form triangles. Press the edges firmly together; then press with the tines of a fork to seal securely. Brush the tops with the egg white. Pierce each top in the center with a small paring knife to allow steam to escape. Arrange pies 1 inch apart on cookie sheets.
**4.** Preheat the oven to very hot (450°). Immediately lower the temperature to hot (400°). Bake for 20 minutes.
**5.** Top each baked pie with Mock Hollandaise Sauce.

**Mock Hollandaise Sauce:** Combine 1 cup dairy sour cream, 2 egg yolks, 2 tablespoons lemon juice, 1 teaspoon Dijon-style mustard and ½ teaspoon salt in top of double boiler. Cook, stirring constantly, over simmering water until thick and hot.

# 6

# Appetizers

Appetizers are the overture to a meal, for they set the mood and are an introduction to the courses that follow. They should be tempting, light and attractive, and for these reasons chicken is an ideal choice.

Appetizers are often served in the living room with drinks, or when the weather permits, outdoors on the porch or terrace. Small savory tidbits, sometimes called finger foods, can be offered informally, with paper napkins instead of plates. These could include Chicken Picadillo Empañadas or Chicken Pillows.

But on more formal occasions, when appetizers are presented at the dining table as the first course, they are usually a little more elegant and sometimes downright impressive. Chicken Pâté with Port Wine Aspic is a good example.

The recipes in the chapter reflect the range of possibilities—from crisp Sesame Chicken Wings to a silky-smooth Fine Chicken and Chicken Liver Pâté.

# CHICKEN-FILLED PASTRY BOATS

A zesty chicken mixture fills these crispy make-ahead pastry shells.

*Bake at 400° for 8 minutes.*
*Makes about 2 dozen.*

½ package (about 11 ounces) piecrust mix
¾ cup finely diced cooked chicken
2 tablespoons finely chopped celery
2 tablespoons chopped green onions
1½ teaspoons finely chopped canned hot chili peppers

½ teaspoon lime or lemon juice
½ teaspoon salt
¼ cup dairy sour cream
2 hard-cooked egg yolks, sieved
Parsley sprigs

**1.** Prepare the piecrust mix following label directions. Roll out, half at a time, to an ⅛-inch thickness on a lightly floured surface.

**2.** Using 3-inch barquette pans or tiny tart pans, invert the pans onto the pastry and cut the pastry ½ inch wider than the pans. Press the pastry into the pans and trim the edges so they are even with the pans. Arrange the pans on cookie sheets; prick the pastry with a fork.

**3.** Bake in a hot oven (400°) for 8 minutes or until golden. Cool in the pans on a wire rack for 5 minutes. Ease out of the pans; cool completely.

**4.** Place in foil or plastic boxes; cover, label and freeze.

**5.** To serve, combine the chicken, celery, onion, chili pepper, lime juice, salt and sour cream in a small bowl; toss to mix well; spoon into the shells. Garnish with sieved egg yolks and small sprigs of parsley. Cover; refrigerate until serving time.

# CHICKEN PILLOWS

These crisp and garlicky chicken pastries can be put together way ahead of time and frozen, unbaked. Remove from the freezer just before baking.

*Bake at 400° for 15 minutes.*
*Makes about 24 pastries.*

2 whole chicken breasts (about 1 pound total weight), skinned, boned and halved
3 tablespoons lemon juice
2 tablespoons olive or vegetable oil
1 teaspoon finely chopped garlic
1 teaspoon leaf oregano, crumbled
½ teaspoon salt
½ cup (1 stick) butter
½ pound phyllo or strudel pastry leaves

**1.** Cut the chicken into 1-inch cubes.
**2.** Combine the lemon juice, oil, garlic, oregano and salt in a small bowl; mix well. Add the chicken pieces and coat with the marinade. Cover and refrigerate overnight.
**3.** Melt the butter over low heat. Unwrap the phyllo and place it on a piece of wax paper. Keep the phyllo covered with another piece of wax paper at all times to prevent it from drying out. Halve the pastry lengthwise with scissors, forming 2 long strips, about 6 inches wide. Take one strip of phyllo, fold it in half crosswise and brush it with butter. Place 2 pieces of chicken at one short end and roll up in pastry to the midpoint. Fold the left and right edges toward the center over the filling and continue rolling, forming a neat package. Brush all over with butter and place seam-side down on a jelly-roll pan. Repeat with the remaining chicken and phyllo.
**4.** Bake in a hot oven (400°) for 15 minutes or until golden brown.

*To Freeze Ahead:* Place the filled and buttered phyllo rolls on a large cookie sheet and freeze. When they are frozen, transfer them to large plastic bags and seal.

*To Bake:* Place the rolls in a single layer in 2 jelly-roll pans, brush with additional melted butter. Bake in a hot oven (400°) for 20 minutes.

# CHICKEN PICADILLO EMPAÑADAS

*Bake at 450° for 8 minutes.*
*Makes 12 servings.*

| | | | |
|---|---|---|---|
| 1 | whole chicken breast (about 10 ounces), skinned and boned | ½ | cup tomato sauce |
| | | ½ | cup chicken broth |
| 1 | tablespoon butter or margarine | 2 | tablespoons raisins |
| | | 1 | tablespoon finely chopped stuffed green olives |
| 1 | tablespoon olive or vegetable oil | 1 | tablespoon finely chopped capers |
| 1 | small onion, minced (¼ cup) | 1 | teaspoon salt |
| | | ¼ | teaspoon pepper |
| 1 | small sweet green pepper, minced (½ cup) | ¼ | teaspoon leaf oregano, crumbled |
| 1 | clove garlic, minced | 1 | package piecrust mix |

**1.** Slice the chicken breast into thin strips; cut the strips into very small pieces. (Or put through medium-coarseness blade of meat grinder.)
**2.** Heat the butter and oil in a large skillet. Sauté the onion, green pepper and garlic until soft, about 5 minutes. Add the chicken; sauté until the meat is white, about 5 minutes.
**3.** Add the tomato sauce, chicken broth, raisins, green olives, capers, salt, pepper and oregano. Bring to boiling; lower the heat. Simmer for about 10 minutes or until most of the liquid has evaporated. Cool to room temperature.
**4.** Prepare the piecrust mix following label directions. Roll out the pastry on a lightly floured surface to a 12 x 16-inch rectangle. Square off the sides. Cut into twelve 4-inch squares.
**5.** Place 1 tablespoon of the filling at one corner of the pastry square. Dampen the edges with a pastry brush dipped in water. Fold into a triangle and press down with the tines of a fork. Place on a large cookie sheet. Repeat with the remaining pastry squares.
**6.** Bake in a very hot oven (450°) for 8 minutes or until golden brown.

*To Serve Cold:* Present at room temperature. If the empañadas must be chilled, remove at least 1 hour before serving.

*To Reheat:* Place the empañadas on an ungreased cookie sheet. Bake in a moderate oven (350°) for 5 minutes or until thoroughly heated.

# CHICKEN, WATER CHESTNUTS AND HERB-CHEESE TRIANGLES

Neat, crisp little packets filled with a savory cheese mixture.

*Bake at 400° for 15 minutes.*
*Makes 2½ dozen.*

| | |
|---|---|
| 1 | pound skinned and boned chicken breasts |
| 1 | can (5 ounces) water chestnuts, drained and finely chopped |
| 1 | package (5 ounces) appetizer cheese with garlic and herbs |
| ¼ | teaspoon salt (optional) |
| 1 | package (1 pound) phyllo or strudel pastry leaves, thawed |
| ½ | cup (1 stick) butter, melted |

**1.** Cut the chicken breasts into small pieces; place one third of the pieces in the container of an electric blender; cover; whirl to a pastelike consistency. Remove to a medium-size bowl; repeat with the remaining chicken pieces. (Or chicken pieces may be *very finely* chopped.)

**2.** Add the water chestnuts, cheese and salt, if used. Blend thoroughly.

**3.** Preheat the oven to hot (400°).

**4.** Stack two leaves of phyllo pastry on the work surface; cover the remaining phyllo with a damp towel to prevent them from drying. For each triangle, cut the phyllo lengthwise into 3-inch-wide strips, cutting through both leaves; brush with butter.

**5.** Place a tablespoon of filling on one end of the strip. Fold one corner to the opposite side, forming a triangle. Continue folding to the other end, keeping a triangle shape. Repeat with the remaining pastry and filling until all are used. Arrange the pastries on a buttered jelly-roll pan. Brush with butter.

**6.** Bake in a preheated hot oven (400°) for 15 minutes or until golden brown. Serve hot.

*Note:* If you wish, the pastries may be filled and shaped and then wrapped and frozen in a single layer until ready to serve. Bake the frozen pastries as directed above.

# SESAME CHICKEN WINGS

Miniature "drumsticks" in a cream and crumb coating "fry" with ease
in the oven. Delicious hot or cold.

*Bake at 375° for 40 minutes.*
*Makes about 36.*

| | | | |
|---|---|---|---|
| 3 | pounds chicken wings (about 18) | 1 | teaspoon paprika |
| 2 | tablespoons toasted sesame seeds* | ½ | teaspoon salt |
| | | ⅓ | cup heavy cream |
| ¾ | cup packaged unseasoned bread crumbs | ½ | cup (1 stick) butter |
| | | | Bottled duck sauce |

**1.** Remove the tips of the chicken wings; save them for making soup.
Cut each wing into two sections.
**2.** Combine the sesame seeds, bread crumbs, paprika and salt in
a shallow dish.
**3.** Dip the chicken pieces in the cream, using a brush to coat them
completely; roll in the crumb mixture. Refrigerate for 1 hour.
**4.** Place the butter in a 13x9x2-inch baking pan. Melt in the oven
while the oven preheats to 375°. Remove from the oven; turn the
chicken pieces in the butter to coat completely.
**5.** Bake in a moderate oven (375°) for 40 minutes. Serve with duck
sauce.

*Shake sesame seeds in a small skillet over low heat until they are golden.

# SWEET AND SOUR
# ORANGE CHICKEN WINGS

*Makes 12 servings.*

3 pounds chicken wings (about 18)
1½ cups all-purpose flour
1½ tablespoons baking powder
1 teaspoon ground ginger
½ teaspoon salt

1 cup water
½ cup vegetable oil
Vegetable oil for frying
Sweet and Sour Orange
Sauce (recipe follows)

**1.** Cut the tips from the chicken wings. Cut each wing into two sections.
**2.** Combine the flour, baking powder, ginger and salt in a medium-size bowl; stir in the water and oil until well blended.
**3.** Using a pastry brush, coat the chicken pieces evenly with the batter.
**4.** Preheat the oven to very slow (250°). Pour oil into a large deep, heavy skillet or deep-fat fryer to a 2-inch depth. Heat to 350° on a deep-fat frying thermometer or until a 1-inch cube of bread turns golden brown in about 65 seconds.
**5.** Fry the chicken wings a few at a time in the hot oil, turning frequently, for about 5 minutes or until golden brown. Remove with a slotted spoon to paper toweling to drain. Keep warm in the preheated very slow oven (250°) until all the pieces are cooked.
**6.** Prepare the Sweet and Sour Orange Sauce.
**7.** To serve, arrange the wings on a platter; garnish with green onion brushes, orange slices and sweet red pepper strips, if you wish. Serve with the Sweet and Sour Orange Sauce for dipping.

**Sweet and Sour Orange Sauce:** Combine 1½ cups orange juice, ¼ cup cider vinegar, ¼ cup soy sauce, ⅓ cup firmly packed light brown sugar, ½ teaspoon ground ginger and 1 clove garlic, finely chopped, in a medium-size saucepan. Combine 2 tablespoons cornstarch and 2 tablespoons dry sherry in a cup; stir into the saucepan. Cook, stirring constantly, until the mixture thickens and bubbles. Makes about 2¼ cups.

# SAVORY CHICKEN WINGS

Mini "drumsticks" rolled in a buttery mixture of fresh herbs
and toasty sesame seeds.

*Makes 36.*

3  pound chicken wings (about 18)
¾  cup (1½ sticks) butter or margarine
2  tablespoons sesame seeds
2  tablespoons finely chopped parsley

2  tablespoons finely chopped green onion
1  tablespoon finely chopped chives
   Peach Sauce (recipe follows)

**1.** Remove the tips of the chicken wings; save for making soup. Cut each wing into two sections.
**2.** Melt the butter with sesame seeds, parsley, green onions and chives in a small skillet.
**3.** Dip the chicken wings on both sides in the butter mixture. Place on the grill.
**4.** Grill for 10 to 15 minutes, turning once, or until the chicken wings are done. Serve as is or with Peach Sauce.


# PEACH SAUCE

*Makes ½ cup.*

½  cup peach preserves
2  tablespoons cider vinegar

¼  teaspoon dry mustard

Combine the peach preserves, vinegar and mustard in a small saucepan. Heat just to boiling, but do not boil. Cool; pour into a small bowl; chill well. The recipe can be doubled.

# ORIENTAL CHICKEN WINGS

*Makes 24.*

| | | | |
|---|---|---|---|
| 2 | pounds chicken wings (about 14) | ⅓ | cup dry sherry |
| 2 | tablespoons vegetable oil | 2 | tablespoons lemon juice |
| 1 | clove garlic, minced | ⅓ | cup light corn syrup |
| ¼ | cup soy sauce | ¼ | teaspoon ground ginger |
| | | 1 | lemon, cut into wedges |

**1.** Remove the wing tips and save for making soup. Cut the wings apart at the joint. Heat the oil in a skillet; brown the wings on both sides. Remove the wings with a slotted spoon; pour off the excess oil.
**2.** Stir in the garlic, soy sauce, sherry, lemon juice, corn syrup and ginger. Add the wings; bring to boiling; lower the heat. Cover; simmer, turning the wings once, for 20 minutes or until the chicken is tender.
**3.** Remove the cover; raise the heat; cook for 10 minutes longer, stirring frequently, or until the sauce thickens and the wings are nicely glazed. Garnish with lemon wedges.

# BARBECUED CHICKEN DRUMETTES

*Bake at 350° for 40 minutes.*
*Makes 36.*

| | | | |
|---|---|---|---|
| 3 | pounds chicken wings (about 18) | 2 | cloves garlic, chopped |
| ½ | teaspoon salt | 1 | cup catsup |
| ¼ | teaspoon pepper | ½ | cup apricot preserves |
| ¼ | cup vegetable oil | 1 | tablespoon Worcestershire sauce |
| 1 | large onion, chopped (1 cup) | ¼ | teaspoon liquid red-pepper seasoning |

**1.** Remove the tips of the chicken wings. Cut each wing into 2 pieces; sprinkle with salt and pepper. Place the pieces side by side in a shallow glass dish.
**2.** Heat the oil in a large skillet; sauté the onion and garlic until golden, about 5 minutes. Stir in the remaining ingredients; simmer for 5 minutes. Cool and pour the mixture evenly over the chicken wings; chill for several hours or overnight.
**3.** When you are ready for final cooking, place the wings in a single layer in a shallow baking pan. Bake in a moderate oven (350°) for 40 minutes or until the wings are tender. Serve hot.

# CHICKEN LIVER-AND-APPLE BROCHETTES

An easy-to-prepare hors d'oeuvre for a dinner party.

*Makes about 2 dozen.*

½ cup cider or apple juice
3 tablespoons soy sauce
¼ teaspoon leaf thyme, crumbled
¼ teaspoon ground cinnamon
⅛ teaspoon ground cloves
½ pound chicken livers
1 eating apple
½ pound sliced bacon (about 12 slices)

**1.** Mix the apple cider, soy sauce, thyme, cinnamon and cloves; pour over the livers in small bowl; cover and marinate in the refrigerator for several hours.
**2.** Cut each liver into 2 or 3 pieces. Quarter and core the apple; cut into bite-size chunks; halve bacon crosswise. Wrap a piece of liver and a piece of apple in each half-slice of bacon; secure with wooden picks. Arrange on a rack in the broiler pan; brush with the marinade.
**3.** Broil 3 to 4 inches from the heat for 5 minutes, turning once or twice, until the bacon is crisp and the livers are well cooked.

# RUMAKI

Polynesian restaurants often feature these kabobs of chicken livers, water chestnuts and bacon as an appetizer. They're perfect to grill on a hibachi.

*Grill for 10 minutes.*
*Makes 24.*

1 can (5 ounces) water chestnuts, drained and sliced
1 pound chicken livers, halved
½ pound bacon, halved
1½ cups soy sauce
½ cup sake or dry sherry
1 clove garlic, halved
Light brown sugar

**1.** Place a water chestnut slice on either side of each chicken liver half; wrap with a piece of bacon; thread on a small wooden skewer.
**2.** Combine the soy sauce, sake and garlic in a large shallow glass dish; add the kabobs, basting with the marinade. Cover the dish with plastic wrap. Refrigerate at least 2 hours.
**3.** Grill 4 inches from the heat, turning and basting with the marinade several times, for 8 minutes. Sprinkle brown sugar in a large metal pan. Dip the kabobs in the sugar to coat them evenly.
**4.** Grill for 2 minutes longer or until glazed. Serve the remaining marinade in tiny cups as a dipping sauce.

# FINE CHICKEN AND CHICKEN LIVER PÂTÉ

*Bake at 350° for 2 hours.*
*Makes 2 loaves, about 1 pound, 11 ounces each.*

| | | | |
|---|---|---|---|
| 1 | large onion, chopped (1 cup) | 1 | tablespoon salt |
| 2 | cloves garlic | 1 | teaspoon leaf thyme, crumbled |
| 2 | tablespoons butter | ½ | teaspoon pepper |
| 1½ | pounds boneless pork shoulder | ½ | teaspoon ground allspice |
| 1 | pound chicken breasts | ¼ | cup brandy |
| 1 | pound chicken livers | 2 | tablespoons chopped black olives |
| ½ | cup heavy cream | 1 | pound bacon |
| 2 | eggs | 4 | bay leaves |

**1.** Sauté the onion and garlic in the butter in a small skillet until soft but not brown. Cut the pork into 2-inch pieces. Bone and skin the chicken breasts. Cut into 2-inch pieces.

**2.** Put the onion, pork, chicken and chicken livers through a food grinder twice, using the finest blade.

**3.** Combine the ground mixture with the cream, eggs, salt, thyme, pepper, allspice, brandy and olives in a large bowl. Beat the mixture with a wooden spoon until it comes together and is smooth and well mixed.

**4.** Line two 7⅜ x 3⅝ x 2¼-inch loaf pans with strips of bacon. Don't overlap the bacon or it will make ridges in the pâté. Each pan will take about 7 strips. Cut to fit where necessary and let the ends hang down over the sides of the pan.

**5.** Divide the mixture between the pans, pressing it firmly; smooth the tops. Press the bay leaves on top of each loaf. Fold the bacon ends over the mixture; then add additional strips to completely cover the mixture. Cover the pans tightly with heavy-duty aluminum foil.

**6.** Put the pans in a larger pan and place on an oven shelf. Pour boiling water into the outer pan to come halfway up the sides of the loaf pans.

**7.** Bake in a moderate oven (350°) for 2 hours or until the juices run yellow with no tinge of pink.

**8.** Remove the pans from the oven to a wire rack; remove the aluminum foil. Let cool, wrap in fresh aluminum foil and then refrigerate. Pâté will keep, refrigerated, for a week.

# DANISH LIVER PÂTÉ

*Bake at 350° for 1½ hours.*
*Makes 6 servings.*

| | |
|---|---|
| ½ pound chicken livers | ½ teaspoon pepper |
| 1 small onion, chopped (¼ cup) | ¼ teaspoon dry mustard |
| ¼ cup packaged unseasoned bread crumbs | ¼ teaspoon ground nutmeg |
| | 1 cup light cream |
| 2 eggs, separated | 2 tablespoons bacon fat, melted and cooled |
| ¾ teaspoon salt | |

**1.** Generously grease an aluminum foil-lined 8½ x 4½ x 2½-inch (6-cup) loaf pan.
**2.** Combine the chicken livers, onion and bread crumbs in the container of an electric blender and blend until the mixture is a smooth paste.
**3.** Beat the egg yolks in a bowl with salt, pepper, mustard and nutmeg. Add the cream and bacon fat and beat again. Fold in liver the mixture; mix thoroughly.
**4.** Beat the egg whites until soft peaks form; fold into the liver mixture. Pour into the prepared loaf pan.
**5.** Bake in a preheated moderate oven (350°) for 1½ hours. Cool in the pan on a wire rack to room temperature. (Loaf will shrink on cooling.) Remove from the pan; peel off the foil, wrap tightly and store for at least 1 day before serving. Keeps about 4 days.

# CHOPPED LIVERS NEW YORK-STYLE

*Makes about 3 cups.*

| | |
|---|---|
| 1 pound chicken livers | ½ teaspoon pepper |
| 2 medium-size onions, chopped | Chopped egg (optional) |
| | Parsley sprigs (optional) |
| ⅓ cup rendered chicken fat | Lettuce cups (optional) |
| 2 hard-cooked eggs | Minced onion (optional) |
| 1 teaspoon salt | |

**1.** Sauté the chicken livers and onions in the chicken fat in a large skillet until no pink remains in the livers and the onions have turned a golden-brown.

**2.** Chop the livers, onions and eggs coarsely and evenly, or put through a food grinder using the coarsest blade. (Do not use an electric blender.) Gently stir in salt and pepper; refrigerate.

**3.** Serve garnished with additional chopped egg and parsley sprigs, if you wish, or serve in lettuce cups and garnish with minced onion and chopped egg. Chopped liver is also good spread on crisp thin crackers or toast or stuffed in celery stalks.

## FESTIVE CHICKEN LIVER PÂTÉ

Easy to make within minutes.

*Makes about 3 cups.*

| | | | |
|---|---|---|---|
| ⅓ | cup chopped onion | ¼ | cup chopped parsley |
| ¼ | cup (½ stick) butter | ¾ | teaspoon salt |
| 1 | pound chicken livers | ¼ | teaspoon pepper |
| 3 | hard-cooked eggs, quartered | | Brandied Aspic |
| 1 | package (8 ounces) cream cheese, cut into 6 or 8 chunks | | (recipe follows) |

**1.** Sauté the onion in the butter in a large skillet until soft; remove with a slotted spoon to the container of an electric blender. Add the livers to the skillet and cook over medium heat for about 10 minutes.

**2.** Add the livers gradually to the onions in the blender; whirl the mixture, a little at a time, until smooth. Add the eggs and cream cheese gradually. Continue to whirl until the mixture is smooth. Stir in the parsley, salt and pepper.

**3.** Transfer the mixture to a 3-cup crock or attractive container. Cover with plastic wrap. Chill in the refrigerator.

**4.** While the pâté is chilling, prepare the Brandied Aspic.

**5.** Decorate the pâté with pimiento cutouts, parsley and pickles. Spoon the chilled aspic over the pâté and refrigerate until firm.

**Brandied Aspic:** Sprinkle 2 teaspoons (from an envelope) of unflavored gelatin over ½ cup canned beef broth in a small saucepan. Stir; let stand to soften for 5 minutes. Heat over very low heat, stirring constantly until gelatin dissolves. Remove from the heat; add 1 tablespoon brandy; pour into a small bowl. Chill until syrupy. Spoon the chilled aspic over the pâté and refrigerate until firm.

# CHICKEN PÂTÉ WITH PORT WINE ASPIC

Shimmery wine aspic covers a savory pâté.
*Bake at 350° for 1 hour and 30 minutes.*
*Makes 12 servings.*

| | |
|---|---|
| 1 chicken breast half (about 8 ounces), skinned and boned | 1 teaspoon ground coriander |
| ½ cup port wine | ½ teaspoon leaf thyme, crumbled |
| 2 tablespoons butter or margarine | ½ teaspoon pepper |
| ½ pound chicken livers | 2 eggs |
| 1 pound ground turkey, pork or veal | ¾ cup heavy cream |
| 1 medium-size onion, minced (½ cup) | 3 tablespoons pistachio nuts or almonds |
| 2 teaspoons salt | 2 bay leaves |
| | Port Wine Aspic Topping (recipe follows) |

**1.** Cut the chicken breast into long thin strips. Place in a small bowl; add the port wine; let marinate several hours. Drain, reserving the wine. Sauté the chicken in butter in small skillet just until no pink remains. Transfer to a plate. Deglaze the pan with the wine; cook until reduced to ¼ cup.

**2.** Chop the chicken livers fine. Combine with the ground turkey, onion, salt, coriander, thyme and pepper in a large bowl. Beat with a wooden spoon until well blended. Gradually beat in the eggs and cream. Stir in the nuts and wine mixture from the skillet.

**3.** Layer the pâté mixture with the chicken breast pieces in a 1½-quart baking dish or loaf pan. Arrange the bay leaves on top; cover with aluminum foil. Set the dish in a larger pan on the oven shelf; fill the pan half full with boiling water.

**4.** Bake in a moderate oven (350°) for 1 hour and 30 minutes or until the juices are no longer pink. Remove to a wire rack. Cool; then chill overnight in the refrigerator. Prepare the aspic.

## PORT WINE ASPIC TOPPING

| | |
|---|---|
| 1 cup chicken broth | Lemon peel |
| 1 envelope unflavored gelatin | Parsley stems and sprigs |
| ½ cup port wine | 2 bay leaves |
| 1 pimiento | |

**1.** Pour the chicken broth through a paper filter or double layer of cheesecloth into a small saucepan; sprinkle the gelatin over. Let stand for 5 minutes to soften. Heat, stirring constantly, until the gelatin is completely dissolved; remove from the heat; stir in the wine. Place the pan in a larger pan of ice and water to speed thickening. Chill, stirring occasionally, until syrupy.

**2.** Remove the pâté from the pan and place it on a rack over a platter to catch the gelatin that drips down. Spoon a thin coating of aspic over the pâté.

**3.** Cut pointed ovals from the pimiento; arrange on top of the pâté to form a poinsettia; cut tiny rounds from the lemon peel for the center of the flower. Add parsley stems and sprigs and bay leaves.

**4.** Brush or spoon several layers of aspic over the decorations. Chill for several hours. Chill the remaining aspic in a shallow bowl or pie plate; chop and spoon around the pâté before serving.

# CHICKEN-WALNUT STRIPS

*Bake at 425° for 15 minutes.*
*Makes 6 to 8 servings.*

| | |
|---|---|
| **2** whole chicken breasts (about 1 pound total weight), skinned, boned and halved | ¼ teaspoon pepper |
| | **1** cup fine dry bread crumbs |
| **2** eggs | **1** cup very finely chopped walnuts |
| Peanut or vegetable oil | Mustard Mayonnaise Dip |
| ½ teaspoon salt | (recipe follows) |

**1.** Cut the chicken breasts into ½ x 3-inch strips with a very sharp knife.

**2.** Beat the eggs with 1 tablespoon of the oil, salt and pepper in a shallow bowl. Place the crumbs and nuts on a plate and blend well.

**3.** Dip the strips, one at a time, in the egg mixture and then coat with the crumbs. Arrange half the strips in a single layer in a jelly-roll pan and pour ¼ cup oil around, not over, them. Repeat with the remaining chicken, arranging in a second pan.

**4.** Place one pan in the center and one in the upper third of a hot oven (425°); bake for 15 minutes, reversing pan positions after 8 minutes.

**5.** Turn out onto a serving plate and serve with Mustard Mayonnaise Dip.

**Mustard Mayonnaise Dip:** Stir 2 tablespoons Dijon mustard into 1 cup mayonnaise. Cover and chill for 1 hour before serving.

# COCONUT CHICKEN

The ambrosial flavor of the tender juicy chicken with its crisp coconut coating is worth the little extra fussing.

*Makes about 36.*

6 skinned and boned chicken breast halves (2 pounds total weight)
⅓ cup lemon juice
1 teaspoon salt
2 teaspoons curry powder
¼ teaspoon ground ginger
2 cups *sifted* all-purpose flour
2 teaspoons baking powder
1½ cups milk

Curry Sauce (recipe follows)
All-purpose flour for dredging
¾ pound desiccated coconut (available in health food section of supermarket) OR:
2 packages (7 ounces each) cookie coconut
3 cups vegetable oil

**1.** Cut each chicken breast half into 6 pieces. Combine the lemon juice, salt, curry powder and ground ginger in a medium-size bowl. Add the chicken; stir to coat well. Marinate for 30 minutes.

**2.** Combine the flour, baking powder and milk in a medium-size bowl; beat until the batter is smooth. (It will be very thick.)

**3.** Make the Curry Sauce.

**4.** Drain any excess marinade from the chicken, stirring the marinade into the batter. Dredge the chicken pieces with flour; dip in the batter; then roll in the coconut.

**5.** Heat the oil in a large skillet to 375° on a deep-fat frying thermometer, or when a pinch of the coated chicken dropped into the oil will sizzle and pop to the surface. The oil should not be so hot it burns the coconut chicken. Fry the chicken until it is golden brown, about 2 minutes on each side. Do not crowd the skillet. As they brown, remove the pieces to paper toweling.

**Make-ahead Tip:** Chicken can be frozen. Freeze in a single layer; remove to plastic bag; seal. Defrost in single layer on cookie sheet. Heat in a moderate oven (350°) for 15 minutes. Can also be refrigerated for up to 4 days. Heat as for frozen chicken.

# CURRY SAUCE

*Makes about 2½ cups.*

1 medium-size onion, finely chopped (½ cup)
1 small sweet red or green pepper, halved, seeded and finely chopped
2 tablespoons butter
1 tablespoon curry powder
½ teaspoon salt
4 tablespoons all-purpose flour
2 cups chicken broth

**1.** Sauté the onion and pepper in the butter in a medium-size saucepan for 5 minutes or until the onion is tender. Stir in the curry powder, salt and flour.

**2.** Gradually add the chicken broth; cook, stirring constantly, until the mixture thickens and bubbles. Lower the heat; cover and simmer, stirring occasionally, for 15 minutes. Pour into a serving bowl.

*Make-ahead Tip:* Sauce can be frozen in a tightly covered container. Defrost, reheat in saucepan over low heat, stirring often. Or refrigerate, covered, for up to 4 days. Reheat as for frozen.

# 7

## Soups

For many believers there's nothing quite like a bowl of chicken soup for keeping the bleak, cold world at bay. In spite of all the jokes about it, chicken soup is still one of the great dishes of the world. Recipes may vary from place to place, but a good chicken soup is sustaining, nutritious and easy to digest. While it may not always cure what ails you, it can bring a warm glow of contentment with each spoonful.

In this chapter there are old-fashioned chicken soups, such as Chicken-Rice Soup, the kind that mother used to make, and modern versions. There are also several turkey soups, most of them using up the last little scraps of the holiday bird. Rich Cream of Turkey Soup and Turkey-Noodle Soup are tasty examples.

# CHICKEN BROTH

Just like mother used to make. Keep some in the freezer for special dishes.

*Makes 12 cups.*

| | | | |
|---|---|---|---|
| 2 | broiler/fryers (3 to 3½ pounds each) | 2 | celery stalks |
| 2 | medium-size carrots, pared and chopped | | Handful of celery leaves |
| | | 3 | sprigs parsley |
| 1 | large parsnip, pared and chopped | 1 | leek, trimmed and well washed (optional) |
| 1 | large onion, chopped (1 cup) | 12 | cups cold water |
| | | 1 | tablespoon salt |
| | | 12 | whole black peppercorns |

**1.** Combine the chicken (with the giblets but not with the livers), carrots, parsnip, onion and celery in a large kettle. Tie the celery leaves, parsley and leek, if used, together with string; add to the kettle. Add cold water to cover the chicken.

**2.** Heat slowly to boiling; skim; add the salt and peppercorns; lower the heat; cover the kettle. Simmer very slowly for 1 to 1½ hours or until the meat falls off the bones; cool the chicken to lukewarm in the broth. Remove the meat and vegetables from the broth; discard the greens.

**3.** Strain the broth through cheesecloth into a large bowl. (There should be about 12 cups.) Use this broth in any recipes calling for chicken broth.

**4.** When the meat is cool enough to handle, remove and discard the skin and bones from the chicken; cut the meat into bite-size pieces; use in recipes that call for cooked chicken. To store in the refrigerator up to 3 to 4 days, keep in a covered container. To freeze, pack in 1- or 2-cup portions in plastic bags or plastic freezer containers.

**5.** To store the broth in the refrigerator up to 4 days, leave a layer of fat on the surface of the broth until ready to use; then lift the fat off and discard it or use it in other cooking. To freeze, transfer the broth to plastic feezer containers, allowing space on top for expansion. Freeze until ready to use (3 to 4 months maximum).

# TURKEY BROTH

*Makes 8 cups.*

Carcass of 12- to 14-pound turkey
2 quarts water
2 celery stalks, broken in half
1 carrot, pared and quartered
1 onion, quartered
6 whole black peppercorns
1 large bay leaf
1 tablespoon salt

**1.** Combine all the ingredients in a large kettle. Bring to boiling; lower the heat to simmer. Cook, uncovered, for 2 to 3 hours. Strain.
**2.** When the bones are cool enough to handle, remove the meat and use in recipes. Chill the broth in the refrigerator. Remove the fat.

# HEARTY GIBLET SOUP

Don't throw out the giblets. Keep in frozen packets until you have 2 cups; then make this meal-in-a-bowl soup.

*Makes 6 servings.*

1 pound chicken giblets
3 tablespoons butter or margarine
½ cup all-purpose flour
8 cups Chicken Broth (page 128) OR: 8 envelopes or teaspoons instant chicken broth and 8 cups water
2 teaspoons salt
¼ teaspoon pepper
1 bay leaf
1 teaspoon leaf sage, crumbled
2 cups cooked rice
½ cup chopped celery
Chopped parsley

**1.** Sauté the giblets in the butter in a large kettle.
**2.** Stir in the flour; cook, stirring constantly, for 5 minutes, or until the flour browns.
**3.** Combine the chicken giblets with the chicken broth, salt, pepper, bay leaf and sage in the kettle; cover.
**4.** Bring to bubbling; lower the heat; simmer for 1 hour and 30 minutes or until the giblets are tender. Stir in the rice and celery and cook for 15 minutes to heat the rice. Serve in heated soup bowls topped with chopped parsley.

# RICH CREAM OF TURKEY SOUP

One of the best parts of a turkey is the soup you can make.

*Makes 6 servings.*

| | | | |
|---|---|---|---|
| 1 | large leek, well washed and chopped OR: 2 large onions, chopped (2 cups) | 8 | cups Chicken Broth (page 128) OR: 8 envelopes or teaspoons instant chicken broth and 8 cups water |
| 1 | cup chopped celery | | Carcass of turkey plus neck and giblets |
| ¼ | cup (½ stick) butter or margarine | | |
| 2 | tablespoons all-purpose flour | 1 | tall can evaporated milk |
| | | 3 | egg yolks |

**1.** Sauté the leeks and celery in the butter in a large kettle until golden. Stir in the flour and brown lightly, stirring constantly.

**2.** Add the chicken broth, carcass, neck and giblets. Bring to boiling; lower the heat; cover the kettle.

**3.** Simmer for 2 hours or until the mixture is rich in flavor. Turn off the heat under the kettle and allow the carcass to rest in the liquid until cool enough to handle. Strain the liquid in the kettle into a large saucepan and discard the bones. Dice any tidbits of meat.

**4.** Beat the evaporated milk and egg yolks together in a large bowl with a wire whisk; beat in about 2 cups of the hot broth; return to the saucepan. Heat gently, stirring often, just until hot; taste and season with salt and pepper; add the diced meat.

# PURÉED CREAM OF TURKEY SOUP

*Makes 6 servings.*

| | | | |
|---|---|---|---|
| 1 | teaspoon salt | 1 | small parsnip, pared and chopped (½ cup) |
| ⅛ | teaspoon pepper | | |
| 5 | cups Turkey Broth (page 129) or canned chicken broth | 1 | tablespoon dry sherry (optional) |
| 1 | large carrot, pared and chopped (½ cup) | ½ | cup light cream |
| ½ | cup chopped celery | 1 | cup chopped cooked turkey |
| 2 | medium-size leeks, washed well and chopped (1 cup) | 2 | tablespoons chopped parsley or watercress |

**1.** Add the salt and pepper to the broth in a large saucepan; heat to boiling. Add the carrot, celery, leeks and parsnip. Lower the heat; simmer until the vegetables are barely soft, about 20 minutes. Remove from the heat.

**2.** Pour the soup through a strainer into a bowl. Purée the vegetables in an electric blender. Return the purée and broth to the pan. Add the sherry, cream and turkey to the soup.

**3.** Heat just to simmering over medium heat. Do not boil. Add the parsley; serve.

## CORN 'N' CHICKEN CHOWDER

Leftover turkey can be used in place of the chicken in this recipe.

*Makes 4 servings.*

| | |
|---|---|
| 4 slices bacon | 1 can (1 pound) cream-style |
| 1 large onion, chopped | corn |
| (1 cup) | 1 tall can evaporated milk |
| 2 large potatoes, pared and | Salt and pepper |
| sliced | Chopped parsley |
| 2 cups chicken broth | |
| 2 cups diced cooked chicken | |
| or turkey | |

**1.** Brown the bacon in a large saucepan; remove with tongs and crumble onto paper toweling; reserve.

**2.** Pour off all but 3 tablespoons bacon fat. Sauté the onion in the bacon fat for 5 minutes; add the sliced potatoes and chicken broth to the pan.

**3.** Bring to boiling; lower the heat; cover the pan; simmer for 15 minutes or until the potatoes are tender.

**4.** Add the diced chicken, cream-style corn and evaporated milk. Bring to bubbling; taste and season with salt and pepper. Ladle into a heated soup tureen and top with the crumbled bacon and parsley just before serving.

# SPRINGTIME CHICKEN SOUP

If you want a fresh vegetable taste in soup, add them just before serving.

*Makes 6 servings.*

| | | | |
|---|---|---|---|
| 1 | large onion, sliced | 6 | medium-size boiling |
| 1 | white turnip, pared and | | potatoes, pared and sliced |
| | diced | 2 | large carrots, pared and |
| 2 | celery stalks with leaves, | | sliced |
| | chopped | 2 | large zucchini, trimmed and |
| 2 | envelopes or teaspoons | | sliced |
| | instant chicken broth | 1 | small yellow squash, |
| 2 | teaspoons salt | | trimmed and sliced |
| 6 | whole black peppercorns | 1 | cup frozen green peas |
| 8 | cups water | | (from a 1-pound bag) |
| 1 | broiler/fryer (3 pounds), | ⅓ | cup cornstarch |
| | cut up | ¾ | cup cold water |

**1.** Combine the onion, turnip, celery, instant chicken broth, salt, peppercorns and water in a large kettle; cover.

**2.** Bring to boiling; lower the heat; simmer for 45 minutes; add the cut up chicken and simmer for 30 minutes or until the chicken is tender; remove the kettle from the heat; allow the chicken to cool in the liquid.

**3.** Slip the skin from the chicken and cut the meat into bite-size pieces. Place in a medium-size bowl; strain the chicken broth into a large bowl; cover with plastic wrap; refrigerate along with the chicken pieces.

**4.** At serving time, pour the broth into the kettle; bring to boiling; add the potatoes and cook for 10 minutes; add the carrots, zucchini and yellow squash; simmer for 10 minutes; add the peas and chicken pieces; simmer for 10 minutes longer or until the chicken is heated through. Bring to boiling.

**5.** Combine the cornstarch and cold water in a cup; stir into the boiling liquid; cook, stirring constantly, until the liquid thickens and bubbles for 3 minutes. Ladle into heated soup bowls.

# HEARTY BEEF AND CHICKEN SOUP

This man-pleasing soup is truly a meal in a soup bowl.

*Makes 12 servings.*

1½ pounds chuck steak, cut into 1-inch cubes
1 large onion, chopped (1 cup)
1 broiler/fryer (about 2½ to 3 pounds)
1 cup chopped celery
2 teaspoons salt
1 teaspoon seasoned salt
¼ teaspoon pepper
1 teaspoon leaf rosemary, crumbled
1 teaspoon leaf thyme, crumbled
1 bay leaf
10 cups water
2 cups uncooked medium noodles
Grated Parmesan cheese (optional)
Chopped parsley (optional)

**1.** Brown the beef in its own fat in a kettle or Dutch oven; stir in the onion and sauté lightly until it is soft.

**2.** Add the chicken, celery, salt, seasoned salt, pepper, rosemary, thyme, bay leaf and water to the kettle; bring to boiling; cover. Simmer for 45 minutes or until the chicken is tender; then remove the chicken from the kettle. Continue cooking the beef for 20 minutes longer or until it is tender.

**3.** While the beef finishes cooking, pull the skin from the chicken and take the meat from bones; cut the meat into cubes. Return to the kettle; bring to boiling.

**4.** Stir in the noodles. Cook for 10 minutes or the until noodles are tender.

**5.** Ladle into soup plates. Sprinkle with Parmesan cheese and chopped parsley, if you wish.

# SAVORY LIMA BEAN SOUP

It's as thick as a stew and as rich as a soup. Here is the perfect way to make chicken giblets into a low-cost main dish.

*Makes 8 servings.*

| | | | |
|---|---|---|---|
| 1 | pound dried lima beans | 3 | envelopes or teaspoons |
| | Cold water | | instant beef broth |
| 1 | pound chicken giblets | 2 | teaspoons salt |
| ½ | pound breakfast sausage links | 1 | teaspoon leaf thyme, crumbled |
| 1 | large onion, chopped (1 cup) | 1 | sweet red pepper, halved, seeded and diced |
| 1 | clove garlic, minced | | |
| 1 | small yellow turnip, pared, sliced and diced | | Chopped parsley (optional) |

**1.** Wash the beans in a strainer under cold running water; place in a kettle and add cold water to cover the beans by 2 inches.

**2.** Bring to boiling; cover the kettle; turn off the heat; allow to stand for 1 hour.

**3.** While the beans soak, brown the giblets and sausages in a large skillet; remove with a slotted spoon.

**4.** Sauté the onion, garlic, and turnip in the pan drippings; stir in the instant beef broth, salt and thyme; cook for 1 minute, stirring constantly.

**5.** Add the giblets, sausages, onion mixture and diced red pepper to the beans in the kettle; stir well with a wooden spoon and add water, if needed, to just cover the beans.

**6.** Simmer, stirring several times, for 2 hours, or until the beans are tender. Ladle into a heated soup tureen, and just before serving sprinkle with the chopped parsley, if you wish.

# LAST-MINUTE CHOWDER

Here is a flavorful way to extend the holiday bird in a substantial soup.

*Makes 6 servings.*

| | | | |
|---|---|---|---|
| 1 | medium-size onion, chopped (½ cup) | 1 | can (about 1 pound) cream-style corn |
| 2 | tablespoons butter or margarine | 1 | small can evaporated milk |
| 2 | cans (10¾ ounces each) condensed chicken noodle soup | 2 | cups diced cooked turkey |
| | | ¼ | teaspoon pepper |
| 1¼ | cups water | 2 | tablespoons chopped parsley |

**1.** In a medium saucepan, sauté the onion in the butter until soft.
**2.** Stir in the chicken noodle soup, water, cream-style corn, evaporated milk, turkey and pepper. Bring to boiling.
**3.** Pour into heated soup bowls or mugs; sprinkle with the parsley.

# HEARTY WINTER SOUP

You don't have to spend all day in the kitchen to perpare this hearty soup.

*Makes 6 servings.*

| | | | |
|---|---|---|---|
| 1 | medium-size onion, chopped (½ cup) | 1 | can (26 ounces) tomato juice |
| 2 | medium-size potatoes, pared and chopped | 1½ | teaspoons salt |
| 1 | can (1 pound) whole-kernel corn, drained | ¼ | teaspoon pepper |
| | | 1 | tablespoon butter or margarine |
| 1 | package (10 ounces) frozen lima beans, cooked and drained | 1 | tablespoon Worcestershire sauce |
| 2 | cans (13¾ ounces each) chicken broth | 3 | cups diced cooked chicken |

**1.** Combine the onion, potatoes, corn, lima beans, chicken broth, tomato juice, salt, pepper, butter and Worcestershire sauce in a kettle or Dutch oven.
**2.** Bring slowly to boiling; lower the heat; cover the kettle; simmer for 30 minutes. Add the chicken and cook for 5 minutes longer or until the vegetables are tender.

# GINGERROOT CHICKEN WING SOUP

This recipe transforms the lowly chicken wing into banquet fare.

*Makes 4 servings.*

8    chicken wings
     (about 1½ pounds)
1    tablespoon peanut or
     corn oil
4    ½-inch-thick slices fresh
     gingerroot, peeled
¼    cup dry sherry
5    cups boiling water OR:
     2 cans (13¾ ounces each)
     chicken broth diluted with
     water to make 5 cups

1    green onion
     Salt to taste
     Soy Sauce Dip (optional,
     recipe follows)
     Chopped green onion
     (optional)

**1.** Remove the tips of the chicken wings. Cut each wing into two sections.

**2.** Heat a large saucepan or skillet; add the oil and gingerroot; stir-fry for 1 minute. Add the chicken wing sections; brown on both sides, stirring constantly. Add the sherry; cover immediately and let sizzle for 1 minute.

**3.** Add the boiling water and green onion. Bring to boiling again; lower the heat; cover. Simmer slowly, for 30 minutes or until the chicken wings are tender. Remove the green onion; skim off any fat. The gingerroot pieces retain their flavor and may be left in the soup. Taste; add salt if needed. Ladle into soup plates; garnish with additional chopped green onion, if you wish. Soy Sauce Dip may be served with the chicken wings for additional flavor.

# SOY SAUCE DIP

*Makes about ½ cup.*

¼    cup light or regular soy
     sauce
1    tablespoon sesame, peanut
     or corn oil

½    teaspoon sugar
2    tablespoons chicken broth
     or water (optional)

Combine the soy sauce, oil and sugar in a small bowl. Serve in individual dip dishes. The sauce is concentrated and should be used sparingly. You may add 2 tablespoons chicken broth or water to dilute the sauce, if you wish.

**Variation:** Add 2 teaspoons minced green onion and 1 teaspoon fresh garlic paste. (Chop the garlic, then mash with the flat of a broad knife.)

# CHICKEN AND DUMPLING SOUP

Here is a soup that makes many think of Mom's good home cooking.
*Makes 6 servings.*

### Chicken Dumplings
1   cup diced cooked chicken
1   cooked chicken liver
    (optional)
1   egg
½   cup all-purpose flour
¼   cup water
1   teaspoon salt
    Pinch of pepper
    Pinch of ground nutmeg
1   tablespoon chopped parsley
2   cups water

### Soup
¼   cup sliced green onion
¼   cup butter or margarine
¼   cup all-purpose flour
6   cups Chicken Broth
    (page 128)
1   package (10 ounces) frozen
    mixed vegetables
½   teaspoon salt
1½ cups diced cooked
    chicken

**1.** Make the Chicken Dumplings: Combine the chicken, liver (if used), egg, flour, water, salt, pepper and nutmeg in an electric food processor fitted with a steel blade. Process on medium speed until the mixture is smooth. Turn into a small bowl; stir in the parsley; cover the bowl with plastic wrap.

**2.** Bring the water to boiling in a large saucepan. With a teaspoon, shape the chicken mixture, half at a time, into ¾-inch balls. Drop one by one into the boiling water. Simmer gently, uncovered, for 8 to 10 minutes; remove with a slotted spoon; keep warm.

**3.** Make the Soup: In a kettle or Dutch oven, sauté the onion in the butter for 3 to 4 minutes or until soft but not brown. Stir in the flour gradually until smooth; add the chicken broth, stirring constantly. Bring to boiling; add the vegetables and salt; cover. Cook for 10 minutes or until the vegetables are tender.

**4.** Add the chicken dumplings and 1½ cups chicken and heat for 5 minutes. Ladle into soup bowls.

# FRENCH CHICKEN GUMBO

Varying a little from the original, this good main-dish soup recipe was brought to this country by French refugees.

*Makes 8 servings.*

| | | | |
|---|---|---|---|
| 2 | slices bacon, diced | 1 | teaspoon liquid red-pepper seasoning |
| 2 | tablespoons vegetable oil | | |
| 2 | tablespoons all-purpose flour | 1 | can (16 ounces) stewed tomatoes |
| 1 | large onion, chopped (1 cup) | 4 | whole chicken breasts (3 pounds total weight), halved |
| 1 | sweet green pepper, halved, seeded and chopped | 4 | cups water |
| 2 | cloves garlic, chopped | 1 | package (10 ounces) frozen okra |
| 1 | teaspoon salt | 2 | teaspoons filé powder (optional) |
| ¼ | to 1 teaspoon black pepper | | |
| 2 | teaspoons Worcestershire sauce | 2 | cups long-grain white rice |

**1.** Cook the bacon, stirring occasionally, until the edges curl and the bacon is browned. Combine the oil and flour in a heavy kettle or Dutch oven. Cook and stir over medium heat until the mixture is golden brown.

**2.** Add the onion, green pepper and garlic. Cook for 4 to 5 minutes or until the vegetables are wilted.

**3.** Add the salt, pepper, Worcestershire, tomatoes, chicken and water. Bring to boiling; lower the heat; simmer for 45 minutes, basting the chicken occasionally with the liquid in the kettle.

**4.** Remove the chicken breasts from the kettle; cool, skin and bone. Cut the chicken meat into large pieces.

**5.** Remove the fat from the surface of the liquid. Bring to boiling; add the okra; cook, stirring occasionally, for 15 minutes. Return the chicken to the kettle; heat until thoroughly hot. A few minutes before serving, stir in filé, if you wish.

**6.** While soup is cooking, cook the rice following label directions.

**7.** Spoon a serving of rice into a large soup bowl and ladle the gumbo over it.

# CHICKEN-RICE SOUP

A stick-to-the-ribs kind of soup, great for cool days.

*Makes 12 one-cup servings.*

**For Broth**
1    broiler/fryer (2 pounds)
4½  cups water
1    onion, quartered
1    bay leaf
6    sprigs parsley
     Celery tops

**For Soup**
2    cans (1 pound each) tomatoes

1    potato, diced (1 cup)
1    large onion, diced (1 cup)
1    sweet green pepper, diced (1 cup)
2    carrots, diced (1 cup)
½    cup long-grain white rice
1    tablespoon salt
½    teaspoon pepper
2    envelopes instant chicken broth

**1.** To make the broth, put the chicken in the water in a Dutch oven. Add the onion, bay leaf, parsley and celery tops. Cover and cook for 1 hour or until the chicken is tender. Remove the solids from the broth to a bowl; strain the broth; return the broth to the Dutch oven.

**2.** While the chicken is cooling, prepare the vegetables. Add the tomatoes, potato, onion, green pepper, carrots, rice, salt, pepper and instant chicken broth to the broth in the Dutch oven. Simmer, covered, for 30 minutes.

**3.** When the chicken is cool enough to handle, skin and bone and cut the meat into small pieces (about 2½ cups). Add to the soup. Cover and cook for 15 minutes or until the vegetables and rice are tender.

# CURRIED APPLE AND CHICKEN SOUP

Versatile curry combines well with apple for a smooth colorful soup.

*Makes 6 servings.*

1    medium-size onion, chopped
4    tablespoons butter or margarine
2    to 3 apples
2    teaspoons curry powder

1    can (10¾ ounces) condensed cream of chicken soup
2    cups water
½    teaspoon salt
1    cup light cream
1    tablespoon lemon juice

**1.** Sauté the onion in the butter in a large saucepan until soft, about 5 minutes. Coarsely shred enough apple to make about 1 cup; add to the saucepan; stir in the curry powder. Cook and stir for 1 to 2 minutes. Add the soup; gradually stir in the water.

**2.** Bring to boiling, stirring often. Lower the heat; cover. Simmer, stirring often, for 10 minutes. Purée, half at a time, in the container of an electric blender. Return to the saucepan. Add the salt and cream and heat through.

**3.** Shred the remaining apple to make about 1 cup; toss with the lemon juice; add to the soup just before serving.

**Chilled Soup:** Add the salt and cream to the puréed mixture; cool; then chill for several hours. Just before serving add the shredded apple tossed with the lemon juice. Garnish with a green onion and a thin slice of apple, if you wish.

## TURKEY SOUP WITH EGG DUMPLINGS

*Makes 6 servings.*

| | |
|---|---|
| ½ cup *sifted* all-purpose flour | ⅛ teaspoon turmeric (optional) |
| ¼ teaspoon salt | 1 medium-size onion, chopped (½ cup) |
| 2 tablespoons butter or margarine, softened | |
| 2 eggs, beaten | 1 package (10 ounces) frozen corn |
| 6 cups Turkey Broth (page 129) or canned chicken broth | 1 package (10 ounces) frozen baby limas |
| 1 teaspoon salt | 1 cup chopped cooked turkey |
| ⅛ teaspoon pepper | Chopped parsley (optional) |
| ½ teaspoon leaf thyme, crumbled | |

**1.** Sift the flour with the salt. Stir into the butter in a medium-size mixing bowl. Add the eggs, beating until well blended.

**2.** Bring the broth to boiling in a large saucepan or kettle with the salt, pepper, thyme and turmeric. Add the onion, corn, limas and turkey. Return the soup to boiling.

**3.** Drop the dumpling batter by teaspoonfuls into the boiling soup to make 12 dumplings. Lower the heat to keep the soup simmering; cover and cook for 20 minutes or until the dumplings are cooked through.

**4.** Serve in warm soup plates or bowls. Sprinkle with finely chopped parsley, if you wish.

# PENNSYLVANIA CHICKEN AND CORN SOUP

*Makes 12 servings.*

| | | | |
|---|---|---|---|
| 1 | stewing chicken (about 5 pounds), cut up | 2 | celery tops |
| 8 | cups water | 2 | packages (10 ounces each) frozen whole-kernel corn |
| 1 | tablespoon salt | ⅛ | teaspoon crumbled saffron threads |
| 10 | whole black peppercorns | | |
| 1 | bay leaf | 2 | tablespoons chopped parsley |
| 2 | small onions, peeled | | |

**1.** Combine the chicken, water, salt, peppercorns, bay leaf, onions, and celery tops in a large kettle. Bring slowly to boiling; lower the heat. Simmer slowly for 2 to 2½ hours or until the meat falls off the bones. Remove the meat from the broth.

**2.** Strain the broth through cheesecloth into a large bowl. When the meat is cool enough to handle, remove the skin and bones from the chicken; cut the meat into bite-size pieces. Skim as much fat as possible from the broth or refrigerate until the fat solidifies.

**3.** To serve, return the chicken to the broth; bring to boiling. Add the corn and saffron; simmer for 10 minutes or until the corn is tender. Taste and add more salt and pepper if necessary. Stir in the parsley.

---

## INSTANT SOUPS FOR FLAVOR DIVIDENDS

Canned chicken broth, instant chicken broth in jars or envelopes and chicken bouillon cubes streamline the preparation of some dishes and enhance the taste of others. Any variety of chicken broth can be the basis of homemade soup. Broth also adds fuller and richer flavor to main dishes when it's used as a cooking liquid in casseroles and stews. Accompaniments such as rice and vegetables also taste much more flavorful when they are simmered in chicken broth.

# GRANDMOTHER'S CHICKEN SOUP

*Makes about 10 servings.*

| | | | |
|---|---|---|---|
| 1 | whole chicken (about 3½ to 4 pounds) | 2 | tablespoons chopped fresh dill OR: 2 teaspoons leaf dillweed |
| 1 | large clove garlic | 1 | lemon slice |
| 1 | whole yellow onion | 2 | teaspoons salt |
| 2 | whole cloves | 10 | whole black peppercorns |
| 1 | large carrot, quartered | 2 | cans (13¾ ounces each) chicken broth |
| 1 | celery stalk with leaves, broken | 10 | cups water |
| 1 | medium-size turnip, pared and roughly chopped | | Matzo Balls (recipe follows) |
| 1 | large parsnip, pared and roughly chopped | | Vegetable Garnish: Pare and chop 1 onion, 1 turnip, 1 carrot and 1 parsnip |
| 2 | parsley sprigs | | |

**1.** Remove all fat and excess skin from the cavity and neck of the chicken with scissors. Cut off the wing tips; skin neck and scrape off the fat. Reserve all the skin, the wing tips and the fat. (You should have about ⅔ cup.)

**2.** Put the chicken in a large kettle or Dutch oven. Add the garlic, onion, cloves, carrot, celery, turnip, parsnip, parsley, dill, lemon slice, salt, peppercorns, chicken broth and water. Heat to boiling; lower the heat; cover. Simmer for about 1 hour or until the chicken is tender. Remove the scum and fat with a spoon as it rises to the surface.

**3.** When the chicken is tender, remove it from the pot; boil the broth for 20 minutes; strain; cool and refrigerate for several hours or overnight.

**4.** Put the reserved chicken fat, wing tips and skin into a small saucepan. Simmer with ⅓ cup water for about 30 minutes. Watch carefully—the water will be replaced by melting chicken fat. When the fat begins to sizzle, it is rendered. Remove 3 tablespoons of the fat; chill and reserve for Matzo Balls. (If you don't have enough fat, skim the congealed fat from the chilled broth.)

**5.** Prepare the Matzo Balls; refrigerate until ready to finish the soup.

**6.** To serve, skim the fat from the top of the chilled broth. Heat the broth to boiling; add the chopped Vegetable Garnish. Lower the heat; simmer until tender, about 20 minutes. Taste; add salt and freshly ground pepper, if needed. Add the matzo balls and continue to simmer for 10 minutes. Ladle into soup bowls with 1 matzo ball to each bowl.

*Note:* The chicken can be used in a salad, sandwiches or any other recipe calling for cooked chicken.

# MATZO BALLS (Knaidlich)

*Makes 10.*

3  eggs
6  tablespoons cold club soda
3  tablespoons reserved
 rendered chicken fat

½  teaspoon salt
 Pinch of white pepper
¾  cup matzo meal

**1.** Beat the eggs slightly in a medium-size bowl. Stir in the club soda, chicken fat, salt and pepper.

**2.** Add the matzo meal slowly, about 2 tablespoons at a time. Cover; refrigerate for about 5 hours.

**3.** Heat 3 quarts of water to boiling in a large saucepan. Shape the matzo mixture into balls with wet hands, using a rounded tablespoon for each. Drop into boiling water; lower the heat; simmer for 25 minutes. Remove with a slotted spoon; cool; refrigerate until about 30 minutes before heating in soup.

---

**STORING SOUP**

• You can put hot soup directly in the refrigerator if it doesn't raise the refrigerator's temperature to 45°. Cool large quantities by putting the container of hot soup in a bowl or basin of ice water.

• Remove any congealed fat from surface before reheating.

# CHINESE CHICKEN WITH HAM SOUP

The few ingredients in this easy-to-make recipe produce
a full-flavored soup.

*Makes 6 servings.*

| | |
|---|---|
| 1 broiler/fryer (3½ to 4 pounds), quartered | 1 green onion |
| ½ pound Smithfield ham, trimmed, rinsed well, skin left on OR: ½ pound prosciutto ham OR: ½ pound boiled ham | 1 celery cabbage (1 pound), cut into 1-inch pieces |
| | Hot cooked rice (optional) |

**1.** Combine the chicken and ham in a kettle or Dutch oven; add
enough cold water to cover (about 8 cups).
**2.** Heat slowly to boiling; skim; add the green onion; lower the heat;
cover. Simmer slowly for 1 to 1½ hours or until the chicken is tender.
Remove the chicken and ham from the kettle.
**3.** When the meat is cool enough to handle, remove and discard the
skin and bones from the chicken; cut the meat into bite-size pieces;
cut the ham into thin strips.
**4.** Return the chicken, ham and celery cabbage to the kettle; cover;
cook for 15 minutes or until the celery cabbage is tender. Serve with
hot cooked rice, if you wish.


# TURKEY AND BEEF OVEN SOUP

*Cook at 200° for 8 to 9 hours.*
*Makes 12 servings.*

| | |
|---|---|
| 3 pounds beef shank | 1 large onion, unpeeled, cut in half and studded with 6 cloves |
| 6 carrots | |
| 4 parsnips | |
| 4 celery stalks | 2 to 3 celery tops |
| 3 to 4 pounds turkey legs, thighs and wings, thawed | 8 whole black peppercorns |
| | 1 bay leaf |
| | Pinch of leaf thyme |
| 3 quarts cold water | 1 tablespoon salt |

**1.** Trim the fat from the beef. Place the beef in a Dutch oven or heavy kettle (large enough to accommodate all the ingredients with at least 3 inches of water to cover). Brown the beef on all sides.
**2.** Pare the carrots and parsnips; wash the celery and add the vegetables to the pot; cook and stir for 1 minute.
**3.** Add the turkey parts, water, onion, celery tops, peppercorns, bay leaf, thyme and salt.
**4.** Bring to boiling; remove from heat; skim off any foam; cover the pot and cook in a very slow oven (200°) for 8 to 9 hours.
**5.** Remove the meat, turkey and vegetables with a slotted spoon; arrange on a platter. Skim and strain the broth. Taste; add additional salt and pepper, if needed. Serve some broth with some of the meat, turkey and vegetables. Reserve the remaining broth to make additional soup.

*Note:* If the dish is not ready at the end of the longest cooking time, raise the oven temperature to moderate (325°) and continue cooking until done, about 15 minutes.

## TURKEY-NOODLE SOUP

*Makes 6 servings.*

| | | | |
|---|---|---|---|
| 5 | cups Turkey Broth (page 129) | 2 | bay leaves |
| 1 | cup diced cooked turkey | 1 | teaspoon leaf oregano, crumbled |
| 1 | can (16 ounces) tomatoes with liquid | ½ | teaspoon leaf basil, crumbled |
| 2 | large onions, diced | 1 | teaspoon salt |
| 1 | large celery stalk, diced | ¼ | teaspoon pepper |
| 2 | tablespoons chopped parsley | 1 | package (10 ounces) frozen mixed vegetables |
| 2 | large cloves garlic, minced | 1 | cup broken spaghetti |
| ¼ | cup catsup | | |

**1.** Remove the fat from the broth. Add the turkey, tomatoes, onion, celery, parsley, garlic, catsup, bay leaves, oregano, basil, salt and pepper. Bring to boiling; cover; lower the heat; simmer for 30 minutes.
**2.** Add the frozen vegetables and bring back to boiling. Add the spaghetti; lower the heat and simmer for 15 minutes.

# 8

## Salads and Sandwiches

**N**othing could be more appealing at the end of a hot summer's day than a cold, delicious salad filled with slivers of tender chicken. Because it blends so well with other ingredients, chicken can be found in salads with a wide variety of vegetables and salad greens, fruits, nuts, spices, herbs, dairy foods, dressings and all kinds of grains. There's just no limit to the salad potential for this versatile bird.

On the following pages are recipes for shimmering molds, such as Creamy Chicken Mousse, several pasta salad variations and some interesting salads that include potatoes or rice, like Buffet Russian Chicken-Potato Salad and Curried Turkey-Rice Salad. They are all ideal for those times when a light, nutritious and quickly served main course is called for.

Chicken and turkey sandwiches are always special, even when they are as basic as thin slices of white meat between two slices of bread with butter or mayonnaise. This chapter has several savory versions—some hot and some cold. It also includes tips on making and freezing sandwiches.

# HOW TO MAKE A BETTER CHICKEN SALAD

When you're preparing a chicken salad, these pointers will help you make it tastier and more nutritious.

### For health:
● When selecting greens, keep in mind that the darker the leaves, the more vitamin A and C they contain.
● The best greens for iron are spinach and beet; spinach is the highest in potassium and calcium content; the top sources for vitamin A are spinach, beet greens and watercress; for vitamin C, beet greens. All go well with chicken.
● To healthy-up a simple chicken salad, add a sprinkling of nuts or sunflower seeds, some raisins, bean sprouts or avocado slices.
● If you're counting calories, avoid dressings made with dairy sour cream, mayonnaise or cheese; instead opt for simple oil and vinegar or low-fat yogurt-based dressings—especially good with chicken.
● Instead of using olive oil in your dressing, try the higher-in-polyunsaturates vegetable, peanut, corn, soy, safflower and sunflower oils.

### For zest:
● Use a wide variety of greens for an interesting flavor. Consider escarole, chicory or endive mixed with the more traditional Boston, Bibb, iceberg or romaine lettuce.
● One of the following can easily be added to chicken salad to make it more delicious: bean sprouts, grapes, capers, cauliflowerets, olives, apples, pimientos, green beans, macaroni.
● To zip up a bland dressing, add a few drops of lemon juice. Or try a dash of dry mustard or curry powder.

## SALAD EXTRAS

**Pasta:** There are over 150 different kinds of pasta to choose from, and they all pair tastefully with chicken. Elbow macaroni is still a popular choice for everyday salads made with chicken and lots of vegetables, while shell macaroni is nice served with combinations of chicken and seafood in more exotic salads. Look for different-shaped pasta like cappelletti (little hats), farfalle (bow ties), or rigatoni for more interesting salads.

*Rice:* Like pasta, rice is a low-cost ingredient that teams well with chicken in salads. There are numerous varieties available: white, brown, precooked, converted, plus packaged mixes of seasoned rice. Wild rice, actually the seed of a water grass, adds a distinctive flavor to chicken and turkey salads.

## *TOSSED SALADS*

# CHICKEN AND CHINESE CABBAGE SALAD

*Makes 4 servings.*

| | | | |
|---|---|---|---|
| 1 | chicken breast (about 12 ounces) | ¼ | cup sliced green onion |
| 1 | package frozen snow peas | 1 | cup bean sprouts |
| ¼ | cup peanut or vegetable oil | 1 | medium-size head Chinese cabbage |
| 2 | tablespoons cider vinegar | 1 | tablespoon toasted sesame seeds |
| 4½ | teaspoons soy sauce | | |
| ¾ | teaspoon ground ginger | ½ | cup coarsely chopped walnuts |
| | Pinch *each* of sugar and salt | | |

**1.** Simmer the chicken breast in salted water until tender, about 10 minutes. Skin, bone and cube (1½ cups).

**2.** Defrost the snow peas; dry on paper toweling.

**3.** For the dressing, shake the oil, vinegar, soy sauce, ginger, sugar and salt in a screw-top jar.

**4.** Toss the chicken, snow peas, green onion and bean sprouts with the soy dressing; cover and refrigerate.

**5.** Slice enough cabbage to make 4 cups. Place in a bowl; arrange the chicken mixture on top. Sprinkle the sesame seeds and walnuts over the top. Toss lightly.

# CHICKEN AND CHERRY TOMATO SALAD
## WITH AVOCADO DRESSING

*Makes 4 servings.*

| | | | |
|---|---|---|---|
| 2 | tablespoons lemon juice | 1 | small very ripe avocado |
| ½ | teaspoon salt | 1 | green onion, minced |
| ½ | teaspoon sugar | ⅓ | cup olive oil |
| 2 | teaspoons leaf basil, crumbled | 3 | to 4 cups cubed cooked chicken |
| 2 | dashes liquid red-pepper seasoning | 1 | head Bibb lettuce |
| | | 1 | pint cherry tomatoes, halved |

**1.** For the dressing, combine the lemon juice, salt, sugar, basil and red-pepper seasoning in a cup. Peel, pit and mash the avocado with a fork in a small bowl and gradually stir in the lemon juice mixture and the onion. Slowly beat in the oil with a fork or whisk.
**2.** Toss the chicken with the dressing and spoon it into the center of a platter. Arrange the lettuce around the edge. Surround the chicken with tomatoes.

# MACARONI AND CHICKEN SALAD
## WITH TUNA DRESSING

Macaroni plus chicken and tuna make a filling main dish.
*Makes 6 servings.*

| | | | |
|---|---|---|---|
| 2 | cups small shells | 1 | can (7 ounces) water-packed tuna, drained |
| ¼ | cup light cream or milk | | |
| 1 | envelope instant chicken broth | ¼ | cup mayonnaise |
| | | ¼ | cup light cream |
| 1 | whole chicken breast (about 12 ounces), cooked | ⅓ | cup vegetable oil |
| | | 1 | tablespoon red wine vinegar |
| 1 | cup finely chopped celery | 1 | clove garlic |
| 1 | small onion, finely chopped (¼ cup) | ¼ | teaspoon leaf tarragon, crumbled |
| ½ | cup minced parsley | ¼ | teaspoon salt |
| | | ⅛ | teaspoon pepper |

**1.** Cook the pasta following label directions just until *al dente*; drain; put in a large bowl.

**2.** Combine ¼ cup cream and instant chicken broth in a cup; pour over the hot pasta; toss; let cool.

**3.** Skin and bone the chicken; shred or chop fine. Add the chicken, celery, onion and parsley to pasta; toss lightly.

**4.** Combine the tuna, mayonnaise, remaining cream, oil, vinegar, garlic, tarragon, salt and pepper in the container of an electric blender. Whirl, stopping blender often to scrape down the side, until the dressing is smooth. Pour the dressing over the salad; toss until evenly coated. Serve or cover and refrigerate for up to 24 hours.

## PASTA AND CHICKEN SALAD

The way to get good flavor in any pasta salad is to add the marinade to the hot pasta.

*Makes 6 servings.*

| | |
|---|---|
| **1** package (8 ounces) rotelle or elbow macaroni | **3** cups cubed cooked chicken or turkey |
| **¼** pound snow peas, trimmed (optional) | **1** sweet red pepper, halved, seeded and cut into slivers |
| **1** large zucchini, trimmed and sliced | **1** sweet green pepper, halved, seeded and cut into slivers |
| **¼** cup vegetable oil | **½** cup mayonnaise or salad dressing |
| **½** cup cider vinegar | Green onion fans (optional) |
| **1** small onion, minced | Radish roses (optional) |
| **2** teaspoons salt | |
| **¼** teaspoon pepper | |

**1.** Cook the pasta in boiling salted water following label directions, adding snow peas and zucchini during the last 2 minutes of cooking.

**2.** Drain the pasta and vegetables into a large glass or ceramic bowl; add the oil, ¼ cup of the vinegar, onion, salt and pepper; toss until very well blended.

**3.** Cover with plastic wrap; let stand for at least 2 hours to blend the flavors.

**4.** Add the cooked chicken and red and green pepper slivers. Combine the mayonnaise and remaining ¼ cup vinegar in a cup until smooth. Add to the pasta and chicken mixture and toss until well blended. Cover with plastic wrap and refrigerate until serving time.

**5.** Spoon into a large glass or ceramic bowl and garnish with green onion fans and radish roses, if you wish.

# ORIENTAL-STYLE CHICKEN SALAD

A pleasing combination of flavors for a main-dish salad.

*Makes 4 servings.*

½ pound mezzani (macaroni)
1 can (20 ounces) pineapple chunks in pineapple juice
1 envelope instant chicken broth
2 tablespoons sesame seeds
1 whole chicken breast (about 12 ounces), cooked
1 package (10 ounces) frozen snow peas
1 can (8 ounces) water chestnuts, sliced
4 green onions, thinly sliced
1½ tablespoons soy sauce
1 cup dairy sour cream
⅓ cup mayonnaise

**1.** Cook the mezzani following label directions just until *al dente;* drain and put in a large bowl.

**2.** Drain the pineapple, reserving the juice. Combine the chicken broth with 2 tablespoons of the reserved pineapple juice in a cup; pour over the pasta; toss.

**3.** Toast the sesame seeds in a small skillet for about 5 minutes. Transfer to a small bowl. Skin and bone the chicken; cut it into 2-inch strips. Blanch the snow peas in boiling water in a large saucepan for about 2 minutes; drain; cool.

**4.** Add the pineapple chunks, sesame seeds, water chestnuts, chicken, snow peas and green onions to the pasta.

**5.** Combine the soy sauce, sour cream, mayonnaise and 3 tablespoons of the reserved pineapple juice in a small bowl; beat until well mixed. Toss two thirds of the dressing with the salad. Cover; refrigerate for several hours. Add the remaining dressing; toss again just before serving.

# MACARONI SALAD WITH BROCCOLI, TURKEY AND HAM

*Makes 6 servings.*

| | | | |
|---|---|---|---|
| ⅓ | cup mayonnaise or salad dressing | 2 | cups fresh broccoli flowerets |
| 1 | container (8 ounces) dairy sour cream | ½ | pound cooked turkey roll, cubed (1½ cups) |
| 1 | envelope garlic salad dressing mix | 1 | package (4 ounces) sliced boiled ham, cut into ¼-inch-wide strips |
| 2 | pounds macaroni salad, from deli (4 cups) | | Tomato wedges (optional) |

**1.** Combine the mayonnaise, sour cream and salad dressing mix in a large bowl.

**2.** Add the macaroni salad, broccoli and turkey cubes; toss gently. Turn out onto a large serving plate; top with ham. (Salad can be refrigerated at this point, if you wish.) Garnish with tomato wedges, if you wish.

# CHICKEN SALAD CHINOISE

Contrasting flavors and textures make this salad a special lunchtime treat. Serve with whole wheat crackers, tomato juice and a chilled baked apple.

*Makes 3 generous servings (3½ cups salad).*

| | | | |
|---|---|---|---|
| 2 | cups diced cold leftover cooked chicken | ⅓ | cup plain lowfat yogurt |
| ½ | cup halved seedless green grapes | 2 | teaspoons Dijon-style mustard |
| ⅓ | cup chopped sweet green pepper | 1 | teaspoon soy sauce |
| ⅓ | cup sliced water chestnuts | | Salt |
| ¼ | cup chopped walnuts | | Pepper |
| | | | Lettuce leaves |

**1.** Combine the chicken, grapes, green pepper, water chestnuts and walnuts in a medium-size bowl.

**2.** Mix the yogurt with the mustard, soy sauce, salt and pepper.

**3.** Toss the salad with the dressing and serve on a bed of lettuce.

# CURRIED TURKEY-RICE SALAD

This attractive salad includes green peas and is flavored
with sour cream and chutney.

*Makes 6 servings.*

| | |
|---|---|
| 1 cup long-grain white rice | 1½ cups dairy sour cream |
| 1 package (10 ounces) frozen green peas | 1 teaspoon salt |
| | ¼ teaspoon pepper |
| 1 medium-size onion, finely chopped (½ cup) | 3 cups diced cooked turkey |
| | 1 cup minced carrots |
| ¼ cup vegetable oil | 3 tablespoons chutney |
| 1 tablespoon curry powder | Lettuce leaves |
| 3 tablespoons lemon juice | 1 tomato, sliced |

**1.** Cook the rice following label directions. Remove from the heat; cool; spoon into a large bowl. Cook the peas following label directions; drain; add to the rice.

**2.** Sauté the onion in the oil in a small skillet until soft. Add the curry powder and lemon juice and cook, stirring, for several seconds. Remove from the heat and mix with the sour cream, salt and pepper. Add to the rice and peas; mix well. Add the turkey, carrots and chutney; mix well. Refrigerate, covered, for 2 hours or longer.

**3.** To serve, spoon the salad over lettuce leaves on a round platter to form a mound. Top with tomato slices.

# GARNISHED CHICKEN-GRAPE SALAD

An attractive salad for a light weekend meal.

*Makes 6 servings.*

| | |
|---|---|
| 3 cups cubed cooked chicken breast | 2 tablespoons lemon juice |
| | 1 teaspoon salt |
| 1 cup diced sweet green pepper | ¼ teaspoon pepper |
| | Lettuce leaves |
| ½ cup chopped celery | 3 ounces slivered almonds, toasted |
| 2 cups seedless green grapes, halved | |
| | 2 hard-cooked eggs, sliced |
| ⅓ cup mayonnaise | 1 large tomato, cut into wedges |
| ⅓ cup dairy sour cream | |

**1.** Combine the chicken, pepper, celery, grapes, mayonnaise, sour cream, lemon juice, salt and pepper in a large bowl; mix well. Cover and refrigerate for at least 1 hour.

**2.** To serve, unmold the salad onto lettuce leaves on a round platter or into a large bowl. Top with the almonds. Arrange the eggs and tomato around the salad.

# BUFFET RUSSIAN CHICKEN-POTATO SALAD

An attractive salad made with a variety of ingredients.

*Makes 8 servings.*

| | | | |
|---|---|---|---|
| 1½ | pounds potatoes | 1 | cup cooked and diced carrots |
| 1 | cup dairy sour cream | 1 | cucumber, pared, seeded |
| 2 | tablespoons lemon juice | | and diced |
| 2 | tablespoons chopped fresh | 2 | medium-size mushrooms, |
| | dill OR: 2 teaspoons leaf | | diced (¼ cup) |
| | dillweed | 3 | tablespoons chopped sweet |
| 1 | teaspoon salt | | pickle |
| ¼ | teaspoon pepper | ¾ | cup mayonnaise |
| 2 | cups cubed cooked white | 2 | tablespoons drained capers |
| | meat of chicken | 6 | pimiento-stuffed olives, |
| 1 | cup cooked, drained and | | sliced |
| | diced beets | 1 | tomato, sliced |

**1.** Cook the potatoes in boiling salted water to cover in a large saucepan until tender, about 25 minutes. Drain, peel, and cut into ½-inch cubes to make 3 cups.

**2.** Combine the sour cream, lemon juice, salt and pepper in a large bowl. Add the potatoes; toss lightly. Let stand at room temperature for 20 minutes.

**3.** Stir in the chicken, beets, carrots, cucumber, mushrooms and pickles, mixing well. Refrigerate for at least 1 hour.

**4.** Just before serving, mound the salad on a platter. Spread with a thin layer of mayonnaise. Garnish with capers, olives and tomato slices.

# MOLDED TURKEY SALAD

*Makes 6 servings.*

2   **envelopes unflavored gelatin**

3   **cups Turkey Broth (page 129) or canned chicken broth (all fat removed)**

1   **teaspoon salt**

¼   **teaspoon turmeric**

½   **teaspoon leaf tarragon, crumbled**

3   **hard-cooked eggs**

2   **whole pimientos, drained**

¼   **cup sliced green onion**

3   **cups diced cooked turkey**

½   **cup chopped parsley Mayonnaise**

**1.** Sprinkle the gelatin over ½ cup of the turkey broth in a large bowl; let stand for 5 minutes to soften.

**2.** Combine the remaining 2½ cups turkey broth, salt, turmeric and tarragon in a saucepan; heat to boiling. Pour over the softened gelatin; stir to dissolve the gelatin. Chill until cool but still liquid.

**3.** Once cooled, spoon one quarter of the gelatin mixture into a 6-cup mold or 8½ x 3⅝ x 2⅝-inch loaf pan. Slice 1 egg and 1 pimiento. Arrange in the gelatin layer. Refrigerate for 5 minutes to set.

**4.** Combine the onion with the turkey. Dice the remaining eggs and pimiento. Layer the mold with spoonfuls of the turkey mixture; sprinkle with egg, pimiento and parsley. Repeat the layers.

**5.** Carefully pour the cool gelatin mixture into the filled mold, using a spatula to help the gelatin flow through the mold and around the edges. Refrigerate until firm.

**6.** Unmold; pass the mayonnaise separately.

# CHICKEN AND AVOCADO SALAD

Canned chicken makes this creamyTex-Mex salad quick and easy.

*Makes 6 servings.*

| | | | |
|---|---|---|---|
| 1 | envelope unflavored gelatin | ¼ | cup mayonnaise or salad |
| 1 | can (13¾ ounces) chicken | | dressing |
| | broth | 1 | teaspoon salt |
| 2 | cans (5 ounces each) boned | ¼ | teaspoon cayenne pepper |
| | chicken or turkey | | Tomato and Green Chili |
| 3 | medium-size avocados | | Sauce (recipe follows) |
| ¼ | cup lemon juice | | Mixed greens |

**1.** Mix the gelatin with ½ cup of the chicken broth in a saucepan; let stand to soften for 5 minutes; heat slowly over low heat, stirring constantly, just until dissolved.

**2.** Place the chicken in a large bowl; break up the larger pieces of meat with a fork.

**3.** Halve the avocados; remove the pits; peel off the skin. Cut the avocado into large chunks; place in the container of an electric blender; add the lemon juice, mayonnaise, salt and cayenne; cover. Whirl at high speed, adding a little chicken broth if necessary, just until the mixture is smooth.

**4.** Turn the blender to low speed; add the remaining chicken broth and the gelatin mixture. Pour over the chicken in the bowl; mix well. Pour the mixture into a 4- or 5-cup mold; chill for several hours or until firm.

**5.** Loosen the mold around the edge with a thin-bladed knife; dip quickly in and out of a pan of hot water. Invert onto a chilled serving plate; lift off the mold. Spoon the Tomato and Green Chili Sauce onto the plate around the mold or serve separately. Serve with a bowl of crisp mixed greens.

# TOMATO AND GREEN CHILI SAUCE

*Makes about 1¾ cups.*

| | | | |
|---|---|---|---|
| 2 | medium-size tomatoes, | ½ | cup chopped green onions |
| | chopped (1½ cups) | 1 | tablespoons red wine |
| 1 | canned hot green chili pepper, | | vinegar |
| | chopped (2 tablespoons) | 1 | tablespoon vegetable oil |

Combine the ingredients in a small bowl; toss to mix well. Chill for 30 minutes or until serving time.

# CURRIED SALAD INDIENNE

Chicken and ham top a curried rice layer.

*Makes 10 servings.*

**First Layer**

2 envelopes unflavored gelatin
3 cups chicken broth
1 bay leaf
¼ cup fresh lemon juice
1 cup fresh or frozen peas, cooked and chilled
2¼ cups diced cooked chicken
1 cup slivered boiled ham (about 6 ounces)
½ cup chopped celery
1 shallot, minced

**Second Layer**

1 envelope unflavored gelatin
½ cup bottled French dressing
1 can (8 ounces) crushed pineapple
1 tablespoon minced onion
½ cup slivered sweet red pepper
½ cup mayonnaise or salad dressing
1 to 3 teaspoons curry powder
2 cups cold *cooked* rice (⅔ cup raw)
 Green grape clusters
 Plum wedges

**1.** For the first layer, soften the gelatin in 1 cup of the chicken broth in a small saucepan. Add the bay leaf; cook over moderate heat, stirring constantly, until the gelatin dissolves. Pour into a large bowl; add the remaining 2 cups of broth; cool; remove the bay leaf.

**2.** Add the lemon juice to the cooled gelatin mixture. Pour about ¼ cup of mixture into an 8-cup mold; add ¼ cup peas to make the top layer. Refrigerate until the layer is sticky-firm.

**3.** Stir the chicken, ham, remaining peas, celery and shallot into the remaining gelatin; pour over the peas in the mold. Refrigerate until the layer is sticky-firm.

**4.** For the second layer, soften the gelatin in the dressing in a small saucepan; cook over moderate heat, stirring until the gelatin dissolves; cool. Add the pineapple with juice; let cool.

**5.** Combine the onion, red pepper, mayonnaise and curry powder in a medium-size bowl; add the rice; toss well. Add the cooled mixture; mix.

**6.** Spoon the rice mixture over the first layer. Press to pack firmly. Chill until firm.

**7.** To unmold, loosen the gelatin around the side of the mold with a long sharp knife. Quickly immerse the mold in a bowl of hot water; invert onto a plate moistened with cold water. Garnish with grape clusters and plum wedges.

# CREAMY CHICKEN MOUSSE

*Makes 6 servings.*

| | | | |
|---|---|---|---|
| 2 | envelopes unflavored gelatin | 1 | can (6¾ ounces) chunk chicken, drained and chopped |
| 1¼ | cups cold water | ½ | cup chopped celery |
| 1 | envelope or teaspoon instant chicken broth | 1 | tablespoon chopped green onion |
| | Radish slices | 1 | tablespoon lemon juice |
| | Halved black olives | | Pinch of pepper |
| 1 | can (10¾ ounces) condensed cream of chicken soup | ½ | cup heavy cream |
| | | | Boston lettuce |

**1.** Sprinkle the gelatin over 1 cup of the water in a small saucepan. Let stand for 5 minutes to soften. Stir over very low heat until the gelatin is dissolved. Stir in the chicken broth.

**2.** Remove ¼ cup of the gelatin mixture to a 1-cup glass measure; stir in the remaining ¼ cup water. Pour into an 8 x 4 x 3-inch loaf pan; refrigerate until syrupy. Arrange the radish slices and olive halves in a decorative pattern in the gelatin; refrigerate until firm.

**3.** Meanwhile, combine the remaining gelatin mixture, cream soup, chicken, celery, green onions, lemon juice and pepper in a medium-size bowl; refrigerate until slightly thickened.

**4.** Whip the cream in a small bowl until stiff; fold into chicken mixture. Carefully pour over the set layer in the loaf pan. Cover; refrigerate about 3 hours or until set. Unmold onto a lettuce-lined serving plate.

# MOLDED ASPARAGUS AND CHICKEN SALAD

An elegant, cool, molded entrée to highlight a summer buffet.

*Makes 8 servings.*

|   | | | |
|---|---|---|---|
| | Poached Chicken Breast (recipe follows) | 4 | tablespoons chopped parsley |
| 1 | small bunch asparagus (1½ to 2 pounds) | 2 | tablespoons chopped green onion |
| 2 | envelopes unflavored gelatin | ½ | cup mayonnaise |
| ½ | cup cold water | | Lettuce |
| 1 | hard-cooked egg, sliced | | |

**1.** Prepare the Poached Chicken Breast.

**2.** Wash and trim the asparagus spears. Tie into bundles and cook whole in boiling salted water just until tender, 10 to 13 minutes. Lift the asparagus from the water; run under cold water to stop the cooking. Drain on paper toweling. Reserve 1 cup of the cooking water.

**3.** Sprinkle the gelatin over the cold water in a small saucepan; let stand to soften for 5 minutes. Heat, stirring constantly, over very low heat until the gelatin is dissolved; remove from the heat. Strain the reserved chicken broth and reserved asparagus liquid through several layers of cheesecloth into a medium-size bowl. Add the gelatin; taste; add salt if needed.

**4.** Set a 6-cup mold or loaf pan in a larger pan with ice and water to chill. Pour about ½ cup of the gelatin mixture into the pan to make a thin layer. When just set, arrange the egg slices and reserved pieces of cooked carrot (from the Poached Chicken Breast) over the gelatin; spoon about ¼ cup of the gelatin over. Cut the asparagus tips to fit the mold; arrange over the eggs. Spoon in another ¼ cup of the gelatin mixture.

**5.** Stir the parsley, onion and reserved diced chicken into the remaining gelatin mixture; pour 1½ cups over the asparagus in the mold. Chill. Chop enough asparagus stalks to make 1 cup; add to the remaining gelatin. Blend in the mayonnaise. Pour over the green chicken layer. Chill for 4 hours or overnight.

**6.** Unmold onto a chilled platter; garnish with lettuce.

# POACHED CHICKEN BREAST

*Makes 2 cups broth and 1½ cups diced chicken.*

| | | | |
|---|---|---|---|
| 1 | whole chicken breast (about 14 ounces) | 1 | celery stalk with leaves, cut up |
| 1 | can (13¾ ounces) chicken broth | 1 | carrot, cut up |
| ¼ | cup dry vermouth or dry white wine | 3 | parsley sprigs |
| 1 | medium-size onion, quartered | ½ | teaspoon leaf tarragon, crumbled |
| | | ¼ | teaspoon salt |
| | | | Pinch of pepper |

**1.** Combine the chicken, broth, vermouth, onion, celery, carrot, parsley, tarragon, salt and pepper in medium-size saucepan. Bring to boiling. Cover; lower the heat; simmer for 30 minutes or until the chicken is tender. Remove and reserve the chicken and carrot; cool. Strain the broth; reserve. (There should be about 2 cups broth.)
**2.** When the chicken is cool, remove from the bone; dice the chicken. Measure and reserve 1½ cups.

# MOCK HEADCHEESE

Colorful with tiny cubes of pink ham in a shimmering gelatin.

*Makes 6 servings.*

| | | | |
|---|---|---|---|
| 2 | cans (13¾ ounces each) chicken broth | 1 | pound cooked turkey breast, cut into ¼-inch cubes |
| 1 | bay leaf | ½ | pound cooked ham, cut into ¼-inch cubes |
| 2 | teaspoons whole black peppercorns | 2 | tablespoons chopped pimiento |
| ¼ | teaspoon leaf thyme, crumbled | 3 | tablespoons chopped parsley |
| | Handful of leafy celery tops | | Pickled beets |
| 1 | carrot, diced | | Lettuce |
| 1½ | envelopes unflavored gelatin | | Potato salad |
| ¼ | cup cold water | | |

**1.** Skim the fat off the chicken broth; pour the broth into a medium-size saucepan. Tie the bay leaf, peppercorns and thyme in cheesecloth; add to the broth along with the celery and carrots. Simmer for 30 minutes. Strain the broth into a large bowl.

**2.** Soften the gelatin in the cold water in a cup for 5 minutes; dissolve over boiling water for 3 to 4 minutes. Add to the broth. Chill the broth mixture until it is as thick as unbeaten egg white.

**3.** Grease an aluminum foil-lined 8½ x 4½ x 2½-inch (6-cup) loaf pan. Fold the turkey, ham, pimiento and parsley into the thickened gelatin mixture; pour into the loaf pan. Refrigerate until set, several hours or overnight. Unmold. Serve, sliced, with pickled beets, lettuce and potato salad.

## MOLDED TURKEY AND POTATO SALAD

An unusual salad that holds its shape without gelatin.

*Makes 8 servings.*

| | | | |
|---|---|---|---|
| 2 | pounds potatoes | 1 | cup sliced radishes |
| 1 | cup bottled French dressing | 3 | cups chopped cooked white meat of turkey (1 pound) |
| ½ | teaspoon salt | | |
| ¼ | teaspoon pepper | ¼ | cup slivered almonds |
| 2 | tablespoons lemon juice | ½ | cup mayonnaise |
| 1 | cup diced celery | | Lettuce |
| 2 | cups chopped unpared red apple | | Green pepper rings |

**1.** Cook the potatoes in boiling salted water to cover in a large saucepan until tender, about 25 minutes. Drain, peel and cut them into ½-inch cubes to make 4 cups.

**2.** Combine the French dressing, salt, pepper and lemon juice in a large bowl. Add the warm potatoes; toss lightly. Let stand at room temperature for 20 minutes.

**3.** Add the celery, apple, radishes, turkey, almonds and mayonnaise; toss. Press into a 2½-quart round bowl. Refrigerate for 2 hours or overnight.

**4.** To serve, unmold onto the platter; garnish with lettuce. Arrange the pepper rings over the top.

# PEPPERY CHICKEN LOAF

Serve this loaf as part of a salad platter with tomatoes, green bean and almond salad and hot biscuits.

*Bake at 350° for 40 minutes.*
*Makes 6 servings.*

| | | | |
|---|---|---|---|
| 3 | hot or sweet Italian sausages | 1½ | pounds chicken breast fillets |
| 1 | small onion, diced (¼ cup) | 1 | medium-size onion, chopped (½ cup) |
| 1 | small sweet green pepper, halved, seeded and diced | ¾ | cup dry white wine |
| ½ | medium-size sweet red pepper, halved, seeded and diced | 2 | eggs |
| | | 1 | teaspoon leaf rosemary, crumbled |
| 2 | tablespoons olive oil | 1 | teaspoon salt |
| 1 | ripe tomato, peeled, seeded and finely chopped | 1½ | cups soft white bread crumbs (about 3 slices) |

**1.** Grease an aluminum foil-lined 9 x 5 x 3-inch (8-cup) loaf pan.

**2.** Simmer the sausages in a small skillet with ½ cup water, turning frequently, until the water disappears and the sausages are lightly browned; cool.

**3.** Sauté the onion, green and red peppers in the oil in a small skillet until quite soft, about 10 minutes. Add the tomato to the sautéed mixture; cook until the moisture disappears; cool.

**4.** Cut the chicken into ¼-inch dice and place in the container of an electric blender with the onion, wine, eggs, rosemary and salt. Blend until the ingredients become a purée, scraping down the side of the blender and rearranging the solid pieces from the top to the bottom of the container as often as necessary. Place the chicken the mixture in a bowl; stir in the bread crumbs; gently fold in the cooled vegetables.

**5.** Arrange half of the chicken mixture in the prepared loaf pan. Trim the ends of the sausages and line them down the center end to end, pressing them lightly into the mixture. Add the remaining chicken mixture and smooth the top of the loaf.

**6.** Bake in a moderate oven (350°) for 40 minutes or until the top begins to brown. Cool for 30 minutes; turn the loaf out of the pan; peel off the foil. When it is cold, wrap and store in the refrigerator for at least 1 day before slicing and serving.

# LAYERED CHICKEN SALAD

*Makes 4 servings.*

| | |
|---|---|
| 2 large potatoes, cooked, drained and cooled Parslied Vinaigrette (recipe follows) | 3 large tomatoes, sliced |
| | 2 tablespoons drained capers |
| | 3 cups diced cooked chicken |
| 1 large red onion, sliced | 2 large celery stalks, sliced on the diagonal |

**1.** Peel the potatoes and cut them into slices. Place in a shallow dish.
**2.** Drizzle half of the Parslied Vinaigrette over the potatoes; let stand for at least 30 minutes to blend flavors.
**3.** Layer the potatoes, red onion and tomatoes in a large salad bowl. Drizzle part of the remaining dressing over. Sprinkle with the capers. Arrange the chicken and celery on top.
**4.** Pass the remainder of the dressing separately.

# CLASSIC VINAIGRETTE DRESSING

*Makes 1 cup.*

| | |
|---|---|
| ¼ cup red wine vinegar | ⅛ teaspoon pepper |
| ¼ teaspoon salt | ¾ cup olive or vegetable oil |

**1.** Place the vinegar, salt and pepper in a jar with tight-fitting lid; cover; shake well.
**2.** Add the oil; cover the jar tightly; shake well.

**Parslied Vinaigrette:** Prepare Classic Vinaigrette Dressing, adding 1 tablespoon chopped parsley and 2 cloves crushed garlic.

# GREAT HERO

Americans have raised sandwich making to an art and the hero is probably the most famous.

*Makes 8 servings.*

| | | | |
|---|---|---|---|
| 1 | loaf whole wheat or white French or Italian bread Prepared mustard | 1 | can (2 ounces) anchovy fillets, drained |
| ½ | pound sliced salami | 4 | mushrooms, sliced |
| ½ | pound sliced turkey breast | 2 | ripe tomatoes, sliced |
| ½ | pound sliced corned beef | | Roasted Red Peppers (recipe follows) |
| ½ | pound sliced Swiss cheese Leaf lettuce | 1 | small zucchini, sliced Pimiento-stuffed green olives Red wine vinegar |
| 3 | hard-cooked eggs, sliced | | Bottled Italian dressing |

**1.** Cut the bread in half lengthwise with a sharp serrated knife. Spread with prepared mustard.

**2.** Arrange the sliced salami, turkey breast, corned beef and Swiss cheese with leaf lettuce, egg slices, anchovies, mushroom and tomato slices, Roasted Red Peppers, zucchini slices and stuffed green olives on the bottom layer of bread. Drizzle with red wine vinegar and Italian dressing. Cover with the top of the bread and cut into thick slices with a sharp knife.

**Roasted Red Peppers:** Makes 8 servings. Halve and seed 4 sweet red peppers. Arrange, cut-sides down, in a single layer on a jelly-roll pan. Broil, 6 inches from the heat, for 30 minutes, turning several times, or until skins blister. Cool and peel off the skins; cut into thick wedges.

# SOME SANDWICH-MAKING TIPS

• For variety, take advantage of all the inviting types and shapes of breads, rolls and buns that are available today. And once in a while, put some fun in your cooking by using two kinds of bread for a sandwich: Whole wheat and home-style, or pumpernickel and rye, for example all go well with chicken. Just be sure to choose slices of the same size and shape so the edges of the sandwich will fit together neatly.

• To keep chicken fillings from soaking into the bread, spread softened butter or margarine all the way to the crusts of each slice.

• For easy spreading without tearing bread, always soften regular or whipped butter or margarine first, or depend on soft margarine. Another trick is to freeze the slices of bread before spreading.

• No need to trim the crust from bread except on the daintiest sandwiches. Crust will help keep the edges of bread from drying out and curling.

• For speed when you're making a big batch of sandwiches, use the assembly-line technique by lining up the bread slices, two by two, in rows on a wooden board, keeping them in order as they come from the loaf.

• When making chicken sandwiches for picnics or brown-bag lunches, pack the lettuce and cucumber slices separately in plastic bags so they'll stay crisp and fresh and the sandwiches won't get soggy. Come lunchtime, they can be added to the sandwich. Raw relishes also travel neatly in a plastic bag or plastic container.

• For easy eating, cut sandwiches for youngsters into 4 small wedges, squares or strips with a sharp French knife.

• Set aside a shelf in your kitchen cabinet to hold lunch-packing materials—wax paper, aluminum foil, pastic wrap and bags and paper napkins; a variety of plastic containers and heatproof paper and plastic cups in various sizes and shapes; and plastic knives, forks and spoons.

# TOMATO SALAD SANDWICH

Thick slices of garden-ripened tomatoes replace bread in these beauties.

*Makes 4 servings.*

| | | | |
|---|---|---|---|
| 4 | large tomatoes | 8 | slices crisp bacon |
| | Salt and pepper | 4 | slices Swiss cheese |
| | Mayonnaise or salad | | Stuffed green and black |
| | dressing | | olives |
| | Leaf lettuce | | Bottled blue cheese salad |
| 8 | slices cooked chicken | | dressing |
| | or turkey | | |

**1.** Peel the tomatoes and cut out the stem ends; cut each into 3 thick slices, season with salt and pepper; reshape, keeping slices in order.
**2.** Place each stem-end slice of tomato on a plate; spread with the mayonnaise; top with the lettuce and chicken; top with the middle tomato slice. Spread with the mayonnaise, then the lettuce, crisp bacon and Swiss cheese. Top with the remaining slice and secure with a toothpick. Top with the olives. Serve with the blue cheese dressing.

---

## HOW TO FREEZE SANDWICHES

• Choose a time when your kitchen is not busy and make and wrap enough sandwiches for a week or two. (After that, frozen sandwiches start to lose their flavor.)
• All breads and rolls freeze well. As a rule of thumb, figure about 16 slices of bread in a 1-pound loaf.
• Be sure to butter bread to the edges. When sandwiches are to be frozen, it is especially importanat to prevent the filling from soaking into the bread.
• Avoid chicken fillings with watery, raw vegetables—such as lettuce, tomato, celery or cucumber.
• Dairy sour cream, pineapple juice, applesauce and cream cheese are all good binders for chicken sandwich fillings to be frozen.
• Cut each sandwich into convenient pieces for eating and package tightly in heavy-duty aluminum foil or plastic sandwich bags; label, date and freeze.
• Pack sandwiches into the lunch box directly from the freezer. They will be thawed and fresh-tasting by lunchtime.

# TURKEY BONANZA SANDWICH

This "something different" sandwich has just about everything in it—turkey, Monterey Jack cheese, chicken liver, lettuce, tomato and radishes.

*Makes 4 sandwiches.*

| | | | |
|---|---|---|---|
| 2 | tablespoons butter or margarine, softened | ⅓ | cup chopped radishes Romaine lettuce leaves |
| 8 | slices cracked wheat or oatmeal bread | 1 | medium-size ripe tomato, thinly sliced |
| ¼ | cup mayonnaise or salad dressing | 2 | packages (6 ounces each) sliced turkey breast roll |
| 2 | tablespoons bottled chili sauce | | Salt and pepper |
| ¼ | pound deli-style chopped chicken liver | 1 | package (6 ounces) sliced Monterey Jack cheese, halved |

**1.** Lightly butter each of the bread slices. Combine the mayonnaise and chili sauce in a small bowl; spread on each of the buttered bread slices.

**2.** Combine the chopped liver and radishes; spread on 4 slices of the bread; top with the romaine leaves and tomato slices.

**3.** Alternate slices of turkey, sprinkled lightly with salt and pepper, and cheese. Top with remaining bread slices, dressing-side down.

# OPEN HOT TURKEY SANDWICH

*Bake at 425° for 4 minutes.*
*Makes 4 servings.*

| | | | |
|---|---|---|---|
| 4 | slices toast, buttered and cut in half | ¼ | teaspoon salt |
| 8 | slices cooked turkey | ⅛ | teaspoon pepper |
| 2 | tablespoons butter or margarine | 1½ | cups milk |
| 2 | tablespoons all-purpose flour | 4 | ounces Cheddar cheese, shredded (1 cup) |
| | | 4 | slices bacon, cooked and halved |

**1.** Put 1 slice of toast in each of 4 au gratin dishes. Arrange 2 turkey slices on the toast.

**2.** Melt the butter in a medium-size saucepan; stir in the flour, salt and pepper. Heat for 1 minute. Pour in the milk; cook, stirring constantly, until the sauce thickens and bubbles; cook for 3 minutes longer. Add the cheese; stir until the cheese melts. Remove from the heat; spoon ½ cup over the turkey in each dish.
**3.** Bake in a hot oven (425°) just until the sauce starts to bubble around the edges, about 4 minutes. Top with bacon.

# GRILLED TURKEY, CHEESE AND TOMATO SANDWICHES

*Makes 4 servings.*

| | | | |
|---|---|---|---|
| 8 | slices bread | 2 | eggs |
| | Butter or margarine | ½ | cup milk |
| 4 | slices cooked turkey | ¼ | teaspoon salt |
| 2 | slices Swiss cheese | | Pinch of cayenne pepper |
| | (1 ounce each) | 2 | tablespoons butter or |
| 8 | thin tomato slices | | margarine |
| | Salt and pepper | | |

**1.** Spread the bread on one side with butter. Arrange 1 slice of turkey, ½ slice cheese and 2 tomato slices on 4 of the buttered sides. Sprinkle with salt and pepper. Top with the remaining 4 slices of bread, buttered-sides down.
**2.** Beat the eggs with the milk, salt and cayenne in a shallow dish. Melt the 2 tablespoons butter in a large skillet or griddle. Dip the sandwiches in the egg mixture to coat both sides, using a flat spatula.
**3.** Brown the sandwiches in the butter, turning to brown both sides and melt the cheese.

# 9

## Party Dishes

**I**f a poll could be taken of the most popular main course served at parties, chicken would win hands down. When a hostess wonders if her guests can eat this food or that or whether they have diet restrictions or allergies to certain proteins, chicken is the answer to her menu problem.

In addition to its universal appeal, chicken offers enormous versatility. It combines well with many other foods, can be cooked in dozens of different ways and is delicious either dressed up or served very simply.

The recipes selected for this chapter include hot and cold dishes for small, intimate brunches, such as Chicken Breasts with Blueberries in Orange Sauce, and dinner parties or large buffet gatherings, such as Coulibiac of Turkey. All of them are a little out-of-the-ordinary, with that special touch of glamor reserved for dishes served on festive occasions.

To help make parties even more enjoyable, this chapter starts off with a dozen tips for planning a perfect party.

# A DOZEN TIPS
## TO HELP YOU PLAN A PERFECT PARTY

**1.** Before you do anything else, sit down with a pencil and paper and plan the entire party menu. Use the plan as a blueprint from which to shop, prepare food, assemble utensils and serving pieces, and set up table decorations. Then mentally act out the preparing, serving and eating of the meal from start to finish.

**2.** Prepare a countdown list of cooking times, oven temperatures, serving directions and so on, and tape it to the refrigerator or other prominent place for easy reference during the party.

**3.** Don't crowd a small freezer by stockpiling homemade ice. It may be worth the added expense to buy ice right before the party and not sacrifice the storage space.

**4.** Don't assume paper is cheaper; sometimes the cost of renting dishes, glassware and the like is about the same as—or even less than—buying paper. If you don't own enough place settings in one pattern, mix several different ones for an eclectic, personal look.

**5.** Avoid last-minute confusion by setting out all serving dishes ahead of time and tagging them with the name of the dish they will contain.

**6.** Plan your regular weekly food shopping to include family food along with the party food. But remember, when refrigerator and kitchen space will be needed for party preparations, it may not be the week to stock up on extra orange juice, coffee or bulky staples.

**7.** Clear counters of all nonessentials like the toaster, coffeepot, cookie jar and such. This will give you valuable extra work space.

**8.** Be inventive about seating. Picnic benches, wicker love seats, stools can all be arranged around a dining table or used to augment seating at a buffet. If you entertain often, invest in cheap, comfortable folding or stacking chairs for reliable extra seating. Tag-sale finds can be scrubbed, stripped or spray-painted and fitted with ribbon-tied seat cushions.

**9.** Always start the evening with an empty dishwasher into which used dishes can disappear between courses. If between-course scraping isn't your style, hide undealt-with dishes in a tub filled with soap and water placed beneath the sink.

**10.** Make sure you have enough coat hangers and ashtrays to accommodate a crowd.

**11.** If space is limited, plan a movable feast. Try hors d'oeuvres in the living room, dinner in the dining room, with as few extra plates per person as possible, and dessert and coffee served buffet-style from the kitchen.

**12.** To make the party more fun, plan a menu that *you* enjoy cooking and eating, and invite the people you really like to be with.

# STUFFED BREAST OF TURKEY BALLOTTINE

The turkey breast can be boned and the dressing prepared the day before and refrigerated separately, or the stuffed breast can be prepared through step 5 early in the day and held in the refrigerator until 3 hours before serving time. Buttered broccoli and carrots go well with this.

*Makes 12 servings.*

| | |
|---|---|
| ½ pound mushrooms | 1 slice cooked ham, cut about |
| 4 tablespoons (½ stick) butter | ½ inch thick (½ pound) |
| or margarine | 2 cans (13¾ ounces each) |
| 3 packages (10 ounces each) | chicken broth |
| frozen chopped spinach, | 1½ cups dry white wine |
| thawed | 1 large onion, quartered |
| 3 eggs, beaten | 2 celery stalks, cut into |
| 1 teaspoon leaf thyme, | 1-inch-long pieces |
| crumbled | 2 carrots, cut into 1-inch |
| 1 teaspoon salt | pieces |
| ¼ teaspoon pepper | 6 whole black peppercorns |
| 1½ cups fresh bread crumbs | 1 large bay leaf |
| (about 3 slices) | Creamy Mustard Gravy |
| 1 whole turkey breast (about | (recipe follows) |
| 6½ to 7 pounds), thawed | |
| if frozen | |

**1.** Reserve two mushroom caps for garnish; finely chop the remaining mushrooms. Sauté the chopped mushrooms in the butter in a small skillet just until tender and lightly browned, about 5 minutes.
**2.** Drain the thawed spinach thoroughly, pressing out any excess liquid against the side of a strainer. Combine the sautéed mushrooms, drained spinach, eggs, thyme, salt, pepper and bread crumbs; mix well. Set aside.
**3.** Place the turkey breast skin-side down on board. With a sharp thin-bladed knife, carefully remove breastbone and ribs from meat without piercing the skin; reserve bones. Split through thickest part of breast, but do not cut all the way through; fold out, flatten with hand. (This will give you a larger amount of breast meat to enclose stuffing.
**4.** Spoon one third of the spinach mixture down the center of the boned breast. Cut the ham slice into 6 half-inch-wide strips. Place 3 strips on the dressing. Carefully spoon one third of the dressing over the ham strips. Repeat with the remaining three ham strips and remaining dressing. Fasten the overlapped meat with skewers to aid rolling.

**5.** Wrap the skewered breast tightly in cheesecloth. Remove the skewers. Tie at 1-inch intervals with string.

**6.** Place the rolled and wrapped turkey breast atop the bones in a Dutch oven or roasting pan. Add the chicken broth, wine, onion celery, carrots, peppercorns and bay leaf. Bring to boiling; lower the heat; cover. Simmer, turning once, for about 2 hours or until tender or until the juices from the meat run clear with no trace of pink when pierced with a two-tined fork. Cool in the broth for 1 hour.

**7.** Remove the turkey breast from the broth; unwrap from the cheesecloth. Slice and serve with Creamy Mustard Gravy.

**Creamy Mustard Gravy:** Melt 4 tablespoons (½ stick) butter or margarine in a medium-size saucepan. Gradually stir in ¼ cup all-purpose flour. Cook, stirring constantly, over medium heat until bubbly; cook for 1 minute longer. Gradually stir in 1 cup milk, 1 cup heavy cream and 2 to 3 tablespoons Dijon-style mustard. Continue to cook over medium heat, stirring constantly, just until sauce thickens, about 5 minutes.

## STUFFED TURKEY BREAST GALANTINE

*Makes 10 servings.*

| | | | |
|---|---|---|---|
| ¼ | pound chicken livers | 1 | whole turkey breast |
| 4 | tablespoons (½ stick) butter | | (about 6½ pounds) |
| | or margarine | 5 | cups water |
| ¼ | pound mushrooms, finely | 1 | carrot, quartered |
| | chopped | 1 | onion, halved |
| ½ | cup chopped green | ½ | teaspoon leaf thyme, |
| | onions | | crumbled |
| ¼ | cup chopped parsley | 1 | bay leaf |
| 1 | cup soft bread crumbs, | | Chaud-Froid Glaze |
| | slightly dried (2 slices) | | (recipe follows) |
| 1 | tablespoon salt | | Tomato peel, lemon peel, |
| ¼ | teaspoon ground pepper | | green onion tops, for garnish |
| 1 | egg | | Watercress |

**1.** Sauté the chicken livers in the butter in a small skillet just until firm; remove with slotted spoon to wooden board and chop fine. Add the mushrooms to the remaining butter in the same skillet; sauté until tender, stirring for about 5 minutes. Add the onion; sauté for 2 minutes longer. Remove to a bowl; add the chicken livers, parsley, bread crumbs, 1 teaspoon of the salt, pepper and egg.

**2.** Place the turkey breast skin-side down on a board. With a sharp, thin-bladed knife, carefully remove the breastbone from the meat without piercing the skin. Spoon the dressing onto the center of the boned breast. Press the meat around the stuffing; fasten with skewers; then wrap tightly in cheesecloth. Tie with string.

**3.** Place the rolled turkey and the bones in a Dutch oven or large kettle. Add the water, carrot, onion, remaining salt, thyme and bay leaf. Bring to boiling; lower the heat; cover. Simmer, turning once, for about 2 hours or until tender. Cool in the broth for 1 hour.

**4.** Remove the turkey roll from the broth; unwrap from the cheesecloth. Place in the shallow dish; cover; refrigerate overnight. Strain the broth; refrigerate.

**5.** Several hours before serving (or the day before), glaze and decorate. Place the cold turkey roll on a cookie sheet or jelly-roll pan, skin-side up. Spoon Chaud-Froid Glaze over it several times until heavily and evenly coated. Chill between each coating. Arrange on a serving platter. Decorate with green onion tops, tomato and lemon peels. Garnish with watercress.

**Chaud-Froid Glaze:** Boil 1½ cups of the reserved broth and ⅛ teaspoon leaf tarragon until reduced to 1 cup; stir in 1 envelope gelatin, softened in ¼ cup cold water, until dissolved. Add ¾ cup heavy cream and strain into a small bowl. Chill until syrupy.

# LEMON AND SAGE CHICKEN BREASTS

*Makes 12 servings.*

| | | | |
|---|---|---|---|
| 16 | small chicken breast halves, boned and skinned (about 4 pounds total weight) | ¼ | cup (½ stick) butter or margarine |
| 2 | cups all-purpose flour | ¼ | cup vegetable oil |
| 2 | teaspoons salt | | Lemon Dressing (recipe follows) |
| ¼ | teaspoon pepper | | Parsley sprigs |
| 2 | teaspoons leaf sage, crumbled | | Tomatoes |
| 1 | teaspoon paprika | | Pickled Cranberries (recipe follows) |

**1.** Trim the excess fat from the chicken. Combine the flour, salt, pepper, sage and paprika in a plastic bag. Shake the chicken pieces in the mixture to coat them.

**2.** Sauté the chicken, a few pieces at a time, in the butter and oil in a large skillet over medium heat until lightly browned, about 4 minutes on each side. Don't overcook. Check the chicken to be sure no pink remains; cool.

**3.** Prepare the Lemon Dressing.

**4.** Cut each cooked breast in half lengthwise and then into 4 long thick strips. Put the strips in a shallow baking dish; pour the dressing over; let marinate in the refrigerator until ready to serve.

**5.** To serve, arrange the marinated chicken on a chilled large platter; garnish with parsley and tomatoes; serve with Pickled Cranberries.

**Lemon Dressing:** Combine 1 cup vegetable oil, 2 tablespoons slivered lemon rind (no white), ½ cup lemon juice, ¼ cup sugar, 1 teaspoon salt, ¼ teaspoon pepper and 2 tablespoons chopped chives in a screw-top jar; shake well. Makes about 1⅔ cups.

# PICKLED CRANBERRIES

*Makes 5 half-pints.*

| | | | |
|---|---|---|---|
| 4 | cups fresh or frozen cranberries (1⅓ packages) | 3 | cups sugar |
| ½ | cup cider vinegar | 2 | 3-inch pieces cinnamon stick |
| ⅓ | cup water | 12 | whole cloves |
| | | 12 | whole allspice |

**1.** Pick over and wash the cranberries. Divide among 5 clean half-pint canning jars with 2-piece lids.

**2.** Combine the vinegar, water, sugar, cinnamon, cloves and allspice in a large saucepan. Bring to boiling; lower the heat; simmer for 5 minutes.
**3.** Pour the hot syrup over the cranberries, filling the jars to the top. Divide the whole spices among the jars. Seal the jars; cool; refrigerate for up to 3 weeks. Sometimes the syrup in the jars will crystalize, coating some of the cranberries with crunchy sugar crystals. Nothing is wrong if this happens; the cranberries taste just as good.

## CHICKEN BRAISED IN CHAMPAGNE

For a festive occasion, bubbly delicate champagne adds its special flavor to the chicken.

*Roast at 400° for 50 minutes; then braise at 325° for 1 hour.*
*Makes 6 servings.*

| | | | |
|---|---|---|---|
| 1 | roasting chicken (about 5 pounds) | 4 | tablespoons (½ stick) butter or margarine, softened |
| 1½ | teaspoons salt | 4 | small yellow onions, quartered |
| ¼ | teaspoon pepper | 2 | pounds small new potatoes |
| 1 | teaspoon lemon juice | 1¾ | cups champagne, leftover or half bottle |
| ½ | teaspoon leaf tarragon, crumbled | 2 | tablespoons all-purpose flour |
| 2 | tablespoons chopped parsley | | |

**1.** Wash the chicken; pat it dry with paper toweling. Sprinkle the inside with 1 teaspoon of the salt and the pepper. Beat the remaining salt, lemon juice, tarragon and parsley into the butter in a small bowl.
**2.** Loosen the breast skin from the chicken; place about 1 tablespoon of the butter mixture under the skin on each side; tie the legs of the chicken together. Rub the remaining butter mixture over the chicken. Place in a small roasting pan.
**3.** Roast, uncovered, in a hot oven (400°) for 50 minutes. Add the onions and potatoes to the roasting pan. Pour 1½ cups of the champagne over. Cover the pan tightly with foil. Lower the oven temperature to 325°. Braise, covered, basting several times, for 1 hour longer or until the chicken and vegetables are tender.
**4.** Remove the chicken to a heated platter. Make a smooth paste with the flour and the remaining ¼ cup of champagne. Pour into the pan liquid. Cook over low heat, stirring constantly, until thickened and bubbly. Cook for 2 minutes; taste and add more salt, if needed. Serve with the chicken.

# STUFFED CHICKEN BREASTS

*Bake at 400° for 15 minutes.*
*Makes 12 servings.*

| | | | |
|---|---|---|---|
| 3 | medium-size onions, finely chopped (1½ cups) | 6 | whole chicken breasts (about 12 ounces each), boned, skinned and split (12 pieces) |
| 7 | tablespoons butter or margarine | ½ | teaspoon salt |
| ½ | pound mushrooms, finely chopped (2 cups) | ⅛ | teaspoon pepper |
| 1 | tablespoon lemon juice | ½ | cup dry white wine |
| ½ | teaspoon salt | | Mornay Sauce (recipe follows) |
| ¼ | teaspoon pepper | ¼ | cup grated Parmesan cheese |
| 1 | cup soft bread crumbs (2 slices) | | Watercress (optional) |
| | | | Steamed broccoli (optional) |
| | | | Cooked brown rice (optional) |

**1.** Sauté the onions in 5 tablespoons of the butter in a large skillet, until tender, about 5 minutes. Add the mushrooms, lemon juice, ½ teaspoon salt and ¼ teaspoon pepper. Sauté, stirring constantly, until the liquid accumulated in the skillet has evaporated, about 5 minutes. Stir in the bread crumbs; cool.

**2.** Pound the chicken breasts between sheets of wax paper to about an ⅛-inch thickness. Place on work surface. Divide the mushroom mixture among the chicken pieces; roll up. Fasten with toothpicks.

**3.** Heat the remaining 2 tablespoons of butter in a large skillet. Brown the chicken breasts, half at a time, on all sides, removing to a plate as they brown. Return all to the skillet; sprinkle with the remaining salt and pepper. Add the wine; bring to boiling; cover. Lower the heat; simmer for 20 minutes or just until tender.

**4.** While the chicken cooks, prepare the Mornay Sauce.

**5.** Transfer the chicken to a large shallow oblong or oval baking dish. You should have about ½ cup cooking liquid; if necessary, boil to reduce to that amount. Pour over the chicken. Spoon the Mornay Sauce over the chicken. Sprinkle with the Parmesan cheese.

**6.** Bake in a hot oven (400°) for 15 minutes or until the sauce is bubbly and the top is browned. Garnish with watercress and serve with broccoli and brown rice, if you wish.

**Mornay Sauce:** Melt 3 tablespoons butter or margarine in medium-size saucepan. Blend in 4 tablespoons all-purpose flour; cook for 1 minute. Gradually stir in 1 can (13¾ ounces) chicken broth. Cook, stirring constantly, until sauce thickens and bubbles; cook for

2 minutes. Stir in 1 cup light cream or milk. Simmer, stirring occasionally, on low heat for 5 minutes. Remove from heat. Add ¾ cup shredded cheese.

## GOLDEN HARVEST CASSEROLE

*Bake at 350° for 45 minutes.*
*Makes 8 servings.*

| | | | |
|---|---|---|---|
| 2 | broiler/fryers (about 2½ to 3 pounds each), cut up | 1 | teaspoon leaf thyme, crumbled |
| ½ | cup all-purpose flour | ¼ | teaspoon cayenne pepper |
| 2 | teaspoons salt | 1 | bay leaf |
| 1 | teaspoon pepper | 1 | can (16 ounces) Italian plum tomatoes |
| ½ | cup vegetable oil | 1 | cup dry white wine |
| 2 | cloves garlic, minced | 2 | tablespoons tomato paste |
| 1 | large onion, diced (1 cup) | ½ | pound frozen, uncooked, peeled and deveined shrimp (optional) |
| 1 | cup sliced celery | | Chopped parsley (optional) |
| 1 | small sweet green pepper, seeded and cut into strips | | Hot cooked rice |
| ½ | pound mushrooms, sliced | | |

**1.** Shake the chicken pieces, a few at a time, in a plastic bag with the flour, 1 teaspoon of the salt and ½ teaspoon of the pepper; reserve the remaining seasoned flour mixture.
**2.** Brown the chicken, a few pieces at a time, in the oil in a large skillet. Place the browned chicken in a 10-cup casserole.
**3.** Remove all but 2 tablespoons of the oil from the skillet. Sauté the garlic and onion until soft; add the celery, green pepper and mushrooms; sauté just until crisp-tender.
**4.** Add the remaining 1 teaspoon salt, ½ teaspoon pepper, 2 table-spoons of the reserved seasoned flour mixture, thyme, cayenne and bay leaf; toss to coat vegetables.
**5.** Add the plum tomatoes plus can liquid, wine and tomato paste. Stir just to mix; bring to boiling. Pour over the chicken in the casserole; cover.
**6.** Bake in a moderate oven (350°) for 25 minutes. Uncover; add the shrimp, pushing the shrimp down into the liquid. Cover; bake an additional 20 minutes or until the chicken and shrimp are tender. Uncover; gently stir to mix the ingredients. Serve over rice. Garnish with chopped parsley, if you wish.

# MINCED CHICKEN AND PORK PIE

A great dish for a picnic and a refreshing change from fried chicken.

*Bake at 425° for 15 minutes; then at 375° for 45 minutes.*

*Makes 6 servings.*

| | |
|---|---|
| 2 cups *sifted* all-purpose flour | 1 large onion, chopped (1 cup) |
| 1 teaspoon salt | 1 clove garlic, minced |
| 6 tablespoons butter or margarine | ¾ pound lean ground pork |
| 6 tablespoons vegetable shortening | 1 teaspoon salt |
| 1 egg | ¼ teaspoon pepper |
| ⅓ cup cold water | ½ teaspoon ground ginger |
| 1 whole chicken breast (about 14 ounces), skinned and boned | ½ teaspoon leaf thyme, crumbled |
| 2 tablespoons butter or margarine | 2 eggs |
| | ½ cup dry white wine |
| | ½ cup chopped parsley |

**1.** Sift together the flour and salt in a medium-size bowl; cut in the butter and shortening with a fork or pastry blender until the mixture is crumbly. Beat the egg and water slightly in a small bowl. Sprinkle over the mixture; mix lightly with a fork, just until pastry holds together and leaves side of bowl clean. Cover; refrigerate for 1 hour.

**2.** Slice the chicken breast in thin strips; cut the strips into very small pieces. (Or put through the medium-size blade of a meat grinder.)

**3.** Melt the butter in a large skillet; add the onion and garlic; sauté for 1 minute. Add the chicken, pork, salt, pepper, ginger and thyme. Cook the mixture, stirring occasionally, until the pork has lost all of its pink color, about 15 minutes. Cool slightly.

**4.** Beat the eggs and wine slightly in a small bowl; add to the meat mixture with parsley; mix thoroughly.

**5.** Divide the pastry in half. Roll out half on a lightly floured surface to a 13-inch round and fit into a 9-inch pie plate. Trim the overhang to ½ inch. Fill with the chicken mixture.

**6.** Roll out the remaining pastry to a 12-inch round; cut several slits near the center (to let steam escape); trim the overhang to ½ inch, even with bottom pastry. Turn the edge up and in; press with the tines of a fork or flute the edges.

**7.** Bake in a hot oven (425°) for 15 minutes. Lower the oven temperature to 375° and continue to bake for 45 minutes. Remove the from oven. Let stand for 15 minutes. Serve with cranberry sauce. To serve cold, remove from refrigerator about 30 minutes before serving.

# CHICKEN WITH CHEESE FONDUE

One of the simplest of the wine recipes to serve at a small, informal gathering.

*Makes 6 servings.*

1¼ pounds Jarlsberg or Swiss cheese, shredded (5 cups)
1 tablespoon cornstarch
½ teaspoon dry mustard
½ teaspoon ground coriander
½ teaspoon caraway seeds, crushed
⅛ teaspoon salt
2 cups dry white wine

1 clove garlic
2 whole cloves
2 tablespoons aquavit, kirsch or vodka
1 loaf Italian or rye bread
Firm flowerets of broccoli and cauliflower, blanched
Cooked chicken breast, cubed

**1.** Toss the shredded cheese with the cornstarch, mustard, coriander, caraway seeds and salt in a large bowl.

**2.** Heat the wine with the garlic and cloves in a fondue dish or flameproof casserole until bubbles start to rise from bottom. Remove the garlic and cloves with a slotted spoon.

**3.** Gradually add the cheese mixture, stirring constantly with a wooden spoon after each addition, until the cheese melts. Do not boil. Stir in the aquavit. Set the dish over an alcohol burner to keep hot white serving.

**4.** Cut the bread into bite-size pieces. (Mix 2 or 3 different kinds of breads.) Place in a basket or on serving plates. Arrange the blanched vegetables and chicken cubes on plates. Set out fondue or regular forks so everyone can spear a piece of bread, vegetable or meat and then twirl it into the hot cheese sauce.

# CHICKEN BREASTS AND MUSHROOMS IN MADEIRA SAUCE

Perfect for a pleasant company dinner.
*Braise at 400° for 20 minutes.*
*Makes 6 servings.*

3  tablespoons butter or
   margarine
3  whole chicken breasts
   (2½ to 3 pounds total
   weight), split
1  teaspoon salt
¼  teaspoon pepper
¾  pound medium-size
   mushrooms
2  teaspoons lemon juice

2  tablespoons chopped shallots
1  tablespoon flour
¾  cup dry Madeira wine
¾  cup heavy cream
¾  cup shredded Swiss cheese
   Hot cooked brown rice or
   steamed new potatoes
   (optional)
   Salad (optional)

**1.** Heat 2 tablespoons of the butter in a large skillet; add the chicken breasts to brown over medium high heat, about 10 minutes on each side; sprinkle both sides with salt and pepper. Transfer to an 11¾ x 7½ x 1¾- inch baking dish or heatproof serving dish.
**2.** Meanwhile trim the mushrooms; toss with the lemon juice. Add the remaining butter to the skillet; stir in the shallots; sauté for 3 minutes. Add the mushrooms; cook, stirring often, for 5 minutes or until slightly browned. Blend in the flour; pour in the Madeira and then the cream. Cook, stirring constantly, until thickened and bubbly; mix in ½ cup of the cheese. Spoon the sauce and mushrooms over the chicken; sprinkle with the remaining cheese.
**3.** Bake in a hot oven (400°) for 20 minutes or until the chicken is tender. Serve with cooked brown rice or new potatoes and a salad, if you wish.

# CHICKEN BREASTS WITH ALMONDS

*Bake at 350° for 25 to 30 minutes.*
*Makes 6 servings.*

| | | | |
|---|---|---|---|
| **3** | whole chicken breasts, halved and boned | **2** | tablespoons all-purpose flour |
| **3** | tablespoons butter | **1** | cup chicken broth |
| ½ | cup almonds, blanched and slivered | ¼ | cup dry white wine or dry vermouth |
| **2** | tablespoons brandy | ¼ | teaspoon salt |
| **1** | tablespoon chopped green onion | | Pinch of ground nutmeg |
| **1** | teaspoon tomato paste | ¼ | teaspoon pepper |
| | | ½ | teaspoon leaf tarragon, crumbled |

**1.** Wash the chicken breasts and pat them dry.

**2.** Melt the butter in a skillet over moderate heat; add the almonds and cook, stirring, until the almonds begin to brown. Remove with a slotted spoon; reserve.

**3.** Brown the chicken breasts lightly on both sides in the same skillet over medium heat. Pour the brandy over and set it aflame. When the flame burns out, remove the chicken to a shallow baking dish. Add the onion to the juices remaining in the skillet; cook over low heat for 30 seconds, stirring constantly. Stir in the tomato paste and flour. Gradually stir in the chicken broth and white wine and cook, stirring, until the sauce is slightly thickened and bubbles, 1 minute. Add the salt, nutmeg, pepper and tarragon. Pour over the chicken. Sprinkle the sautéed almonds over the chicken in the baking dish.

**4.** Bake in a moderate oven (350°) for 25 to 30 minutes.

# ITALIAN CHICKEN ROLL

*Bake at 350° for 1 hour.*
*Makes 8 servings.*

| | | | |
|---|---|---|---|
| 2 | sweet Italian sausages, each about 5 inches long | 2 | cups fresh Italian or French bread crumbs |
| 3 | whole chicken breasts (about 14 ounces each), skinned and boned | ½ | cup grated Parmesan cheese |
| | | ¼ | cup chopped parsley |
| | | ⅔ | cup olive oil |
| ¼ | pound Genoa salami, sliced | 2 | tablespoons dry white wine |
| ¼ | pound prosciutto ham, sliced | 6 | eggs |
| | | | Watercress |
| ¼ | pound mortadella, sliced | | Cherry tomatoes |

**1.** Brown the sausages slowly in a small skillet; drain on paper toweling.

**2.** Arrange the chicken breasts in two rows between two long sheets of parchment or wax paper, overlapping slightly to fill the spaces.

**3.** Pound with the side of a wooden mallet or rolling pin until the chicken meat is thin and as even as possible. Lift up the top sheet of paper occasionally and fill the empty spaces by pushing the chicken meat together. (It may be necessary to replace the top sheet of paper.) You are aiming for a 10 x 15-inch solid sheet of chicken meat. Remove the top sheet of paper.

**4.** Arrange a layer of Genoa salami, then prosciutto, then mortadella over the chicken breasts to within 1 inch of the edges.

**5.** Combine the bread crumbs, Parmesan cheese, parsley, 4 tablespoons of the olive oil and wine in a medium-size bowl. Spread the mixture over cold cuts to 1 inch of edges, pressing down firmly.

**6.** Beat the eggs slightly in medium-size bowl. Heat 2 tablespoons of the olive oil in a large skillet. Add the eggs and scramble softly.

**7.** Arrange the eggs over the bread crumb mixture at a 10-inch edge closest to you and spread upward 6 inches and to within 1 inch of edges. Line up sausages end to end in the center of the eggs.

**8.** Carefully roll up like a jelly roll with the help of the bottom sheet of paper.

**9.** Cut a double thickness of cheesecloth long enough to cover the chicken plus enough on ends to gather and tie. Carefully wrap the cheesecloth around the chicken roll. Tie the ends and tie the roll in 4 or 5 places with kitchen twine. Brush the cheesecloth all over with the remaining olive oil. Place the roll on a rack in a roasting pan.

**10.** Bake in a moderate oven (350°) for 45 minutes. Remove from the oven. Carefully cut the twine and remove the cheesecloth. Brush the chicken roll with the pan drippings; return to the oven and continue to bake for an additional 15 minutes.

**11.** Remove the chicken roll to a serving platter; let rest for 15 minutes before cutting. Garnish with watercress and cherry tomatoes.

**12.** To serve cold, remove from the refrigerator about 30 minutes before serving.

## SWEET AND PUNGENT CHICKEN WINGS

Small but meaty chicken wings are a good choice for this tasty skillet dish.

*Makes 4 servings.*

| | | | |
|---|---|---|---|
| 1 | egg | 4 | tablespoons cornstarch |
| 6 | tablespoons water | 2 | tablespoons cold water |
| ½ | cup all-purpose flour | ½ | cup vegetable oil |
| 1 | teaspoon salt | 1 | large sweet red pepper, |
| 12 | chicken wings, wing tips | | seeded and cut into 1-inch |
| | removed | | chunks |
| 1 | can pineapple chunks | 1 | package frozen pea pods |
| ⅓ | cup cider vinegar | ½ | cup sliced water chestnuts |
| 2 | tablespoons brown sugar | | Hot cooked rice |
| 1 | teaspoon soy sauce | 2 | tablespoons cashews |

**1.** Beat the egg lightly in a medium-size bowl. Stir in the water, flour and salt; mix well. Add chicken wings, turn to coat. Let stand for 20 minutes.

**2.** Drain the juice from the pineapple into a 2-cup glass measure; add water to make 1 cup liquid; stir in the vinegar, brown sugar and soy sauce. Combine the cornstarch and water in a small cup.

**3.** Heat the oil in a large skillet. Lift the chicken wings from the batter. Fry the wings, a few at a time, for 10 minutes on each side or until brown and tender. Remove to paper toweling to drain. Keep warm on a serving platter. Pour the fat from the skillet into 1-cup measure; return 2 tablespoons to the skillet.

**4.** Add the red pepper, pea pods and water chestnuts; stir-fry for 3 minutes or until the vegetables are crisp-tender. Remove and reserve.

**5.** Pour the pineapple mixture into the skillet; heat thoroughly. Return the vegetables and pineapple to the skillet. Stir the cornstarch mixture again; slowly mix into the skillet. Cook for several minutes or until the vegetables and pineapple glisten and the mixture thickens.

**6.** Arrange the rice on a platter; top with the chicken wings; spoon the vegetables and sauce over wings; sprinkle with cashews.

# TURKEY AND HAM FLORENTINE

A delicious make-ahead casserole that combines your
favorite holiday meats.

*Bake at 350° for 1 hour.*

*Makes 8 servings.*

**Spinach Layer**
3    packages (10 ounces each)
     frozen chopped spinach
1½   teaspoons salt
3    tablespoons butter
1    medium-size onion,
     chopped (½ cup)
¾    cup light cream
½    cup grated Parmesan cheese
¼    teaspoon ground nutmeg

**Turkey and Ham Layer**
1    medium-size onion,
     chopped (½ cup)
2    tablespoons vegetable oil

2    pounds uncooked turkey,
     ground
1    pound cooked ham, cut into
     ½-inch cubes
¼    cup (½ stick) butter
¼    cup all-purpose flour
2    teaspoons salt
½    teaspoon pepper
1¼   cups light cream
2¾   cups milk
6    ounces Gruyère cheese,
     shredded (1½ cups)
½    cup grated Parmesan cheese
½    pound lasagne noodles

**1.** To prepare the spinach layer, cook the spinach following label directions and using the 1½ teaspoons salt. Drain well, pressing out as much liquid as possible with the back of a spoon.

**2.** Melt the butter in same pan; sauté the onion until tender, about 5 minutes. Stir in the spinach, cream, cheese and nutmeg.

**3.** To prepare the turkey and ham layer, sauté the onion in the oil in a large skillet. Add the turkey and cook, breaking it up with a fork, until it loses its pink color; stir in the ham.

**4.** Melt the ¼ cup butter in a large saucepan; stir in the flour, salt and pepper. Cook, stirring, until smooth and bubbly, about 1 minute. Gradually stir in the cream and then the milk. Cook and stir over medium-high heat until thickened, about 10 minutes. Stir in 1 cup of the Gruyère and ¼ cup of the Parmesan. Stir in the turkey-ham mixture. Combine the remaining Gruyère and Parmesan in a bowl; reserve.

**5.** Cook the lasagne noodles following label directions.

**6.** To assemble, preheat the oven to moderate (350°). Line the bottom of a 13 x 9 x 2-inch baking pan with one third of the lasagne noodles. Spoon one third of the turkey mixture on top. Distribute one third of the spinach mixture evenly over the turkey mixture; repeat layering 2 more times. Top with the reserved Gruyère and Parmesan.

**7.** To prepare and serve the same day, cover and bake in a moderate oven (350°) for 50 minutes or until bubbly-hot; uncover for last 15 minutes of baking. Let stand for 10 minutes before serving.

*To Freeze:* Cover baking pan of uncooked mixture tightly with foil; freeze. To serve, thaw overnight in refrigerator and bake, covered, in a moderate oven (350°) for 1 hour, or until bubbly-hot. Uncover for last 15 minutes of baking. Let stand for 10 minutes before serving.

# CHICKEN BREASTS IN CHAMPAGNE SAUCE

*Makes 6 servings.*

| | |
|---|---|
| 3 whole chicken breasts (2½ to 3 pounds total weight), split | 2 tablespoons all-purpose flour |
| 3 tablespoons butter or margarine | 2 egg yolks |
| 1 teaspoon salt | 1 package (6 ounces) long grain and wild rice mix, cooked |
| ¼ teaspoon pepper | following label directions |
| ½ teaspoon leaf thyme, crumbled | Watercress (optional) |
| ½ cup chicken broth | Seedless green grapes (optional) |
| 1½ cups dry champagne or dry white wine | |

**1.** Brown the chicken breasts in the butter in a large skillet until golden brown, about 20 minutes, turning often.

**2.** Add the salt, pepper, thyme, broth and 1¼ cups of the champagne to the pan drippings in the skillet. Bring to boiling; lower the heat; cover. Simmer for 20 minutes or until the chicken is tender; remove the chicken and keep it warm.

**3.** Stir the flour into the remaining ¼ cup of champagne; stir the mixture into the liquid in the skillet. Cook, stirring constantly, until the mixture is thickened and bubbly.

**4.** Beat the egg yolks in a small bowl; add about ½ cup of the hot sauce; stir back into the skillet. Heat thoroughly, but do not boil.

**5.** To serve, arrange the chicken breasts on a platter with the hot rice; spoon a little sauce over each piece of chicken. Garnish with watercress and green grapes, if you wish.

# CHICKEN BREASTS WITH BLUEBERRIES IN ORANGE SAUCE

*Makes 4 servings.*

| | | | |
|---|---|---|---|
| 2 | whole chicken breasts (about 12 ounces each) | 2 | eggs, lightly beaten |
| 1 | teaspoon butter or margarine | ½ | cup packaged unseasoned bread crumbs |
| 1 | small onion, chopped (¼ cup) | 2 | tablespoons vegetable oil |
| ½ | teaspoon leaf tarragon, crumbled | 2 | tablespoons butter or margarine |
| 4 | ounces Swiss cheese, shredded (½ cup) | 2 | cups orange juice |
| ⅓ | cup all-purpose flour | ½ | cup dry sherry |
| 1 | teaspoon salt | 3 | tablespoons cornstarch |
| ¼ | teaspoon pepper | 3 | tablespoons cold water |
| | | 1 | pint fresh blueberries |
| | | 2 | navel orange, peeled and sectioned |

**1.** Halve, skin and bone the chicken breasts; pound with a mallet or rolling pin until about ¼ inch thick.

**2.** Melt 1 teaspoon of butter in a large skillet; sauté the onion until it is tender, about 3 minutes. Mix the onion, tarragon and cheese in a cup; divide evenly among the chicken breasts. Roll up and tuck in the edges.

**3.** Combine the flour, salt and pepper; dip the chicken into the mixture to coat; then dip into the beaten egg and then into the bread crumbs.

**4.** Heat the oil and 2 tablespoons of butter in the same skillet; brown the chicken breasts well on all sides over medium heat for about 10 minutes. Pour off any excess fat.

**5.** Return the chicken to the skillet; pour in the orange juice and sherry. Cook, covered, over medium heat for 30 minutes, turning once or twice.

**6.** Mix the cornstarch with the water; stir into skillet. Cook, stirring constantly, until the sauce thickens and bubbles. Add the blueberries and orange sections; heat just until the fruit is heated through.

# TURKEY BREAST TETRAZZINI
# WITH GREEN NOODLES

*Bake at 350° for 30 minutes.*
*Makes 8 servings.*

| | | | |
|---|---|---|---|
| 1 | whole frozen turkey breast (about 5 pounds), thawed | 1 | cup heavy cream |
| 6 | tablespoons butter or margarine | ⅔ | cup milk |
| | | ⅔ | cup grated Parmesan cheese |
| ½ | cup all-purpose flour | ⅓ | cup dry sherry |
| 1 | teaspoon salt | 2 | packages (8 ounces each) spinach noodles |
| ¼ | teaspoon white pepper | | |
| ¼ | teaspoon ground nutmeg | 1 | can (4 ounces) slivered almonds |
| 1 | can (13¾ ounces) chicken broth | | |

**1.** Cook the turkey breast following label directions. Cut into ¼-inch-thick slices.

**2.** Melt the butter in a large saucepan. Stir in the flour, salt, pepper and nutmeg. Heat, stirring constantly, for 1 minute. Gradually add the broth, heavy cream and milk. Cook, stirring constantly, until the sauce thickens and bubbles. Continue to cook for 1 minute. Remove from the heat. Stir in ⅓ cup of the Parmesan and the sherry until well blended.

**3.** Cook the noodles following label directions. Drain. Turn into a well-buttered 2-quart baking dish.

**4.** Arrange the turkey slices on the noodles. Pour the sauce over the slices. Sprinkle the remaining ⅓ cup of Parmesan and the nuts over the sauce. The casserole may be refrigerated at this point if made ahead.

**5.** Bake in a moderate oven (350°) for 30 minutes or until bubbly and lightly browned.

# CHICKEN-SPINACH TETRAZZINI

This is a dish of grand proportions, good for a party crowd at any season. Assemble the whole dish ahead and refrigerate. Bring to room temperature and then bake just before serving.

*Bake at 350° for 30 minutes.*
*Makes 16 servings.*

6 whole boneless skinless chicken breasts (3½ pounds total weight)
6 cups water
2 medium-size onions, quartered
2 medium-size carrots, sliced
2 celery stalks, sliced
1 teaspoon leaf thyme, crumbled
2 bay leaves
2 teaspoons salt
8 whole black peppercorns
1 cup (2 sticks) butter or margarine
½ cup all-purpose flour
2 cups heavy cream

1 cup dry white wine
¼ teaspoon pepper
⅛ teaspoon ground nutmeg
½ pound Swiss cheese, shredded (about 2 cups)
1 pound medium-size mushrooms, thinly sliced
2 packages (1 pound each) linguine
2 packages (10 ounces each) frozen chopped spinach, thawed
1¼ cups fresh bread crumbs (3 slices)
⅓ cup melted butter
⅓ cup grated Parmesan cheese
¼ cup chopped parsley

**1.** Place the chicken breasts in a large kettle or Dutch oven. Add the water, onions, carrots, celery, thyme, bay leaves, salt and peppercorns. Bring to boiling; lower the heat; cover; simmer for 30 minutes or until the chicken is tender. Remove the chicken breasts with a slotted spoon to a bowl to cool. Cut into bite-size pieces. Strain the stock; measure 4 cups and set aside. (Save the remainder for soups or sauces. Refrigerate if using within 1 to 3 days or freeze for longer storage.)

**2.** Melt ½ cup of the butter in a large saucepan; blend in the flour. Cook, stirring constantly, for 1 minute. Gradually stir in the 4 cups stock, heavy cream and wine. Cook, stirring constantly, until the sauce thickens and bubbles. Add the pepper and nutmeg. Continue to cook for 1 minute. Remove from the heat. Stir in the shredded cheese until it is melted. Set aside.

**3.** Sauté the mushrooms in the remaining ½ cup butter in a large skillet just until golden brown. Set aside.

**4.** Cook the linguine following package directions. Drain. Press the excess liquid from the thawed spinach. Add the mushrooms, spinach and chicken pieces to the linguine; mix well. Pour the cheese sauce over the linguine; toss gently until well mixed.

**5.** Turn the linguine into a well-buttered 5-quart shallow baking dish, or two 2½-quart shallow baking dishes.

**6.** Combine the bread crumbs, melted butter, Parmesan and chopped parsley in a small bowl; mix well. Sprinkle over the dish evenly.

**7.** Bake in a preheated moderate oven (350°) for 30 minutes or until bubbly and lightly browned.

## BUFFET TURKEY-NOODLE BAKE

An attractive buffet dish that can be made with leftover cooked turkey. It is enriched with a pasta delicacy—green noodles—and vegetables.

*Bake at 350° for 30 minutes.*
*Makes 12 servings.*

| | | | |
|---|---|---|---|
| ⅓ | cup butter or margarine | 5 | cups diced cooked turkey |
| ⅓ | cup all-purpose flour | 1 | jar (1 pound) whole white |
| 1 | teaspoon salt | | onions, drained and rinsed |
| ¼ | teaspoon pepper | | (cut large onions in half) |
| 1 | to 2 tablespoons curry | 1 | package (1 pound, 4 ounces) |
| | powder | | frozen mixed vegetables, |
| 1 | can (10¾ ounces) condensed | | slightly thawed |
| | chicken broth plus water to | 1 | package (8 ounces) spinach |
| | equal 2 cups | | egg noodles |
| 1 | cup light cream or milk | 3 | cups herb-seasoned |
| 2 | tablespoons Worcestershire | | croutons |
| | sauce | | |

**1.** Melt the butter in a large skillet. Stir in the flour, salt, pepper and curry powder to make a smooth paste; cook for 1 minute. Gradually add the chicken broth, stirring constantly, until thickened and smooth. Add the cream, Worcestershire and turkey; cook for 10 minutes to blend the flavors. Pour into a large bowl; add the onions and mixed vegetables.

**2.** Cook the noodles following label directions; drain; add to the turkey mixture. Spoon into a 3-quart shallow baking dish. Top with the croutons.

**3.** Bake in a moderate oven (350°) for 30 minutes or until bubbly-hot. Let stand for 10 minutes before serving.

# COULIBIAC OF TURKEY

This classic Russian main-dish pastry is usually filled with salmon. Ours uses adaptable fresh turkey (ground) and is baked in a free-form design.

*Bake at 400° for 30 minutes; then at 350° for 15 minutes.*
*Makes 8 servings.*

**Butter Pastry**
5   cups *sifted* all-purpose flour
1¼  cups (2½ sticks) chilled
    butter
    About 1 cup ice water
1   egg, beaten

**Turkey Filling**
1   large onion, chopped (1 cup)
6   tablespoons (¾ stick) butter
    or margarine
2   pounds uncooked turkey,
    ground

2   cups chopped fresh
    mushrooms, (½ pound)
1   teaspoon salt
½   teaspoon pepper
1½  cups *cooked* long-grain
    white rice
2   uncooked eggs
3   hard-cooked eggs, chopped
½   cup chopped fresh parsley
¼   cup chopped fresh dill
    OR: 1 tablespoon dried
    dillweed
2   cups dairy sour cream

**1.** To prepare the pastry, place 2½ cups of the flour in a bowl. With a pastry knife or fork, cut in half of the butter until the mixture resembles coarse meal. Sprinkle with up to half the water and toss until the dough holds together. Shape the dough into a flattened ball; wrap in wax paper and refrigerate for at least 3 hours. Repeat with the remaining pastry ingredients. (Pastry can also be made in 2 batches in a food processor.)

**2.** To prepare the filling, sauté the onion in the butter in a large skillet until soft. Add the turkey and cook over a high heat, stirring often, breaking up the meat with a spoon. When the meat loses its pink color, stir in the mushrooms and cook for 2 minutes longer. Stir in the remaining ingredients, except the sour cream. Cover; refrigerate.

**3.** To assemble the coulibiac, roll 1 ball of dough into a 12 x 17 x ⅛-inch rectangle on a lightly floured surface. Center the rolled dough on a buttered 10 x 15-inch cookie sheet and spoon the filling onto the dough, leaving a 3-inch border all around. Trim the excess pastry beyond a 3-inch border; reserve the scraps. Brush the border with beaten egg.

**4.** Roll out the remaining pastry to the same size as the first and trim to a 14 x 9-inch rectangle. Place over the filling and bring the edges of the bottom pastry up over the top. Press to seal. Press the edges of the pastry together decoratively with the tines of a fork and brush the top of the pastry with egg. Roll out the remaining pastry scraps and cut out decorative shapes with cookie cutters or the point of a sharp knife. Press the shapes onto the top of the pastry and brush all over with beaten egg. Cover loosely with aluminum foil and refrigerate the pastry from 1 to 6 hours before baking.

**5.** Preheat the oven to hot (400°). Brush the top of the pastry with beaten egg and bake in the center of the oven for 30 minutes. Lower the oven temperature to 350° and bake for 15 minutes longer or until golden brown. Transfer to a platter and serve the pastry cut in squares with the sour cream.

# CHICKEN AND ARTICHOKE CRÊPES

Ideal for a company dinner.
*Bake at 400° for 15 minutes.*
*Makes 6 to 8 servings.*

| | | | |
|---|---|---|---|
| | Basic Crêpes (recipe follows) | 4 | tablespoons butter or margarine |
| 3 | whole chicken breasts (about 2 pounds total weight) | ¼ | pound small mushrooms, sliced (1½ cups) |
| 3 | cups water | 2 | teaspoons lemon juice |
| 2 | teaspoons salt | ¼ | cup all-purpose flour |
| ¼ | teaspoon pepper | ⅛ | teaspoon ground nutmeg |
| 1 | package (9 ounces) frozen artichoke hearts | ½ | cup light cream |
| 1 | large onion, chopped (1 cup) | ½ | cup shredded Swiss cheese |
| | | | Parsley sprigs (optional) |
| | | | Lemon, thinly sliced (optional) |

**1.** Prepare the Basic Crêpes in a 7- or 8-inch skillet, using 2 to 3 tablespoons of batter for each. (Makes about 16.)

**2.** Combine the chicken breasts, water, salt and pepper in a large saucepan. Bring to boiling; lower the heat; cover. Simmer for 40 minutes or until tender. Remove the chicken from the broth. Boil the broth, uncovered, over a high heat until reduced to 2 cups. Slip the skin from the chicken; remove the meat from the bones; cut it into small pieces; place in a medium-size bowl.

**3.** Cook the artichoke hearts following label directions; drain. Cut each heart into 2 or 3 pieces; add to the chicken in the bowl.

**4.** Sauté the onion in the butter in a large saucepan until soft, about 5 minutes; add the mushrooms and lemon juice. Sauté, stirring often, for 3 to 4 minutes. Stir in the flour and nutmeg; gradually stir in the reduced chicken broth. Cook, stirring constantly, until the sauce thickens and bubbles, 1 minute; add the cream; simmer for 5 minutes. Add about 1½ cups of the sauce to the chicken, reserving the remaining sauce for the top.

**5.** Place about ¼ cup of the filling on each crêpe; roll up. Place the filled crêpes seam-side down in a lightly greased 13 x 9 x 2-inch baking dish, or place in individual baking dishes. Spoon the reserved sauce over the crêpes; sprinkle with the cheese. (Crêpes can be refrigerated for several hours before baking time.)

**6.** Bake in a hot oven (400°) until bubbly hot, about 15 minutes (25 minutes if they have been refrigerated). Garnish with the parsley and lemon, if you wish.

# BASIC CRÊPES

*Makes 12 to 16 small crêpes (6 to 7 inches in diameter) or 10 to 12 large crêpes (8 to 10 inches in diameter).*

| | | | |
|---|---|---|---|
| 3 | eggs | 2 | tablespoons butter or |
| ¾ | cup all-purpose flour | | margarine, melted |
| ¼ | teaspoon salt | | Butter |
| 1 | cup milk | | |

**1.** Combine the eggs, flour, salt and ¼ cup of the milk in a medium-size bowl; beat with a rotary beater until smooth. Beat in the melted butter and then the remaining milk. Refrigerate, covered, for at least 1 hour.

**2.** Slowly heat a skillet until a drop of water sizzles when dropped on the surface. Butter the skillet lightly for the first few crêpes; after that it will be seasoned and the crêpes will not stick. To make small crêpes, use 2 to 3 tablespoons of batter for each and a 7- or 8-inch skillet. To make large crêpes, use 3 to 4 tablespoons of batter for each and an 8- or 10-inch skillet. Measure the amount of batter into a small measuring cup or ladle to make the first crêpe, then scoop up the batter and pour into the skillet all at once for subsequent ones.

**3.** Pour the batter into the hot skillet; quickly rotate the skillet to spread the batter evenly. Cook over a medium heat until lightly browned; turn and brown the other side. Remove to a plate. When the crêpes are cool, stack with aluminum foil or plastic wrap between them.

**Sweet Crêpes:** Follow the recipe for Basic Crêpes, adding 2 tablespoons of sugar to the batter.

# TURKEY CRÊPES WITH CHEESE SAUCE

*Broil 5 minutes.*
*Makes 6 servings.*

2  eggs
⅓  cup plus 2 tablespoons all-purpose flour
3  cups milk
¼  teaspoon sugar
½  teaspoon salt
   Vegetable oil
2  tablespoons butter or margarine

⅛  teaspoon pepper
½  teaspoon dry mustard
1¼  cups shredded pasteurized process Gruyère cheese (five 1-ounce wedges)
2½  cups finely diced cooked turkey

**1.** Beat the eggs in a medium-size bowl; beat in the ⅓ cup flour and then 1 cup of the milk, the sugar and ¼ teaspoon of the salt.

**2.** Heat a small skillet over medium heat; brush with oil. Pour 2 tablespoons of the batter into the center of the pan; quickly tilt the pan so the batter spreads and covers the bottom. Cook until the edges brown and holes appear on top. Turn and heat for 1 minute longer. Repeat with the remaining batter to make 12 crêpes. Remove the crêpes to a plate and separate with wax paper.

**3.** Melt the butter in a medium-size saucepan. Add the 2 tablespoons flour, remaining salt, pepper and mustard. Heat for 1 minute. Stir in 1½ cups of the milk. Cook, stirring constantly, until the sauce thickens and bubbles. Cook and stir for 3 minutes longer. Add 1 cup of the cheese, stirring until it melts. Remove from the heat.

**4.** Combine 1 cup of the cheese sauce with the turkey in a medium-size bowl. Mix the remaining ½ cup of milk into the cheese sauce.

**5.** Place about 3 tablespoons of the filling on each crêpe. Roll to enclose. Fold the ends under and arrange in one layer in a buttered 8-cup shallow flameproof baking dish. Pour the remaining sauce over the crêpes. Sprinkle with the remaining ¼ cup of cheese.

**6.** Broil, about 5 inches from the heat, until the cheese is melted and browned and the sauce is bubbly, about 5 minutes.

# CHICKEN TERRINE À L'ORANGE

Begin this country-style pâté several days ahead of time.

*Bake at 350° for 3 to 3½ hours.*

*Makes about 4½ pounds or 18 servings.*

| | | | |
|---|---|---|---|
| ½ | pound chicken livers | 2 | eggs |
| 2 | tablespoons butter or margarine | ¼ | cup heavy cream |
| | | 4 | teaspoons salt |
| 3 | medium-size onions, finely chopped | 1 | teaspoon pepper |
| | | 1¼ | teaspoon leaf thyme, crumbled |
| 4 | small chicken thighs (about ½ pound) | ½ | teaspoon ground allspice |
| ¼ | cup brandy | 1 | tablespoon grated orange rind |
| ¼ | cup orange juice | | |
| 1½ | pounds boneless pork shoulder | 1 | pound pork fatback |
| | | 2 | bay leaves |
| 1 | pound pork fat | 2 | whole cloves |
| 1 | large chicken breast (about 12 ounces) | 2 | navel oranges, sectioned |
| | | 1 | teaspoon unflavored gelatin |

**1.** Sauté the chicken livers in the butter in a medium-size skillet until firm but still pink inside, 3 to 4 minutes. Remove to a small bowl with a slotted spoon. Sauté the onion in the fat remaining in the skillet until soft, about 5 minutes. Set aside.

**2.** Remove the skin and bones from the chicken thighs, keeping the meat from each in one piece. Add to the chicken livers; add the brandy and orange juice; cover. Refrigerate to marinate overnight.

**3.** Cut the pork shoulder and fat into small pieces; skin and bone the chicken breast; cut the meat into small pieces. Put the pork, fat and chicken breast through a food grinder twice, using the coarse blade, or once through the fine blade.

**4.** Combine the chopped meats with the reserved onion, eggs, cream, salt, pepper, thyme, allspice and orange rind; beat vigorously with a wooden spoon to blend thoroughly. Cover and refrigerate overnight.

**5.** Next day, lift the livers and thigh meats from the marinade; reserve enough livers to make a row lengthwise in the terrine. Chop the remaining livers fine and add to the chopped meat mixture; add the marinade and stir.

**6.** Line an 8-cup terrine or a 9 x 5 x 3-inch loaf pan or baking dish with thin slices of the fatback; spoon one third of the chopped mixture into the terrine; press one or two strips of the fatback lengthwise down the center; arrange the livers on top; fold the fatback over or add more to enclose the livers. Add one third more of the chopped meat mixture, pressing it slightly. Press two more slices of fatback down the center; arrange the thigh meat, wrapping the fat around the meat. Top with the remaining chopped meat mixture, mounding it slightly and smoothing the top with wet hands or a spatula.

**7.** Press the bay leaves and cloves on top; fold the overhanging ends of the fat over the pâté; cover the top with overlapping slices of fat. Cover the terrine or pan with aluminum foil. Put the terrine in a larger pan and place on the oven shelf. Pour boiling water into the outer pan to come halfway up the sides.

**8.** Bake in a moderate oven (350°) for 3 to 3½ hours or until the juices run yellow with no trace of pink (170° to 175° on meat a thermometer.)

**9.** Remove the terrine from the oven to a wire rack; remove the aluminum foil. Let cool; pour the cooking juices into a measuring cup (you should have ⅔ cup; if not, add water); reserve. Cover the terrine; refrigerate overnight.

**10.** Next day, remove the loaf from the pan; remove and discard the fatback slices from the top of the loaf. Arrange thin orange sections on the top of the loaf. Heat the reserved juices to boiling in a small saucepan; soften 1 teaspoon of unflavored gelatin in 1 tablespoon of cold water for 5 minutes. Stir them into the boiling juices; remove from the heat. Strain through a clean paper towel (do not let the fat drip through the towel). Cool the gelatin mixture until slightly syrupy; then brush or spoon evenly over the oranges on top of the loaf until glazed. Refrigerate until the gelatin is set. Cover with plastic wrap and keep refrigerated until serving time. It will keep, refrigerated, for several days.

# 10

## Quick-to-Fix Dishes

**B**ecause of our busy life-style, most people have a limited time to spend on cooking, except for special occasions. Producing an enticing and nutritious dinner quickly every evening can be a challenge for even the most gifted chef. That's where microwave ovens, woks, electric skillets and other time-saving appliances come in handy. For they enable an average cook to whip together delicious meals in an absolute minimum of time, with little effort.

Having reliable and creative recipes on hand is also an important aid. Because chicken cooks so fast, it is an ideal choice for hurry-up main-course dishes. Some recipes, such as Chicken à la King and Chinese Fried Rice and Chicken, take less than fifteen minutes from beginning to end. A good selection is given in this chapter, along with tips and hints on various styles of quick cooking.

# MICROWAVE COOKING

## Microwave How-tos for Chicken

Cooking in a microwave oven.
● Choose *chicken pieces* (breasts, thighs or drumsticks) of equal size, so that they will cook evenly. To cook drumsticks, arrange them in a circle on a baking dish, with thicker ends out.
● Brush a *whole chicken* with melted butter or margarine, or rub with shortening and season with salt and pepper. Place, breast-side down, on a microwave-safe roasting rack in a shallow pan. Cover chicken lightly with wax paper to prevent spattering. Microwave on Medium, 9 minutes per pound, or until the drumstick moves easily, turning chicken breast-side up after half the cooking time has elapsed. Allow to rest for 10 minutes and then carve.

## Browning Microwave-cooked Chicken

One big drawback of microwaving is the difficulty of getting foods to brown. The reason: Microwave-cooked foods are not blasted with direct heat (which browns the surface), but cooked evenly by absorption or heat transference. Poultry over 3 pounds usually will brown. For poultry under that weight, consider these tips.
● Rub with butter and paprika. Or apply a brown sauce (soy or meat sauce) or add a dry or liquid browning aid, especially developed for microwave cooking.
● Use a special browning skillet to give crisp golden color to cut-up chicken.
● Run microwave-cooked food under the broiler of a conventional oven for a quick cosmetic touch-up.
● Investigate some of the newest microwave features, such as variable power, built-in computers, sensing probes and special browning units.

# CHICKEN ROSSO

*Cook on High power for 25 minutes.*
*(Conventional cooking: 45 minutes.)*
*Makes 6 servings.*

2   eggs, beaten
⅔   cup packaged unseasoned
    bread crumbs
⅓   cup grated Romano or
    Parmesan cheese
⅛   teaspoon garlic powder
¼   teaspoon leaf basil,
    crumbled
¼   teaspoon leaf oregano,
    crumbled

½   teaspoon salt
¼   teaspoon pepper
1   broiler/fryer (3 to 3½
    pounds), cut up into 8
    pieces
1   can (15 ounces) tomato
    sauce or tomato herb sauce
2   tablespoons chopped
    parsley

**1.** Pour the beaten egg into a shallow dish; mix the bread crumbs, Romano cheese, garlic powder, basil, oregano, salt and pepper on wax paper. Dip the chicken pieces in the beaten egg; then dredge with the bread crumb mixture.

**2.** Place the chicken in a 3-quart shallow glass baking dish, with the large pieces in the corners, skin-side down. Arrange the smaller pieces in the center. Cook, covered with plastic wrap, on High power for 7 minutes. Turn the pieces over; cook for 7 minutes more. Remove the baking dish from the microwave.

**3.** Pour the tomato sauce into a glass measuring cup; heat until it bubbles, about 4 minutes. Pour it evenly over the chicken. Return the baking dish to the microwave. Cook, covered, for 7 minutes.

**4.** Remove from oven; cover with aluminum foil; let stand for 5 minutes. Serve from the baking dish, garnished with parsley.

# CHICKEN ROSEMARY

*Cook on High power for 16 minutes.*
*(Conventional cooking: 45 minutes.)*
*Makes 4 servings.*

| | | | |
|---|---|---|---|
| 3 | cloves garlic, crushed | 3 | tablespoons fresh lemon juice |
| 1 | teaspoon leaf rosemary, crumbled | 1 | teaspoon salt |
| | | ½ | teaspoon pepper |
| ⅛ | teaspoon chili powder | ⅛ | teaspoon ground cumin |
| ½ | cup dry white wine | 1 | broiler/fryer (3½ to |
| ¼ | cup olive oil | | 4 pounds), cut up |

**1.** Combine the garlic, rosemary, chili powder, wine, olive oil, lemon juice, salt, pepper and cumin in a 3-quart shallow glass baking dish. Add the chicken pieces, turning several times to coat well. Remove the chicken.

**2.** Put the baking dish in center of oven; heat the seasoning mixture for 3 to 4 minutes on High power until it is simmering. Add the chicken, skin-side down, placing the thicker portions near the edge of the dish. Spoon the mixture over the chicken.

**3.** Cook, covered with plastic wrap, for 4 minutes. Turn the chicken over, spooning the mixture over it. Cook for 4 minutes. Rotate the dish one half turn. Cook for 4 minutes.

**4.** Remove from the oven; cover tightly with aluminum foil; let stand for 15 minutes.

# LOUISIANA TURKEY ROYALE

Serving turkey the second time around can be delicious,
when you follow this recipe.

*Microwave on Medium power for 10 minutes.*
*Makes 6 servings.*

| | |
|---|---|
| 1 tablespoon butter or margarine | ¼ cup minced parsley |
| 1 cup sliced mushrooms | 1 can (4 ounces) pimientos, sliced |
| 1 sweet green pepper, halved, seeded and slivered | 1 teaspoon salt |
| 3 cups cubed cooked turkey | ¼ teaspoon pepper |
| Velouté Sauce (recipe follows) | 1 teaspoon paprika |
| ¼ cup dry sherry | ¼ cup almonds, toasted and slivered |

**1.** Heat the butter in a 10-cup microwave-safe casserole on Medium power for 30 seconds.
**2.** Stir in the mushrooms and green pepper; cover with plastic wrap.
**3.** Cook on Medium power for 2 minutes. Add the cubed turkey, Velouté Sauce, sherry, parsley, pimiento, salt, pepper and paprika. Cover the casserole loosely with wax paper.
**4.** Microwave on Medium power for 8 to 10 minutes, turning the dish several times. Stir; let stand for 5 minutes. Sprinkle the top with the almonds.

# VELOUTÉ SAUCE

Also excellent with chicken croquettes.

*Makes 2 cups.*

| | |
|---|---|
| ¼ cup (½ stick) butter or margarine | 1 can (13¾ ounces) chicken broth |
| ¼ cup all-purpose flour | ¼ cup water |
| ⅛ teaspoon pepper | 1 teaspoon lemon juice |

**1.** Melt the butter in a small saucepan. Blend in the flour and pepper; cook, stirring constantly, until the mixture bubbles. Gradually stir in the broth and water until well blended.
**2.** Cook over low heat, stirring constantly, until the sauce thickens and bubbles for 3 minutes. Stir in the lemon juice.

# SPEEDY TURKEY LOAF

Melted mint jelly is the crowning glory on a meatloaf made
with ground turkey.

*Microwave on High power for 30 minutes.*
*Makes 6 servings.*

| | | | |
|---|---|---|---|
| 1 | roll (1½ pounds) frozen ground turkey, thawed | 1 | small onion, minced (¼ cup) |
| 2 | slices rye bread, crumbled (2 cups) | ¼ | cup chopped parsley |
| | | 1½ | teaspoons salt |
| 2 | eggs, beaten | ¼ | teaspoon pepper |
| | | ½ | cup mint jelly, heated |

**1.** Combine the ground turkey, bread crumbs, eggs, onion, parsley, salt and pepper in a medium-size bowl until well blended. Pack the mixture into an 8 x 6 x 2½-inch loaf pan; invert onto a microwave-safe tray; cover lightly with plastic wrap.

**2.** Microwave on High power, turning the tray several times, for 30 minutes or until firm. Remove and spoon the mint jelly over to glaze. Allow the turkey loaf to stand for 10 minutes.

**3.** Transfer the loaf to a heated serving platter with two wide pancake turners.

***Cook's Tip:*** The turkey mixture can be made and shaped the night before and placed on microwave-safe tray. Then refrigerate and add 5 minutes to the cooking time.

## *WOK (STIR-FRY) COOKING*

### How to Stir-fry Chicken

Stir-frying is a great do-it-yourself idea. Chop, slice and cut poultry and vegetables into small pieces, place in bowls, cover with plastic wrap and store in refrigerator. Each person can take out his share and cook a dinner in just a few minutes.

Be sure that the chicken is really cold when cut into tiny pieces with a very sharp knife. Slice all vegetables in small pieces too. (This can be done early in the day and then refrigerated.) Heat peanut or vegetable oil with a clove of garlic (if you wish) in a wok or a large, heavy skillet until very hot. Add the chicken a few pieces at a time if there is a lot, and stir-fry with a large slotted spoon until the chicken is golden. Remove and reserve. Add more oil if necessary; then add the vegetables a part at a time, and stir-fry just until they are well coated and turn a bright color. Return the chicken to the pan and add the chicken broth or other liquid. Cover the pan and steam for 5 minutes, or until the vegetables are crisp-tender.

**Note:** You can substitue slices of raw turkey fillet for the boneless chicken in any recipe for stir-fried chicken.

# CHICKEN AND SNOW PEAS IN ORANGE SAUCE

*Makes 4 servings.*

| | |
|---|---|
| 2 navel oranges | 6 ounces snow peas, washed, trimmed OR: 1 package (6 ounces) frozen ones |
| 2 tablespoons butter or margarine | 1 teaspoon salt |
| ¼ teaspoon ground ginger | ⅛ teaspoon pepper |
| ¼ teaspoon ground cinnamon | 2 teaspoons chili sauce |
| 1 pound boneless chicken breast, sliced ⅛ inch thick | ¼ cup cashews or peanuts |
| | Hot cooked rice |

**1.** Grate 1 tablespoon rind from the oranges; reserve. Section one of the oranges (½ cup); reserve. Squeeze the remaining orange; measure 2 tablespoons juice; reserve.
**2.** Heat the butter in wok or large skillet. Stir-fry the grated orange rind, ginger and cinnamon for a few seconds. Add the chicken; stir-fry 3 to 4 minutes. Stir in the snow peas; cook for 1 minute. Sprinkle with salt and pepper.
**3.** Stir in chili sauce; cook for 1 minute. Stir in the orange sections and juice; cook for 2 minutes. Sprinkle with the nuts. Serve with hot cooked rice.

# CHICKEN PROVENÇALE

*Makes 4 servings.*

| | | | |
|---|---|---|---|
| 2 | tablespoons olive oil | 1 | teaspoon salt |
| 1 | clove garlic, finely chopped | ¼ | teaspoon pepper |
| 1 | pound boneless chicken | 1 | cup cherry tomatoes |
| | breast, sliced ½ inch thick | 1 | can (3½ ounces) pitted |
| 3 | small zucchini (1 pound), | | black olives |
| | sliced | 2 | tablespoons lemon juice |
| 1 | teaspoon leaf basil, crumbled | | French bread (optional) |
| ¼ | teaspoon leaf oregano, | | OR: Garlic toast (optional) |
| | crumbled | | |

**1.** Heat the oil in a wok or large skillet. Stir-fry the garlic, chicken and zucchini over a high heat for 4 to 5 minutes. Add the basil, oregano, salt and pepper; cook for 1 more minute.
**2.** Add the tomatoes and olives. Cook and stir for 2 minutes. Blend in the lemon juice. Serve with French bread or garlic toast, if you wish.

# CHICKEN LIVERS AND PEPPERS

*Makes 4 servings.*

| | | | |
|---|---|---|---|
| 1 | pound chicken livers | ½ | pound medium-size |
| 1 | tablespoon butter or | | mushrooms, sliced |
| | margarine | 4 | green onions, sliced |
| 2 | tablespoons vegetable oil | 1 | teaspoon Worcestershire |
| 2 | teaspoons all-purpose flour | | sauce |
| ½ | teaspoon salt | 2 | tablespoons dry Madeira |
| ¼ | teaspoon pepper | | wine |
| 1 | large sweet green pepper, | 2 | tablespoons chopped |
| | halved, seeded and cut into | | parsley |
| | 1-inch pieces | | Buttered noodles |

**1.** Wash the chicken livers; drain on paper toweling; trim and cut each in half.

**2.** Heat the butter and 1 tablespoon of the oil in a wok or large skillet; add the livers. Combine the flour, salt and pepper in a cup; sprinkle over the livers. Stir-fry over high heat until browned, 4 minutes. Remove to a plate.

**3.** Add the remaining oil, green pepper and mushrooms to the wok; stir-fry for 3 to 4 minutes. Stir in the green onions, Worcestershire sauce and Madeira; cook for 1 minute. Return the livers to the wok. Cook and stir for 2 minutes. Sprinkle with parsley. Serve with cooked buttered noodles.

# SWEET AND PUNGENT CHICKEN BREASTS

You can fix this chicken dish in a jiffy when you start with frozen chicken breasts.

*Makes 4 servings.*

| | | | |
|---|---|---|---|
| 1 | package (1 pound, 6 ounces) frozen breaded chicken breasts | 1 | medium-size sweet green pepper, halved, seeded and cut into slivers |
| 1 | can (8 ounces) pineapple chunks in pineapple juice | 2 | tablespoons vegetable oil |
| ⅓ | cup cider vinegar | 1 | medium-size tomato, cored and cut into wedges |
| 2 | tablespoons light brown sugar | 2 | tablespoons cornstarch |
| 1 | teaspoon soy sauce | 2 | tablespoons cold water |
| ½ | teaspoon red pepper flakes | | Hot cooked rice |

**1.** Prepare the chicken breasts following label directions.

**2.** Drain the juice from the pineapple into a 2-cup glass measure; reserve the pineapple chunks. Add water to the pineapple juice to make 1 cup of liquid. Add the vinegar, brown sugar, soy sauce and red pepper flakes. Stir to dissolve brown the sugar; reserve.

**3.** Stir-fry the green pepper in the oil in a large skillet until crisp-tender, about 2 minutes. Add the pineapple juice-vinegar mixture, reserved pineapple chunks and tomato wedges; bring slowly to boiling. Lower the heat. Combine the cornstarch with the water; stir into the skillet; cook just until thickened.

**4.** Arrange the baked chicken pieces on a serving platter; spoon the vegetables and fruit mixture over the chicken. Serve with rice.

# TURKEY WITH MUSHROOMS AND SNOW PEAS

*Makes 4 servings.*

| | | | |
|---|---|---|---|
| 2 | tablespoons vegetable oil | 2 | teaspoons cornstarch |
| 1 | medium-size onion, cut into 8 wedges | 2 | tablespoons soy sauce |
| ½ | pound medium-size mushrooms, quartered | 1½ | cups cooked turkey, cut into 2-inch-long by ½-inch-wide strips |
| ½ | cup sliced water chestnuts | 1 | package (6 ounces) frozen snow peas, thawed and drained |
| 1 | teaspoon salt | | Hot cooked rice |
| | Pinch of pepper | | |
| ¼ | cup dry sherry | | |
| ½ | cup Turkey Broth (page 129) | | |

**1.** Heat the oil in a large skillet over medium-high heat. Add the onion; stir-fry for about 2 minutes. Add the mushrooms, water chestnuts, salt, pepper and sherry; stir-fry for 1½ minutes.
**2.** Pour the broth over the vegetables; bring to simmering. Combine the cornstarch and soy sauce in a small cup; stir into the broth. Cook for 30 seconds or until the sauce thickens and clears. Add the turkey and snow peas. Stir gently for 1 minute or until heated through. Serve over hot cooked rice.


# STIR-FRIED CHICKEN AND VEGETABLES

*Makes 2 servings.*

| | | | |
|---|---|---|---|
| 3 | teaspoons vegetable oil | ¼ | cup water |
| 1 | package (10 ounces) frozen Chinese-style stir-fry vegetables with seasonings | | Soy sauce |
| | | | Hot cooked rice |
| 2 | chicken breast fillets (about 8 ounces total weight), cut into ¼-inch-thick slices | | |

**1.** Heat 2 teaspoonfuls of the oil in a heavy skillet. Remove and reserve the seasoning envelope from the vegetables. Add the frozen vegetables to the hot oil and stir to break up the pieces. Cover and let cook for 2 minutes. Remove to a small bowl; keep warm.

**2.** Heat the remaining teaspoon of oil in the skillet. Add the chicken; cook, stirring constantly with a wooden spoon, for 5 minutes. There should be no pink left in the chicken.

**3.** Return the vegetables to the skillet; sprinkle the seasonings over and stir in the water until the sauce thickens, about 1 minute. Season to taste with soy sauce and serve with hot cooked rice.

# CHINESE FRIED RICE AND CHICKEN

Preparation time: 4 minutes.
Cooking time: 8 minutes

*Makes 4 servings.*

| | | | |
|---|---|---|---|
| 4 | tablespoons vegetable oil or butter | 3 | cups cooked rice |
| 1 | cup thinly sliced green onions, including green tops | 4 | tablespoons soy sauce |
| | | ½ | teaspoon ground ginger |
| 1 | cup bamboo shoots, drained and sliced | ½ | teaspoon garlic powder |
| | | 2 | eggs, lightly beaten |
| | | 2 | cups cubed cooked chicken |

**1.** Heat the oil in a wok or large skillet. Reserve 2 tablespoons of the onions for garnish. Sauté the remaining onions and bamboo shoots in the oil, stirring constantly for 2 minutes.

**2.** Add the cooked rice, stirring until the rice is coated with oil and heated through.

**3.** Add the soy sauce, ginger, garlic powder, eggs and chicken. Cook, stirring lightly, for 5 minutes more or until the chicken is heated through and the eggs are set.

# CHICKEN CHINOISE

Preparation time: 15 minutes.
Cooking time: 12 minutes.
*Makes 4 servings.*

2 whole chicken breasts, boned and skinned (about 1 pound total weight)
2 tablespoons cornstarch
½ teaspoon salt
½ teaspoon ground ginger
2 tablespoons vegetable oil
2 celery stalks, sliced on the diagonal

1 sweet green pepper, diced
1 can (4 ounces) button mushrooms, undrained
1 can (5 ounces) bamboo shoots, drained
1 tablespoon soy sauce
1 cup chicken broth
¼ cup blanched, toasted and slivered almonds

**1.** Cut the chicken into 2-inch squares.

**2.** Combine 1 tablespoon of the cornstarch, salt and ginger in a bag. Add the chicken to the bag and shake.

**3.** Heat the oil in a wok or skillet and stir-fry the chicken pieces until the chicken turns white, about 2 minutes.

**4.** Add the celery and green pepper; cook for about 2 minutes or until the vegetables are tender.

**5.** Add the mushrooms with liquid and bamboo shoots. Add the soy sauce with remaining 1 tablespoon cornstarch and chicken broth; stir into the skillet. Cook until thickened, about 4 minutes, stirring gently. Top with the almonds and serve.

# CHICKEN BREASTS IN CURRIED CHUTNEY

*Makes 4 servings.*

| | | | |
|---|---|---|---|
| 2 | whole boneless chicken breasts | ⅓ | cup chopped chutney |
| 1 | medium-size onion, sliced | ½ | cup dry white wine |
| ¼ | cup (½ stick) butter or margarine | 1 | cup heavy cream |
| 4 | tablespoons curry powder | ½ | teaspoon salt |
| | | ¼ | teaspoon pepper |

**1.** Halve the chicken breasts; sauté them with the onion in the butter in a large skillet for about 3 minutes on each side. Remove to a warm platter.

**2.** Add the curry, chutney, wine, cream, salt and pepper to the skillet. Cook, stirring frequently, for 5 minutes. Return the chicken to the skillet; heat for 2 minutes until bubbly-hot.

# CHICKEN WITH CREAM SAUCE

*Makes 6 servings.*

| | | | |
|---|---|---|---|
| 3 | whole chicken breasts (about 12 ounces each), skinned, boned and halved | 1 | envelope (1.25 ounces) sour cream sauce mix |
| ½ | teaspoon leaf thyme, crumbled | 1 | cup milk |
| ½ | teaspoon salt | 1 | package (10 ounces) frozen broccoli spears, slightly thawed, cut in half lengthwise |
| ¼ | teaspoon pepper | | |
| 2 | tablespoons butter or margarine | | |

**1.** Rub the chicken breasts with thyme, salt and pepper.

**2.** Sauté the chicken breasts in the butter in a large skillet for about 3 minutes on each side, or just until meat feels firm to the touch. Remove to a serving platter. Drain off the pan drippings.

**3.** Add the sour cream sauce mix; gradually stir in the milk, scraping up the browned bits; heat just until bubbly. Add the broccoli; cover. Cook for 2 minutes or until the broccoli is heated thoroughly. Spoon over the chicken breasts.

# CHICKEN WITH HAM AND MUSHROOMS

Complete menu: Quick-cooking long grain and wild rice, raw zucchini sticks, tomato slices and blueberries with cream.

*Makes 4 servings.*

2　whole chicken breasts
　(14 ounces each), split
2　tablespoons all-purpose flour
½　teaspoon salt
⅛　teaspoon pepper
1　tablespoon butter or
　margarine
1　tablespoon vegetable oil

¼　pound cooked ham,
　finely slivered
1　tablespoon finely chopped
　onion
¼　pound fresh mushrooms,
　sliced
1　tablespoon dry sherry
1　cup light cream

**1.** Skin and bone the chicken. Flatten slightly between sheets of wax paper with a rolling pin or the flat side of a meat mallet. Combine 1 tablespoon of the flour, salt and pepper on one piece of the wax paper; turn the chicken in the flour to coat it on all sides.
**2.** Heat the butter and oil in a large skillet. Sauté the chicken for 3 minutes on each side (do not overcook). Remove from the skillet and keep warm.
**3.** Add the ham to the skillet; stir until lightly browned, about 1 minute. Stir in the onion and mushrooms. Cook until softened, about 3 minutes. Add the sherry; stir for 1 minute. Lower the heat.
**4.** Combine the remaining tablespoon of flour with the cream in a small bowl; stir into the ham mixture. Simmer until the sauce is thickened and bubbly, about 2 minutes.
**5.** Return the chicken to the skillet, turning to coat with the sauce. Heat for 1 minute.

# CHICKEN CUTLETS WITH HOLLANDAISE SAUCE

*Makes 4 servings.*

⅓　cup all-purpose flour
½　teaspoon leaf tarragon,
　crumbled
½　teaspoon salt
¼　teaspoon pepper
2　whole boned chicken
　breasts, halved

¼　cup (½ stick) butter or
　margarine
1　package (10 ounces) frozen
　asparagus spears, thawed
　Quick Hollandaise Sauce
　(recipe follows)

**1.** Combine the flour, tarragon, salt and pepper; coat each chicken half evenly with the mixture. Melt the butter in a large skillet. Sauté the chicken, turning frequently, until browned and tender, about 3 minutes on each side.

**2.** Add the thawed asparagus spears. Continue cooking until the chicken is thoroughly cooked and the asparagus is heated through, 5 to 10 minutes.

**Quick Hollandaise Sauce:** Combine 3 egg yolks, 2 tablespoons lemon juice, ½ teaspoon leaf tarragon and ¼ teaspoon salt in the container of an electric blender. Whirl until smooth. Pour in ½ cup (1 stick) melted butter. Whirl until the sauce thickens, about 30 seconds. Pour over the chicken and asparagus.

## CHICKEN MADEIRA

*Makes 4 servings.*

| | | | |
|---|---|---|---|
| 2 | whole boneless chicken breasts | ½ | teaspoon salt |
| 2 | tablespoons butter or margarine | ¼ | teaspoon pepper |
| 1 | package (6 ounces) frozen mushrooms in butter sauce | ½ | cup dry Madeira wine |

**1.** Cut the chicken into ¼-inch-thick slices. Melt the butter in a medium-size skillet. Sauté the chicken for about 5 minutes or until the chicken turns white. Add the frozen mushrooms, breaking them up with a wooden spoon. Continue cooking until the chicken is tender and the mushrooms are cooked, about 10 minutes.

**2.** Add the salt, pepper and wine. Cook, stirring constantly, until the pan is deglazed.

# STUFFED CHICKEN BREAST DINNER

Preparation time: 10 minutes.
Cooking time: 25 minutes.

*Makes 4 servings.*

2    **chicken breasts (12 to 14 ounces each), boned, skinned and halved**
1    **package (8 ounces) frozen crabmeat stuffing, thawed***
2    **tablespoons butter**

¼    **cup dry white wine or dry vermouth**
1    **package (10 ounces) asparagus spears, thawed* Foolproof Hollandaise Sauce (recipe follows)**

**1.** Flatten the chicken breasts between sheets of wax paper with a meat mallet or rolling pin. Place one quarter of the crabmeat stuffing on each piece of chicken. Fold the long ends of the chicken over the stuffing; fasten with toothpicks.

**2.** Set the heat indicator of the electric skillet at 350° (or use medium heat for a nonelectric skillet). Melt the butter. Sauté the chicken rolls for 5 minutes, until golden.

**3.** Add the wine, scraping up the browned bits with a wooden spoon. Cover; cook for 15 minutes. (If the skillet is getting too hot, lower the heat to 325°.) Add the asparagus; cover and cook for 5 minutes. Serve with Foolproof Hollandaise Sauce.

*Remove from the freezer to the refrigerator in the morning.

***Note:*** If frozen crabmeat stuffing is not available in your area, a package of chicken-flavored stuffing mix plus a can of crabmeat can be substituted. Any extra stuffing can be heated and served with the chicken.

# FOOLPROOF HOLLANDAISE SAUCE

A blender makes this elegant sauce in only 5 minutes.

*Makes ¾ cup.*

| | |
|---|---|
| 3   egg yolks | ½   cup (1 stick) butter, melted |
| 2   tablespoons lemon juice | (keep hot) |
| ¼   teaspoon salt | |

**1.** Rinse the container of an electric blender with hot water. Add the egg yolks, lemon juice and salt. Whirl to combine.

**2.** Remove the lid; pour in the hot butter gradually with the motor still on. Whirl until sauce thickens, about 30 seconds.

**3.** Pour into a small bowl and keep warm over hot water if you are not using immediately.

# CHICKEN LIVERS WITH RICE

*Cook on top of the stove for 12 minutes.*
*Makes 4 servings.*

| | |
|---|---|
| 1⅓ cups packaged precooked rice | ¼   teaspoon pepper |
| 4   slices bacon | 1   pound chicken livers, halved |
| 1   medium-size onion, sliced | ⅓   cup dry red wine |
| 2   tablespoons chopped sweet green pepper | ¼   cup water |
| | Hot cooked rice |
| ¼   cup all-purpose flour | ¼   cup pitted black olives, chopped |
| ½   teaspoon salt | |

**1.** Cook the rice following label directions for 4 servings.

**2.** Cook the bacon in a large skillet until crisp; drain on paper toweling; crumble and reserve.

**3.** Add the onion and green pepper to the fat in the skillet; cook until tender, about 3 minutes.

**4.** Combine the flour, salt and pepper on wax paper. Dredge the livers with the flour mixture, shaking off any excess. Brown the livers quickly.

**5.** Add the wine and water to the skillet; simmer, covered, for 1 minute. Serve the livers on hot rice; top with the bacon and olives.

# CHICKEN LIVERS WITH BACON AND GREEN BEANS

A tasty way to use economical and nutritious chicken livers.

*Makes 4 servings.*

| | | | |
|---|---|---|---|
| 1 | pound chicken livers | ¼ | cup water |
| 4 | slices bacon | 1 | package (9 ounces) frozen |
| 2 | tablespoons all-purpose | | Italian green beans |
| | flour | | Fried rice |

**1.** Trim the livers of any connective tissue or fat. Cook the bacon in a large skillet; remove to paper toweling; crumble and reserve. Pour the bacon drippings into a cup; measure and return 2 tablespoons to the skillet.

**2.** Roll the chicken livers in the flour to coat them. Brown on all sides in the drippings (5 to 10 minutes). Stir in ¼ cup water, scraping up the browned bits from the skillet. Add the beans; cover and cook for 10 minutes or until the beans are tender. The livers should be brown outside and slightly pink inside. Taste; add salt and pepper, if you wish. Sprinkle with the crumbled bacon. Serve with fried rice.

# CHICKEN DIVAN

No one would believe that this is a special leftover poultry dish. It looks and tastes great enough for a party.

*Broil for 10 minutes.*
*Makes 4 servings.*

| | | | |
|---|---|---|---|
| 2 | packages (10 ounces) frozen broccoli spears | 1 | teaspoon salt |
| ¼ | cup (½ stick) butter or margarine | ¼ | teaspoon pepper |
| | | ½ | cup heavy cream, whipped |
| ¼ | cup all-purpose flour | ½ | cup grated Parmesan cheese |
| 2 | cups milk | 12 | slices roasted chicken |
| 2 | tablespoons dry sherry | | OR: 8 slices roasted turkey |

**1.** Cook the broccoli following label directions; drain and arrange in an 8-cup flameproof baking dish.

**2.** Melt the butter in a medium-size saucepan. Stir in the flour and cook, stirring constantly, until the mixture bubbles. Stir in the milk, sherry, salt and pepper. Cook, stirring constantly, until the sauce thickens and bubbles for 2 minutes. Fold in the whipped cream and Parmesan cheese with a wire whisk.

**3.** Arrange the chicken slices over the broccoli in the baking pan; spoon the sauce over to cover completely.

**4.** Broil, 4 inches from the heat, for 10 minutes or until the sauce is bubbly.

# CHICKEN À LA KING

Created by a chef at Delmonico's Restaurant in 1880 New York for Foxhall Keene. Later the name was changed from Keene to King.

*Makes 4 servings.*

| | |
|---|---|
| ¼ cup (½ stick) butter or margarine | ½ teaspoon Worcestershire sauce |
| ¼ pound mushrooms, sliced | 2 cups diced cooked chicken or turkey |
| ¼ cup all-purpose flour | |
| 1 cup chicken broth | 1 jar (4 ounces) pimientos, drained and diced |
| 1 cup light cream or milk | |
| 1 teaspoon salt | Hot cooked rice |

**1.** Melt the butter in a medium-size saucepan; sauté the mushroom slices for 3 minutes; remove with a slotted spoon and reserve.

**2.** Stir the flour into the saucepan and cook, stirring constantly, until the mixture bubbles. Stir in the chicken broth, light cream milk, salt and Worcestershire sauce. Cook, stirring constantly, until the sauce thickens and bubbles.

**3.** Add the sautéed mushrooms, diced chicken and diced pimiento. Simmer for 5 minutes or until heated through. Serve over hot cooked rice.

# ROAST CHICKEN WITH CHERRY SAUCE

For a quick but classy dinner entrée, make this luscious sauce to serve over ready-to-eat chicken.

*Makes 2 servings.*

| | | | |
|---|---|---|---|
| 2 | tablespoons sugar | 1 | tablespoon cornstarch |
| 2 | tablespoons white vinegar | ½ | cup chicken broth |
| 1 | large navel orange | 1 | tablespoon orange liqueur |
| 1 | lemon | | (optional) |
| 1 | can (16 ounces) pitted sour cherries | 1 | deli-roasted whole chicken (about 2½ pounds) |

**1.** Combine the sugar and vinegar in a medium-size saucepan. Heat until the sugar caramelizes and becomes amber in color. (Do not overcook.)

**2.** Cut very thin strips of peel from the orange and lemon with a sharp knife, removing the colored part only (no white). Reserve the fruits for another use. Combine the orange and lemon strips in a saucepan with water to cover; bring to boiling; remove from the heat; let stand for 3 minutes; drain and reserve the rinds.

**3.** Drain the cherries; add the juice to the saucepan containing the caramel. Stir the cornstarch into the chicken broth; stir into the juice in the saucepan. Cook, stirring constantly, until the sauce thickens and clears. Add the drained cherries, reserved rinds and orange liqueur, if used. Heat just until the mixture starts to bubble. Serve with deli-roasted chicken.

***Go-withs:*** Long grain and wild rice mix, green beans almondine and French chocolate pudding mousse.

# TURKEY AND RICE CASSEROLE

Preparation time: 20 minutes
Cooking time: 10 minutes

*Makes 4 servings.*

1 package (8 ounces) chicken-flavored rice and vermicelli mixture
4 green onions, sliced
¼ cup (½ stick) butter or margarine
2¾ cups boiling water
1 teaspoon salt
¼ teaspoon pepper
2 cups cubed cooked turkey
1 cup dairy sour cream
¼ cup shredded sharp Cheddar cheese
½ teaspoon salt
½ teaspoon leaf dillweed
¼ cup toasted and slivered almonds

**1.** Sauté the rice and vermicelli mixture and onions in the butter in a large skillet, stirring frequently until the vermicelli is light brown.
**2.** Add the boiling water, 1 teaspoon salt and ¼ teaspoon pepper. Stir once. Lower the heat; cover; simmer for 15 minutes or until the liquid is absorbed.
**3.** Combine the turkey, sour cream, cheese, ½ teaspoon salt and dillweed.
**4.** Spread the cooked rice mixture evenly over the bottom of a 2-quart shallow baking dish. Top with the turkey mixture. Sprinkle with the slivered almonds.
**5.** Bake in a hot oven (400°) until heated through, about 10 minutes.

# 11

# International
# Dishes

Chicken plays an important part in the cuisine of most countries of the world. Chicken dishes have been named after cardinals (Richelieu) and cities (Marengo), composers (Rossini) and generals (Demidov), and they have graced the tables of emperors, philosophers and kings.

Chicken Tetrazzini, Chicken Kiev, Paella and Chicken Cacciatore are a few of the great international culinary creations included in this chapter. All the recipes are up-to-date adaptations, and all use time-saving American ingredients, such as chicken parts, canned tomatoes and tomato paste. They are organized under the names of their countries of origin.

# PAELLA

Here's a slightly different variation of the Spanish chicken and rice classic.

*Bake at 400° for 50 minutes.*
*Makes 6 servings.*

| | | | |
|---|---|---|---|
| 4 | hot or sweet Italian sausages or a combination of both | 1 | teaspoon leaf oregano, crumbled |
| ¼ | cup olive or vegetable oil | 1 | teaspoon salt |
| 1 | broiler/fryer (3 pounds), cut up | ¼ | teaspoon pepper |
| 1 | large onion, chopped (1 cup) | ¼ | teaspoon powdered saffron |
| 1 | clove garlic, minced | ½ | pound shelled and deveined fresh shrimp OR: 1 package (8 ounces) frozen shrimp, slightly thawed |
| 1½ | cups long-grain white rice | | |
| 1 | can (8 ounces) tomato sauce | | |
| 1 | can (13¾ ounces) chicken broth (1¾ cups) | 1 | package (9 ounces) Italian green beans |
| 2 | cups water | 1 | jar (4 ounces) pimientos, slivered |

**1.** Parboil the sausages in water to cover, for 10 minutes. Drain; cut into ¼-inch-thick slices.

**2.** Heat the oil in a paella pan or a large deep skillet. Brown the chicken pieces a few at a time; remove the pieces as they brown.

**3.** Sauté the onion and garlic in the same skillet until tender, about 5 minutes. Add the rice, tomato sauce, chicken broth, water, oregano, salt, pepper and saffron. Bring to boiling. If you are using a paella pan, place the chicken pieces on top of the rice mixture. (If you are using a skillet, pour the mixture into a 13x9x2-inch baking dish.) Cover with aluminum foil.

**4.** Bake in a hot oven (400°) for 30 minutes. Add the shrimp and sausages to the mixture. Cover; bake for 20 minutes longer or until the chicken, rice and seafood are done.

**5.** Cook the green beans following package directions; drain. Fluff up the rice mixture; stir in the pimiento; garnish with the green beans around the edges of the pan.

# CHICKEN BASQUE STYLE

Flavors from the Basque region of Spain give this chicken dish
a zesty flavor.

*Bake at 350° for 30 minutes.*
*Makes 8 servings.*

2  broiler/fryers (about 3 pounds each), cut up
½  cup all-purpose flour
½  teaspoon pepper
2  teaspoons salt
¼  cup olive oil
2  cloves garlic, minced
2  medium-size onions, each cut into 8 wedges
1  medium-size sweet red pepper, halved, seeded and slivered
1  medium-size sweet green pepper, halved, seeded and slivered

1  small eggplant (about 1 pound), cut into ¾-inch cubes
1½ teaspoons leaf oregano, crumbled
½  teaspoon leaf basil, crumbled
¼  teaspoon red pepper flakes
1  can (16 ounces) whole tomatoes, undrained
1  cup dry white wine
1  can (3¼ ounces) pitted black olives, drained and halved

**1.** Shake the chicken pieces a few at a time in a plastic bag with the flour, pepper and 1 teaspoon of the salt; reserve the remaining flour mixture.
**2.** Brown the chicken pieces in the oil in a large saucepan; remove to a 10-cup baking dish. Pour the pan drippings into a 1-cup glass measure; wipe out the saucepan. Add enough additional olive oil to the pan drippings to make ¼ cup. Pour into the saucepan.
**3.** Add the garlic, onion wedges, red and green peppers and eggplant. Cook, stirring frequently, until the vegetables are crisp-tender, about 3 minutes. Add 2 tablespoons of the reserved flour mixture, the remaining 1 teaspoon salt, oregano, basil and red pepper flakes; toss to coat the vegetables. Add the tomatoes with their liquid, breaking up the large pieces, and the wine. Bring to boiling. Pour the vegetable mixture over the chicken; cover.
**4.** Bake in a moderate oven (350°) for 30 minutes or until the chicken is tender. Uncover; add the olives; stir to mix.

# NORMANDY CHICKEN

*Makes 6 servings.*

| | | | |
|---|---|---|---|
| 2 | tablespoons butter or margarine | ½ | cup chicken broth |
| 3 | whole chicken breasts (2½ pounds total weight), split | ⅛ | teaspoon leaf thyme, crumbled |
| 1 | teaspoon salt | 2 | eating apples, cut into 1-inch chunks |
| ¼ | teaspoon pepper | 1 | teaspoon cornstarch |
| 1 | small onion, sliced | ½ | cup light cream |
| 2 | tablespoons apple brandy or cider | | Chopped parsley (optional) |

**1.** Melt the butter in a large skillet. Add the chicken; sprinkle with the salt and pepper. Cook over medium heat, turning often until nicely browned, about 10 minutes. Lift one or two pieces of the chicken and stir the onion into the drippings in the skillet; cook for 2 to 3 minutes.
**2.** Sprinkle the apple brandy over the chicken; add the chicken broth and thyme; cover. Cook over low heat for 5 minutes. Add the apple pieces, pushing them under and between the chicken pieces to cook evenly. Cook, covered, for 10 to 15 minutes longer or until the chicken is tender.
**3.** Lift the chicken and apples to a heated serving platter; keep warm. Mix the cornstarch and cream; add to the boiling liquid. Cook, stirring constantly, until the sauce thickens and bubbles for 1 minute. Taste and add more salt and pepper if needed. Spoon the sauce over the chicken; sprinkle with the chopped parsley, if you wish.

# POULET MARENGO

This dish originated in the Italian town of Marengo. They say it was created by Napoleon's chef to celebrate his victory over the Austrians there.

*Bake at 350° for 1 hour and 10 minutes.*
*Makes 8 servings.*

| | | | |
|---|---|---|---|
| 6 | slices bacon, cut into 1-inch pieces | 1 | clove garlic, minced |
| 2 | broiler/fryers (about 3 pounds each), cut up | ½ | pound mushrooms, sliced |
| ½ | cup all-purpose flour | 2 | cans (1 pound each) tomatoes |
| 2 | teaspoons salt | ¼ | cup chopped parsley |
| ¼ | teaspoon pepper | | Few drops liquid red-pepper seasoning |
| 1 | large onion, chopped (1 cup) | | Golden Croutons (recipe follows) |

**1.** Fry the bacon until it is almost crisp in a large skillet. Lift out with a slotted spoon; drain on paper toweling and reserve. Leave the drippings in the pan.

**2.** Shake the chicken in the mixture of flour, salt and pepper in a plastic bag to coat well; reserve the remaining flour.

**3.** Brown the chicken, a few pieces at a time, in the bacon drippings; place in a 12-cup shallow casserole.

**4.** Sauté the onion and garlic until soft in same pan; stir in the reserved flour mixture. Stir the mushrooms, tomatoes, parsley and red-pepper seasoning into the pan. Bring to boiling, stirring constantly, until the sauce thickens.

**5.** Spoon over the chicken in the casserole; cover. (The casserole can be put together up to this point and then refrigerated. Increase the baking time by 20 minutes.)

**6.** Bake in a moderate oven (350°) for 1 hour or until the chicken is tender. Uncover; sprinkle with the reserved bacon. Bake for 10 minutes longer or until the bacon is crisp and heated.

**7.** Just before serving, sprinkle Golden Croutons over the top; garnish with more chopped parsley, if you wish.

**Golden Croutons:** Trim the crusts from 2 slices of white bread; cut the bread into 1½-inch cubes. Spread in a single layer in a shallow baking pan. Toast along with the casserole in a moderate oven (350°) for 10 minutes or until golden. Makes 1 cup.

# COQ AU VIN BLANC

Traditionally the chicken is cut into pieces and the wine is red. Here is a delicious new interpretation of the French classic dish.

*Bake at 325° for 1 hour.*
*Makes 8 servings.*

| | | | |
|---|---|---|---|
| 1 | roasting chicken (about 5 pounds) Salt and pepper | 1<br>1 | teaspoon salt<br>teaspoon leaf thyme, crumbled |
| 4 | slices bacon, diced | ¼ | teaspoon pepper |
| 2 | tablespoons olive or vegetable oil | ¼<br>½ | cup cornstarch<br>cup cold water |
| 1 | large onion, chopped (1 cup) | | Vegetable Bouquet (recipe follows) |
| 2 | cloves garlic, minced | | Parsley sprigs (optional) |
| 1 | cup dry white wine | | |
| 1 | cup chicken broth | | |

**1.** Tie the legs and wings of the chicken and season it with salt and pepper.

**2.** Brown the bacon in an ovenproof kettle; remove the bacon with a slotted spoon and reserve. Add the oil to the kettle and heat until hot.

**3.** Brown the chicken well on all sides and remove; reserve. Sauté the onion and garlic in the pan drippings until soft.

**4.** Stir in the white wine, chicken broth, 1 teaspoon salt, thyme and ¼ teaspoon pepper and heat to bubbling. Return the chicken and bacon to the kettle; spoon the liquid over the chicken; cover the kettle.

**5.** Bake in a slow oven (325°) for 1 hour or until the chicken is tender when pierced with a two-tined fork. Remove the chicken to a heated serving platter and keep warm.

**6.** Bring the liquid in the kettle to boiling. Combine the cornstarch and cold water in a cup until smooth. Stir the cornstarch mixture into the bubbling liquid and cook, stirring constantly, until the sauce thickens and bubbles for 2 minutes.

**7.** Arrange the Vegetable Bouquet around the chicken and spoon part of the sauce over the chicken. Garnish with parsley, if you wish. Pass the remaining sauce in a heated sauce bowl.

**Vegetable Bouquet:** In a very large skillet, sauté 1 pound pared baby carrots and 1 pound peeled small white onions in 3 tablespoons butter or margarine for 5 minutes. Add ¾ cup chicken broth; bring to boiling; lower the heat and cover the skillet. Cook for 15 minutes or until almost tender. Push the vegetables to one side; add 1 bunch washed and halved leeks or 2 bunches green onions and 1 pound medium mushrooms, sliced. Cover; cook for 5 minutes longer, or just until tender. (Divide all recipe ingredients between two skillets if you don't have one that is large enough.) Arrange the vegetables in piles around the Coq au Vin Blanc and pour the cooking liquid into the sauce, if you wish. Makes 8 servings.

## CHICKEN ENCHILADAS

A little chicken goes a long way.

*Bake at 350° for 20 minutes.*
*Makes 4 servings.*

| | |
|---|---|
| 1 large onion, chopped (1 cup) | ½ teaspoon salt |
| 1 clove garlic, minced | ¼ teaspoon leaf oregano, crumbled |
| 1 can (4 ounces) green chili peppers, drained, seeded and chopped | 1 package (9 ounces) refrigerated, canned or frozen tortillas |
| 1 tablespoon vegetable oil | 1 cup chopped cooked chicken (from unstuffed roast chicken) |
| 2⅓ cups tomato purée (from a 29-ounce can) | 1 cup dairy sour cream |
| ½ cup water | 1 cup shredded mild Cheddar cheese (4 ounces) |
| ¼ cup chopped pitted black olives | |

**1.** For the sauce, sauté the onion, garlic and chili peppers in oil in a large saucepan until tender, about 3 minutes. Add the tomato purée, water, olives, ¼ teaspoon of the salt and the oregano; bring to boiling. Lower the heat; simmer for 30 minutes.

**2.** Soften the tortillas following label directions.

**3.** Combine the chicken, sour cream, ¾ cup of the cheese and remaining salt in a medium-size bowl. Spoon a rounded tablespoon of the chicken mixture in the center of each tortilla; roll up. Place the filled tortillas, seam-side down, in a greased 12 x 18-inch baking dish. Spoon the sauce over the top; sprinkle with the remaining cheese.

**4.** Bake in a moderate oven (350°) for 20 minutes or until hot.

# CHICKEN FLAUTAS

Flauta means flute in Spanish—the perfect name for this tube-shaped taco variation stuffed with mild chili-flavored chicken and eaten out of hand.

*Makes 12 flautas.*

1 broiler/fryer (about 2½ pounds), cut up
4 cups water
2 tablespoons vegetable shortening
1 medium-size onion, chopped (½ cup)
1 clove garlic, minced
1 tablespoon cornstarch
1¼ teaspoons salt

¼ teaspoon pepper
½ cup canned diced mild green chilies (about 4-ounce can)
Vegetable oil for frying
1 dozen fresh or frozen corn tortillas, thawed
1 cup dairy sour cream
¼ cup milk
Fresh coriander leaves (optional)

**1.** Bring the chicken and water to boiling in a kettle; lower the heat; cover. Simmer until fork-tender, about 25 minutes. Drain; reserve ½ cup of the broth. (Freeze the rest into cubes for use in other recipes.) Cool the chicken until it is easy to handle. Bone and skin the chicken, shred the meat.

**2.** Heat the shortening in a large saucepan until melted. Add the onion and garlic, sauté for 1 minute. Stir in the cornstarch, salt and pepper. Add the reserved ½ cup broth, shredded chicken and chilies. Stir and cook until very thick and bubbly; remove from the heat.

**3.** Heat ⅛ to ¼ inch of oil in a small skillet over medium heat until very hot. Sauté the tortillas one at a time, a few seconds on each side, until limp. This will soften the tortillas so that they will roll up more easily. Do not cook too long or they will become crisp. Drain on paper toweling.

**4.** Fill each tortilla with a heaping spoonful (3 tablespoons) of the chicken mixture across center. Roll the tortilla around the filling. Be sure the filling is 1 inch from the edges or ends of the rolled tortilla to avoid splattering during frying.

**5.** Place 2 or 3 flautas, seam-side down, in hot oil. Sauté, turning on all sides, until crisp. Drain. Keep warm while cooking the rest.

**6.** Combine the sour cream and milk in a small saucepan. Heat over very low heat just until lukewarm. Spoon over the flautas. Garnish with fresh coriander leaves, if you wish.

***Shortcut Tip:*** The chicken can be cooked ahead and refrigerated (see Step 1). Or use 2¼ cups diced or shredded leftover chicken.

# CHICKEN WITH PEPPERS MEXICAN STYLE

*Makes 6 servings.*

1 broiler/fryer (3 pounds), cut up
2 tablespoons vegetable oil
1 large onion, cut lengthwise into eighths, separated
1 clove garlic, minced
¼ pound cooked ham, diced
1 can (1 pound) Italian-style plum tomatoes
1 teaspoon salt
¼ teaspoon pepper
¼ teaspoon leaf oregano, crumbled
¼ teaspoon leaf thyme, crumbled
1 small sweet green pepper, halved, seeded and cut into strips
1 small sweet red pepper, halved, seeded and cut into strips
⅓ cup pimiento-stuffed olives, sliced
⅓ cup pitted black olives, sliced
Hot cooked rice
2 tablespoons chopped parsley

**1.** Brown the chicken in the oil in a large skillet. Remove to a bowl. Drain the drippings into a glass measure; return 2 tablespoons to the skillet. Sauté the onion, garlic and ham. Add the tomatoes, salt, pepper, oregano and thyme. Bring to boiling. Cook over high heat, stirring occasionally, until most of the liquid has evaporated, about 10 minutes.

**2.** Add the chicken; turn to coat with the sauce. Cover. Cook over low heat for 25 minutes or until the chicken is tender.

**3.** Add the green and red peppers and stuffed and black olives. Cover; cook an additional 5 minutes or until the peppers are crisp-tender. Serve over hot cooked rice. Garnish with chopped parsley.

# PORK AND CHICKEN TABLECLOTH STAINER

This Mexican classic has a quaint name and is said to result from the invariable spilling of some of the sauce on the tablecloth during eating. The combination of flavors is intriguing.

*Makes 8 servings.*

| | | | |
|---|---|---|---|
| 2 | pounds boneless lean pork loin, cut into 1-inch pieces | ½ | cup chicken stock or water |
| 2 | tablespoons vegetable oil | 2 | medium-size sweet potatoes or yams (about ¾ pound), pared, cut in half lengthwise, and cut into ¼-inch slices |
| 1 | broiler/fryer (2½ pounds), cut up | | |
| 1 | large onion, chopped (1 cup) | | |
| 1 | clove garlic, minced | 2 | medium-size zucchini (about ¾ pound), cut into ¼-inch-thick rounds |
| 1 | cup shelled walnuts | | |
| 2 | tablespoons sesame seeds | | |
| 2 | teaspoons salt | 2 | small apples, quartered, cored and sliced |
| 2 | teaspoons chili powder | | |
| ¼ | teaspoon ground cinnamon | 1 | can (8 ounces) pineapple chunks, drained |
| ¼ | teaspoon ground cloves | | |
| ¼ | cup chopped parsley | 2 | small bananas, peeled and sliced |
| 1 | can (1 pound) Italian-style tomatoes, undrained | | |

**1.** Brown the pork slowly in the oil in a large Dutch oven; remove with a slotted spoon to a bowl. Brown the chicken; remove to the bowl. Drain the drippings into a glass measure; return 2 tablespoons to the Dutch oven. Sauté the onion, garlic, walnuts and sesame seeds in the Dutch oven until the onion is transparent, about 5 minutes. Add the salt, chili powder, cinnamon and cloves. Cook and stir for 1 minute. Add the parsley, tomatoes with their liquid and chicken stock. Heat thoroughly.

**2.** Purée the sauce, part at a time, in the container of an electric blender. Return the walnut sauce to the Dutch oven. Place the pork in the sauce; arrange the chicken over the top. Bring the sauce to boiling; cover. Cook over medium-low heat for ¾ hour or until the pork is just about fork-tender. Stir occasionally, adding ½ cup of additional chicken stock or water, if necessary.

**3.** Add the sweet potatoes and zucchini to the Dutch oven; cook, covered, for 15 minutes or until the sweet potatoes are firm-tender. Add the apple slices; cook for 5 minutes longer.

**4.** Spoon the meat and vegetable mixture into a deep serving dish. Top with pineapple chunks and banana slices. Serve in soup bowls.

# ARROZ CON POLLO CRIOLLO

This Cuban-style chicken with saffron rice is colorful, fragrant and easy.

*Bake at 375° for 1 hour.*

*Makes 8 servings.*

| | | | |
|---|---|---|---|
| 2 | broiler/fryers (about 2½ pounds each), cut up | ½ | teaspoon ground cumin |
| 2 | teaspoons salt | ½ | teaspoon pepper |
| ¼ | cup olive or vegetable oil | ½ | teaspoon leaf oregano, crumbled |
| 1 | medium-size onion, chopped (½ cup) | | Few strands saffron, crushed (optional) |
| 1 | small sweet green pepper, halved, seeded and chopped | ½ | teaspoon paprika |
| 2 | cloves garlic, minced | 1½ | cups long-grain white rice |
| 1 | can (8 ounces) tomato sauce | 1 | package (10 ounces) frozen green peas |
| 1 | cup dry white wine | 1 | pimiento, chopped (optional) |
| 2½ | cups water | | |

**1.** Sprinkle the chicken with 1 teaspoon of the salt. Brown, part at a time, in the oil in a large skillet; remove.

**2.** Stir the onion, green pepper and garlic into the drippings in the pan; sauté until soft. Stir in the tomato sauce, wine, water, remaining salt, cumin, pepper, oregano, saffron (if used), paprika and rice; bring to boiling. Pour into a 12-cup casserole; arrange the chicken on top; cover the casserole.

**3.** Bake in moderate oven (375°) for 1 hour or until the chicken and rice are tender and the liquid is absorbed.

**4.** While the chicken cooks, cook the peas following label directions; drain. Spoon them around the edge of dish; garnish with the pimiento, if you wish.

# CHICKEN FRA DIAVOLO

*Makes 4 servings.*

1½ pounds chicken breast
fillets, skinned and quartered
¼ cup all-purpose flour
2 tablespoons butter or
margarine
2 tablespoons vegetable oil
1 large sweet green pepper,
seeded and cut into thin
strips

1 large sweet red pepper,
seeded and cut into thin
strips
3 cups Basic Tomato Sauce
(recipe follows)
¼ teaspoon liquid red-pepper
seasoning
¼ cup sliced pitted black
olives

**1.** Dust the chicken pieces with the flour to coat them well.

**2.** Heat the butter and oil in a large skillet; brown the chicken on both sides for 10 minutes adding the pepper strips halfway through the cooking time.

**3.** Lower the heat, add the tomato sauce and red-pepper seasoning; cover; simmer for 10 minutes or until the sauce is heated through and the chicken is tender. Garnish with the black olives.

# BASIC TOMATO SAUCE

A slow-cooked specialty that is the basis for many quick meals.

*Makes 10 cups.*

¼ pound salt pork, finely
chopped
⅓ cup vegetable oil
2 large cloves garlic
3 medium-size onions,
chopped (1½ cups)
1 cup chopped celery
¾ cup chopped carrots
2 medium-size sweet green
peppers, seeded and chopped
2 tablespoons parsley
flakes
2 cans (35 ounces each)
Italian plum tomatoes

2 cans (6 ounces each)
tomato paste
1 can (13¾ ounces) chicken
broth
2 teaspoons salt
½ teaspoon pepper
1 teaspoon leaf basil,
crumbled
1 large bay leaf
1 teaspoon sugar
½ teaspoon leaf thyme,
crumbled
1 pound fresh mushrooms,
sliced

**1.** Cook the salt pork in the oil in a large skillet until brown. Remove the pieces with a slotted spoon. Add the garlic; cook until golden, then remove and discard.

**2.** Add the onions, celery, carrots, peppers and parsley to the drippings in the skillet; cook until tender but not browned. Pour the mixture into a Dutch oven or saucepan. Add the tomatoes, tomato paste, chicken broth, salt pepper, basil, bay leaf, sugar and thyme and pork pieces, stirring to mix well and break up the tomatoes.

**3.** Cover and cook over very low heat, stirring occasionally, for 4 to 6 hours. Taste; add more salt and basil, if you wish.

**4.** Add the sliced mushrooms and cook for 10 minutes longer. Use immediately or refrigerate in tightly covered containers.

## CHICKEN CACCIATORE

*Makes 4 servings.*

⅓ cup plus 1 tablespoon all-purpose flour
2½ teaspoons salt
1 teaspoon pepper
1 broiler/fryer (about 3 pounds), cut up
3 tablespoons olive or vegetable oil
1 large onion, sliced
3 cloves garlic, finely chopped

½ pound fresh mushrooms, sliced
6 medium-size tomatoes, cored and cut into wedges
¼ cup dry red wine
1 tablespoon Italian seasoning
1 can (6 ounces) tomato paste
1 sweet green pepper, thinly sliced

**1.** Combine the ⅓ cup flour, 1 teaspoon of the salt and ½ teaspoon of the pepper in a plastic bag. Add the chicken; shake to coat thoroughly.

**2.** Heat the oil in a heavy kettle or Dutch oven. Brown the chicken, a few pieces at a time, on all sides; remove and keep warm.

**3.** Pour off all but 1 tablespoon of the oil. Add the onion, garlic and mushrooms; cook for 1 minute. Add the tomatoes, wine, remaining salt and pepper and Italian seasoning. Simmer rapidly, stirring often, for 15 minutes.

**4.** Stir in the tomato paste and return the chicken to the kettle.

**5.** Simmer over a low heat for 1 hour or until the chicken is tender.

**6.** Remove the chicken to a heated serving platter; keep warm. Blend the remaining 1 tablespoon of flour with a small amount of cold water in a cup; stir into the sauce. Add the green pepper; bring to boiling. Cook and stir until the sauce is thickened and bubbly. Spoon the sauce over the chicken.

***Note:*** This dish can be frozen. Reduce the cooking time in step 5 to 40 minutes to prevent over cooking while reheating.

# TICINO-STLYE LEMON CHICKEN

Ticino is the Italian-speaking Canton of Switzerland.

*Makes 4 servings.*

| | | | |
|---|---|---|---|
| 1 | broiler/fryer (2½ to 3 pounds), cut into serving pieces | 2 | teaspoons all-purpose flour |
| 1 | teaspoon salt | 1 | cup chicken broth |
| ¼ | teaspoon freshly ground pepper | 2 | egg yolks |
| 1 | tablespoon olive oil | 2 | tablespoons freshly squeezed lemon juice |
| 3 | tablespoons butter or margarine | 2 | tablespoons minced parsley |
| | | | Hot cooked rice |
| | | | Green salad |

**1.** Skin the chicken and trim off any fat; sprinkle on all sides with salt and pepper.

**2.** Heat the oil and butter in a large skillet. Add the chicken pieces and cook over high heat, turning often, until golden brown on all sides. Transfer the chicken to a heavy flameproof casserole or Dutch oven; sprinkle with the flour.

**3.** Pour off the fat from the skillet. Add the chicken broth to the skillet; bring to boiling, scraping and stirring to dissolve the browned bits. Pour the boiling broth over the chicken; simmer, covered, for 30 minutes or until the chicken is tender. Remove the chicken; keep it warm.

**4.** Combine the egg yolks and lemon juice in a small bowl; beat with a wire whisk until frothy. Gradually add ½ cup of the hot juice from the casserole; pour the mixture back into the casserole. Return the chicken to the sauce and heat through, about 2 minutes. (Do not boil.) Taste and add more salt and pepper if necessary. Sprinkle with parsley. Serve with hot cooked rice and a tossed green salad.

# WALNUT CHICKEN WITH BROCCOLI

*Makes 4 servings.*

| | |
|---|---|
| 2 | whole chicken breasts, skinned and boned OR: 1 pound boneless chicken breasts |
| 1 | egg white |
| 1 | tablespoon cornstarch |
| ½ | teaspoon salt |
| ½ | teaspoon sugar |
| ½ | pound broccoli (1 pound) |
| ½ | bunch green onions |
| 8 | tablespoons vegetable oil |
| ¼ | cup chicken broth or water |
| 1 | cup walnut halves or pieces |
| 2 | cloves garlic, crushed |
| 3 | slices fresh gingerroot OR: ¼ teaspoon ground ginger |
| 1 | tablespoon soy sauce |
| 1 | tablespoon dry sherry |
| | Hot cooked rice (optional) |

**1.** Cut the chicken into 1-inch cubes. Place in a bowl; add the egg white, cornstarch, salt and sugar; toss until mixed.

**2.** Pare off the tough outer layer of the broccoli stalks; cut each stalk crosswise in half. Separate the top half into flowerets; cut the lower half into ½-inch lengths.

**3.** Heat a large deep skillet, Dutch oven or wok over high heat. Add 2 tablespoons of the oil; swirl to coat the bottom and side. Add the broccoli and onions; stir-fry with a slotted spoon until coated with oil. Add the broth or water; cover; cook for 2 minutes or until the broccoli is tender-crisp. Remove to a medium-size bowl.

**4.** Reheat the pan. Add the remaining oil. Add the walnuts; stir-fry until lightly browned; remove to paper toweling to drain. Remove all but about 2 tablespoons of the oil from the pan. Add the garlic and ginger; fry until browned to flavor the oil and then discard. Add the chicken; stir-fry until golden brown. Stir in the vegetables, soy sauce and sherry. Taste for salt, add if needed. Spoon the mixture onto a warm platter; sprinkle with the walnuts. Serve with hot cooked rice, if you wish.

# MUSHROOMS AND CHICKEN LO MEIN

*Makes 4 servings.*

| | | | |
|---|---|---|---|
| 2 | whole chicken breasts, skinned and boned OR: 1 pound boneless chicken breasts | | Boiling water |
| | | 2 | tablespoons cornstarch |
| | | 2 | cups cold water or chicken broth |
| ½ | small head bok choy OR: ½ pound Swiss chard | ½ | cup sliced water chestnuts |
| | | 1 | tablespoon soy sauce |
| ¼ | pound snow pea pods OR: 1 package (7 ounces) frozen snow peas, thawed | 1 | can (15 ounces) straw mushrooms, drained (available in Oriental grocery stores) OR: 2 cans (4½ ounces each) whole mushrooms, drained |
| ½ | cup vegetable oil | | |
| 4 | packages (3 ounces each) chicken-flavored Oriental instant noodle soup (also known as ramen noodles) | | |

**1.** Cut the chicken into thin slices. Cut the white part of bok choy or chard stalks into diagonal slices and the green tops into 1-inch lengths. Keep them in separate bowls. Remove the strings from the fresh snow pea pods.

**2.** Heat a large deep skillet, Dutch oven or wok over high heat. Add the oil; heat for 30 seconds. Add the uncooked blocks of instant noodles; fry until browned on broad sides; remove to a large bowl with a slotted spoon, leaving the oil in the pan. Sprinkle 2 seasoning packets from the noodles over the browned noodles; add boiling water to barely cover. Let stand while preparing the sauce, tossing occasionally.

**3.** Combine the cornstarch, water and remaining 2 seasoning packets in a 4-cup measure. If you are using chicken broth, omit the packets. Reheat pan; add the white part of the bok choy or chard and pea pods; stir-fry until just wilted. Remove with a slotted spoon to a medium-size bowl. Add the chicken to the pan; stir-fry until browned. Add the water chestnuts and green leaves; stir-fry for 15 seconds.

**4.** Restir the cornstarch mixture; pour into the pan; bring to boiling. Return the vegetables to the pan; add the soy sauce and mushrooms. Drain the noodles; add to the sauce. Toss and serve in a warm dish.

# VELVET SLICED CHICKEN

A light and delicate dish from the North.

*Makes 4 servings.*

| | | | |
|---|---|---|---|
| 1 | chicken breast (about 14 ounces), split | 1 | tablespoon dry sherry |
| 8 | egg whites (1 cup)* | ½ | teaspoon sugar |
| 3 | tablespoons cornstarch | 2 | tablespoons minced cooked bacon or ham |
| 1 | teaspoon salt | | Chopped green onions for garnish |
| ¾ | cup chicken broth | | |
| 2 | cups peanut or corn oil | | |
| ¼ | pound fresh snow peas, halved OR: ½ a 10-ounce package frozen snow peas | | |

**1.** Skin and bone the chicken. Flatten the pieces between sheets of wax paper to an ⅛-inch thickness using a meat mallet or rolling pin. Cut the breast pieces in half lengthwise, then cut into 1-inch pieces to make 1 x 1 x ⅛-inch slices (about ¾ cup).

**2.** Beat the egg whites in a large bowl with a rotary beater until foamy. Stir in the chicken.

**3.** Combine the cornstarch and salt in a small bowl; stir in the chicken broth slowly until blended. Pour into the chicken mixture.

**4.** Heat the oil in a wok or skillet to 300° on a deep-fat frying thermometer. Stir the chicken mixture; pour it into the hot oil.

**5.** Turn the mixture gently with a slotted spoon as the egg white sets and the chicken turns white (about 2 minutes).

**6.** Pour the oil and chicken into a strainer placed over a bowl to drain.

**7.** Wipe the wok clean. Return 1 tablespoon of the oil to the wok; reheat. Place the chicken mixture and snow peas in the wok; stir-fry for 1 minute. Sprinkle with the sherry and sugar. Stir for 1 more minute. Sprinkle with the bacon; garnish with the green onions.

*Add the egg yolks to your next batch of scrambled eggs with an equal volume of water or use the yolks to make custard.

# CANTONESE-STYLE CHOW MEIN

*Makes 6 servings.*

1 package (10 ounces) frozen mixed Chinese-style vegetables in seasoned sauce
2 teaspoons cornstarch
1 tablespoon soy sauce
2 whole chicken breasts, skinned, boned and cut into thin strips OR: 2 cups slivered cooked chicken
3 to 4 teaspoons vegetable oil
¼ cup chopped green onion
1 can (10¾ ounces) condensed chicken broth
2 tablespoons dry sherry
1½ cups very fine noodles (from an 8-ounce package)
1 package (8 ounces) frozen cooked, shelled and deveined shrimp
2 cups finely shredded romaine lettuce OR: 1 cup bean sprouts
1 can (3 ounces) chow mein noodles

**1.** Remove the vegetables from the package; let thaw in a large bowl until the pieces can be separated with a fork.

**2.** Combine the cornstarch and soy sauce with the chicken in a medium-size bowl.

**3.** Heat a wok or large skillet until very hot. Add the oil and chicken mixture. Stir-fry until the chicken turns white and the pieces separate. (If you are using cooked chicken, stir-fry for 30 seconds until hot.) Remove the chicken to a plate with a slotted spoon.

**4.** Add 1 more teaspoon of oil if necessary; stir in the green onions. Add the broth and sherry; cover; bring to boiling, stir in the noodles; let boil for about 1 minute.

**5.** Stir in the partially thawed vegetables; cook, uncovered, for 1 minute. Add the frozen shrimp and reserved chicken. Stir-fry until the noodles are tender and the chicken and shrimp are heated through.

**6.** Stir in the lettuce; serve immediately. Sprinkle with the noodles.

# GREEK CHICKEN PIE

A deep-dish pie with golden, glazed lattice crust.

*Bake at 400° for 30 minutes.*

*Makes 8 servings.*

| | | | |
|---|---|---|---|
| 1 | broiler/fryer (about 3 pounds), cut up | 6 | tablespoons all-purpose flour |
| 1 | teaspoon salt | 1 | teaspoon salt |
| ¼ | teaspoon pepper | ¼ | teaspoon pepper |
| 3 | cups thinly sliced carrots | ½ | cup light cream |
| 1½ | cups sliced celery | 2 | tablespoons lemon juice |
| 1 | large onion, chopped (1 cup) | 1 | package (about 11 ounces) |
| 1 | package (9 ounces) frozen | | piecrust mix |
| | artichoke hearts | 1 | egg beaten with 1 |
| ½ | cup (1 stick) butter | | tablespoon water |

**1.** Put the chicken in a large kettle or Dutch oven. Add just enough water to cover. Bring to boiling; skim off the foam. Add 1 teaspoon of salt and ¼ teaspoon of pepper; lower the heat; cover. Simmer for 30 minutes or until the chicken is tender. Remove the chicken from the broth to a large bowl; let cool.

**2.** Add the carrots, celery, onion and artichoke hearts to the broth. Simmer until tender, about 15 minutes. Drain; reserve the broth and vegetables. Measure the broth; add water, if necessary, to make 3 cups.

**3.** Skin and bone the chicken; cut into bite-size pieces. Add the vegetables to the chicken.

**4.** Heat the butter in a large saucepan; add the flour and remaining salt and pepper. Cook and stir for 1 minute. Stir in the chicken broth and cream. Cook, stirring constantly, until thickened and bubbly. Stir in the lemon juice, chicken and vegetables. Spoon into a shallow 2-quart or 11 x 7 x 2-inch baking dish. (Can be made ahead and refrigerated at this point.)

**5.** Prepare the piecrust mix following label directions. Roll out on a floured surface; cut into ¾-inch strips. Fit over the filling in a lattice pattern. Join the strips around the edge of the dish with an edging strip. Pinch to seal; flute. Brush the pastry with the egg and water.

**6.** Bake in a hot oven (400°) for 30 minutes or until the pastry is golden and the filling is bubbly-hot. (Add about 10 minutes if the filling has been prepared ahead.)

# INDIAN CHICKEN CURRY

Chicken is a real delicacy in India, where it is served at weddings and other celebrations. This "hot" curry dish is a North Indian specialty.

*Bake at 375° for 1 hour and 15 minutes.*
*Makes 6 servings.*

| | | | |
|---|---|---|---|
| 2 | medium-size onions, quartered | 1 | can (6 ounces) tomato paste |
| 2 | cloves garlic | 2 | to 3 teaspoons curry powder |
| 1 | small piece fresh gingerroot OR: ½ teaspoon ground ginger | 1 | teaspoon turmeric |
| | | 1 | teaspoon salt |
| | | 1 | broiler/fryer (about 2½ pounds), cut up |
| ½ | teaspoon coriander seeds | 1 | teaspoon lemon juice |
| 1¾ | cups water | | Indian Rice Pilaf |
| ¾ | cup vegetable oil | | (recipe follows) |
| 1 | teaspoon cumin seeds | | |

**1.** Place the onions, garlic, ginger, coriander seeds and ¾ cup of the water in the container of an electric blender. Whirl at low speed until smooth.

**2.** Heat 3 tablespoons of the oil in a small skillet. Add the cumin seeds and onion mixture. Cook slowly, stirring occasionally, until the water has evaporated, about 25 minutes. Add 3 more tablespoons of the oil; cook for 10 minutes, stirring occasionally. When the oil starts to separate from the onion mixture, stir in the tomato paste, curry powder, turmeric and salt. Lower the heat; simmer the sauce for about 15 minutes, stirring occasionally.

**3.** Heat the remaining oil in a large skillet. Brown the chicken pieces on all sides, turning frequently; place in a shallow 13 x 9 x 2-inch baking dish.

**4.** Stir the remaining 1 cup water and the lemon juice into the sauce; mix thoroughly; spoon it over the chicken; cover.

**5.** Bake in a moderate oven (375°) for 1 hour and 15 minutes. Serve with Indian Rice Pilaf.

# INDIAN RICE PILAF

*Bake at 375° for 40 minutes.*
*Makes 6 servings.*

2 cups long-grain white rice
4 tablespoons vegetable oil
½ teaspoon cumin seeds
1 2-inch piece cinnamon stick
2 whole cloves
1 whole cardamom seed
1 package (10 ounces) frozen peas and carrots

1 quart cold water
2 teaspoons salt
2 to 3 teaspoons curry powder
Pinch of turmeric
¼ cup salted cashew nuts, broken into pieces

**1.** Cover the rice with cold water; let stand for 30 minutes. Heat the oil in a large saucepan. Add the cumin, cinnamon, cloves and cardamom; heat until the cumin start popping.
**2.** Add the frozen vegetables; stir constantly over medium heat for 10 minutes. Drain the rice; add to the saucepan. Cook over medium heat for 7 minutes, stirring frequently.
**3.** Add the water and salt; bring to boiling. Remove from the heat. Stir in the curry powder, turmeric and nuts.
**4.** Turn the rice mixture into a 10-cup casserole; cover. Bake in a moderate oven (375°) for 35 to 40 minutes or until the rice is tender. Garnish with a generous sprinkling of additional cashews, if you wish.

# ROAST CHICKEN INDIAN STYLE

*An intriguing blend of spices, herbs and yogurt gives the chicken its rich golden color and delicious pungent flavor.*

*Roast at 350° for about 2½ hours or 20 minutes per pound.*
*Makes 8 servings.*

| | |
|---|---|
| ⅛ teaspoon powdered saffron | ¼ teaspoon ground ginger |
| 1 teaspoon hot water | 1 roasting chicken (6 pounds) |
| 1 container (8 ounces) plain yogurt | 3 tablespoons vegetable oil |
| | 3 medium-size onions |
| 3 tablespoons lime juice | Hot couscous or rice |
| 1½ teaspoons salt | 1¼ cups chicken broth |
| 2 cloves garlic, minced | 2 tablespoons all-purpose flour |
| 1 teaspoon curry powder | Parsley (optional) |
| ½ teaspoon ground cumin | Lime wedges (optional) |
| ¼ teaspoon ground cardamom | Kumquats (optional) |

**1.** Soak the saffron in the hot water in a small bowl; stir in 4 tablespoons of the yogurt, lime juice, salt, garlic, curry powder, cumin, cardamom and ginger.

**2.** Rub about 2 tablespoons of the yogurt mixture inside the chicken; rub the remaining over the skin to coat it completely and evenly. Tie the legs together. Leave to marinate for at least 1 hour at room temperature, or several hours refrigerated. Place, breast-side up, in a shallow roasting pan. Brush with the oil.

**3.** Roast in a moderate oven (350°) for 1 hour; brush with the pan juices. Cut each onion into 6 wedges; arrange around the chicken. Continue roasting and basting 1 to 1½ hours longer or until the drumstick moves easily at the joint. Arrange the chicken and onions on a heated platter with hot couscous or rice. Keep warm.

**4.** Add the chicken broth to the roasting pan; set the pan over a burner and heat while stirring to dissolve the browned bits. Strain the pan juices into a 2-cup measure; skim the fat, and measure 2 tablespoons of the fat into a small saucepan. Stir in the flour; cook and stir over medium heat for 1 minute. Stir in the skimmed pan juices; continue cooking and stirring until the sauce thickens and boils for 2 minute. Stir in the remaining yogurt. Taste; add more salt and lime juice if needed. The sauce will look slightly curdled. Serve with the chicken. Garnish the platter with parsley, lime wedges and kumquats, if you wish.

# INDONESIAN SATES WITH PEPPER RELISH

*Makes 27 small skewers.*

¼  cup peanut oil
1  medium-size onion, chopped (½ cup)
2  cloves garlic, minced
1  tomato, peeled and chopped
2  tablespoons peanut butter
1  can (13¾ ounces) chicken broth

1  can (6 ounces) tomato paste
½  teaspoon red pepper flakes
1  teaspoon salt
2  pounds boneless chicken breasts, skinned and cut into ½-inch cubes
   Pepper Relish (recipe follows)

**1.** Heat the oil in a large skillet; sauté the onion, garlic and tomato until very thick. Stir in the peanut butter, chicken broth and tomato paste; stir in the pepper flakes. Simmer, stirring constantly, for 5 minutes. Add the salt; cool.
**2.** Spear 2 cubes of the chicken on each heatproof skewer. Place the skewers side by side in a shallow glass dish. Spoon the sauce over the chicken; cover and let stand in the refrigerator until ready to serve.
**3.** Broil 5 to 6 minutes on each side or until the chicken is lightly browned and hot. Spoon Pepper Relish over each skewer and serve immediately.

# PEPPER RELISH

*Makes 1⅔ cups.*

Half a 16-ounce jar sweet pickled red and green cherry peppers
1  jar (4 ounces) pimiento, drained

½  navel orange, peeled and cubed
½  cup chopped celery
1  teaspoon sugar

Halve the cherry peppers and remove the seeds and stems. Place the peppers and remaining ingredients in the container of an electric blender. Whirl at medium speed until finely chopped. Chill until ready to serve.

# CHICKEN KIEV

*Deep-fat fry at 360° for 5 minutes.*
*Makes 6 servings.*

| | |
|---|---|
| 2 tablespoons chopped parsley | 2 eggs |
| 1 tablespoon chopped chives | 1 tablespoon water |
| ½ teaspoon salt | 1 teaspoon vegetable oil |
| ¼ teaspoon pepper | 3 tablespoons all-purpose |
| ½ cup (1 stick) butter, softened | flour |
| 3 whole chicken breasts | 1 to 1¼ cups packaged |
| (about 12 ounces each), | unseasoned bread crumbs |
| boned, skinned and halved | Vegetable oil for frying |

**1.** Stir the parsley, chives, salt and pepper into the butter in a medium-size bowl. Shape into a 3x2-inch rectangle on wax paper; chill for 20 minutes.

**2.** Place the chicken breasts, one at a time, between sheets of wax paper. Pound with a wooden mallet to a ¼-inch thickness, being careful not to tear the chicken. Remove the wax paper.

**3.** Cut the chilled herb-butter into six equal finger-size pieces. Place each "finger" an inch in from the lower edge of each chicken breast; fold the lower edge over the "finger"; fold in the sides; roll up to enclose the filling completely.

**4.** Beat the eggs, water and oil in a plate; place the flour and crumbs in two separate plates. Roll each chicken bundle in the flour; dip in the egg mixture; roll in the crumbs to coat them evenly. Place them in a pan. Chill for 1 hour to set the coating.

**5.** Into a deep-fat fryer, pour the vegetable oil 2 inches deep. Heat to 360° on a deep-fat frying thermometer. Fry the chicken bundles, two at a time, for 5 minutes, or until the chicken loses pinkness. Drain on paper toweling. Keep warm in a 200° oven.

# INDEX

Appetizers, 109-125
  barbecued chicken drumettes, 117
  chicken, water chestnuts and herb-
    cheese triangles, 113
  chicken-filled pastry boats, 110
  chicken liver-and-apple brochettes, 118
  chicken picadillo empañadas, 112
  chicken pillows, 111
  chicken-walnut strips, 123
  chopped livers New York-style, 120-121
  coconut chicken, 124
  Oriental chicken wings, 117
  rumaki, 118
  savory chicken wings, 116
  sesame chicken wings, 114
  sweet and sour orange chicken wings,
    115
  *see also* Pâté
Apples
  brochette with chicken liver and, 118
  chicken casserole with cheese and, 97
  curried chicken soup with, 139-140
  pear slaw with, 30

raisinberry relish, 31
stuffing
  fruited, 28
  sausage and, 27
Arroz con pollo criollo, 231
Artichokes, crêpes with chicken and,
  193-194
Asparagus and chicken salad, molded, 160
Aspic
  brandied, 121
  port wine topping, 122-123
Avocado
  chicken and cherry tomato salad with
    dressing of, 150
  salad with chicken and, 157

Barbecue
  chicken, 53
    drumettes, 117
    ginger, 57
    herb-grilled, 63
    Johnny Appleseed, 58

Barbecue, chicken *(cont'd)*
    Kansas, 68-69
    lemony kabobs with shrimp and,
        54-55
    orange-ginger-soy, 54
    Pollo di Anna, 56
    Southern, 55
    Texas-style, 68
    glazes, 69-70
    marinades, 55, 69
    procedures, 51, 59-61
    safety tips for, 50, 58
    turkey
        legs, 57
        teriyaki, 62
        wine-basted, 59
    wrapping in, 51-52
Barbecue sauce, 29
    piquant, 53
    Southern, 55
Beans
    chicken livers with bacon and green,
        216
    curried limas and chicken wings, 99
    herbed scaloppine with white, 48
    savory lima bean soup, 134
Beef
    hearty soup with chicken and, 133
    oven soup with turkey and, 144-145
Beer batter fried chicken, 37
Bistro chicken pot pies, 102-103
Boiled turkey dinner, 77
Braised dishes, chicken
    casserole, 73
    in champagne, 177
    chicken and rice deluxe, 78-79
    chicken paprika with spätzle, 86
    chicken rosemary with orzo, 83
    curried corn and chicken, 79
    fricassee, 80
    with grapes and black olives, 81
    jambalaya, 82
    Neapolitan-style, 82-83
    Normandy, 224
    with peppers Mexican style, 229
    plantation, skillet, 84
    thrifty vegetables and, 85
Brandied aspic, 121
Bread stuffing
    cornbread-sausage, 26
    old-fashioned, 24
Breasts
    chicken
        with almonds, 183

with blueberries in orange sauce,
    187
boning of, 12
broccoli au gratin and, 98
in champagne sauce, 188
with cheese fondue, 181
chicken Athena, 42
with cream sauce, 211
in curried chutney, 211
ginger chicken, 57
lemon and sage, 176
and mushrooms in Madeira sauce,
    182
Neapolitan-style, 82-83
poached, 161
stuffed, 178-179
stuffed, dinner, 214
sweet and pungent, 207
*see also* cutlets; Scaloppine,
    chicken
turkey
    carving of, 19
    roast, with barbecue sauce, 29
    stuffed, ballottine, 173-174
    stuffed, galantine, 174-175
    tandoori, 67
    tetrazzini, with green noodles, 189
Broccoli
    au gratin chicken and, 98
    chicken divan, 216-217
    curried turkey and, 90
    macaroni salad with turkey, ham and,
        153
    walnut chicken with, 235
Brochettes, chicken liver-and-apple, 118
Broiled dishes
    chicken
        deviled legs, 66-67
        favorite herb-grilled, 63
        Indonesian sates with pepper relish,
            243
        kabobs, 64
        Kansas barbecued, 68-69
        lemon-butter, 65
        with mustard glaze, 66
        orange, 65
        Texas-style barbecued, 68
    procedures, 63-64
    turkey
        tandoori turkey breasts, 67
        teriyaki, 62
    *see also* Barbecue
Broth
    chicken, 128

instant, 141
turkey, 129
Buffet Russian chicken-potato
 salad, 155
Buffet turkey-noodle bake, 191
Buying tips
 chicken, 5-6, 7
 turkey, 6, 7

Cantonese-style chow mein, 238
Cape Cod relish, 30
Carolina Brunswick stew, 78
Carving tips, 19
Casseroles
 chicken
  with apples and cheese, 97
  arroz con pollo criollo, 231
  baked, with stuffing, 96
  braised, 73
  broccoli au gratin and, 98
  chicken cacciatore, 232
  curried limas and wings, 99
  divan, 216-217
  easy oven, and vegetables, 95
  fricassee, 92
  golden harvest, 179
  paella, 222
  polenta with chicken livers, 89
  pork and chicken tablecloth stainer,
   230
  poulet Marengo, 225
  quick, with noodles, 94-95
  rosso, 201
  Spanish dinner with noodles and, 94
  spinach tetrazzini and, 190-191
  stuffing strata with, 91
  tortilla, 93
 freezing and heating, 88
 turkey
  buffet noodle bake with, 191
  curried broccoli and, 90
  ham and, Florentine, 186-187
  Louisiana turkey royale, 203
  rice and, 219
  soufflé-topped, 90-91
  tetrazzini, with green noodles, 189
Chaud-froid glaze, 175
Cheese
 crêpes with turkey and, 195
 fondue, with chicken, 181
Chicken
 baked
  Basque-style, 223

microwave, 200
rosemary, 202
rosso, 201
barbecued, see Barbecue, chicken
boning breast of, 12
braised, see Braised dishes, chicken
broiled, see Broiled dishes, chicken
buying tips, 5-6, 7
casseroles, see Casseroles, chicken
cutlets
 with hollandaise sauce, 212-213
 Parmesan, 40-41
 sautéed, 41
 cutting up, 8-9
defrosting, 13-15
fried, see Fried chicken
ground
 croquettes Kiev style, 38
nutritional value, 4
pies, see Pies, chicken
poached, 161
roast
 with cherry sauce, 218
 with herbs, 22-23
 Indian style, 242
salads
 avocado and, 157
 buffet Russian, with potatoes, 155
 cherry tomato and, with avocado
  dressing, 150
 Chinese cabbage and, 149
 chinoise, 153
 creamy chicken mousse, 159
 curried, Indienne, 158
 garnished, with grapes, 154-155
 layered, 164
 macaroni and, with tuna dressing,
  150-151
 molded asparagus and, 160
 Oriental-style, 152
 pasta and, 151
 peppery chicken loaf, 163
sandwiches
 tomato salad, 167
sautéed, see Sautéed dishes,
 chicken
scaloppine, see Scaloppine,
 chicken
soup, see Soup(s), chicken
stew, see Stew(s), chicken
stir-fried, see Stir-frying
storage of, 13
stuffed
 breasts, 178-179

Chicken, stuffed *(cont'd)*
    dinner of breast of, 214
    Italian chicken roll, 184-185
    *see also* specific chicken parts
Chinese chicken with ham soup,
    144
Chopped livers, New York-style,
    120-121
Coconut chicken, 124
Coq au vin blanc, 226-227
Corn 'n' chicken chowder, 131
Corn-sausage stuffing, 24
Cornbread-sausage stuffing, 26
Coulibiac of turkey, 192-193
Cranberries
    Cape Cod relish, 30
    mold with, 31
    pickled, 176-177
    raisinberry relish, 31
Creamy chicken mousse, 159
Crêpes
    basic, 194
    chicken and artichoke, 193-194
    turkey, with cheese sauce, 195
Crispy fried chicken, 36-37
Croquettes
    chicken, Kiev-style, 38
    turkey, 39
Croutons, golden, 225
Curry-style dishes
    chicken breasts in curried chutney,
        211
    curried apple and chicken soup,
        139-140
    curried corn and chicken, 79
    curried limas and chicken wings, 99
    curried salad Indienne, 158
    curried turkey and broccoli, 90
    curried turkey-rice salad, 154
    curry sauce, 125
    Indian chicken curry, 240
Cutlets
    chicken
        with hollandaise sauce, 212-213
        Parmesan, 40-41
        sautéed, 41
    turkey
        turkey schnitzel, 42
    *see also* Scaloppine

Danish liver pâté, 120
Deep-frying, 33-34
Defrosting, 13-15, 88

Deviled chicken legs, 66-67
Dip(s)
    mustard mayonnaise, 123
    soy sauce, 136-137
Double crunchy fried chicken, 36
Dressing, salad
    avocado, 150
    classic vinaigrette, 164
    tomato and green chili sauce, 157
    tuna, 151

Easy herb-celery stuffing, 26
Easy oven chicken and vegetables, 95
Empañadas, chicken picadillo, 112
Enchiladas, chicken, 227

Festive chicken liver pâté, 121
Flautas, chicken, 228
Fondue, chicken with cheese, 181
Foolproof hollandiase sauce, 215
Freezing tips, 13, 21
    casserole, 88
    pie, 103
    sandwich, 167
French chicken gumbo, 138
Fricassee, chicken, 80, 92
Fried chicken
    in a basket, 34-35
    beer batter, 37
    crispy, 36-37
    croquettes Kiev style, 38
    double crunchy, 36
    Kiev, 244
    Maryland, with cream gravy and
        biscuits, 35
    oven methods, 37
    sweet and pungent chicken wings,
        185
    tips, 33-34
    *see also* Sautéed dishes, chicken;
        stir-frying
Fruit-wine glaze, 70
Fruited brown rice stuffing, 23
Fruited stuffing, 28

Garnished chicken-grape salad, 154-155
Giblets
    gravy with, 21
    hearty soup with, 129
    savory lima bean soup with, 134
    storage of, 13

see also Liver, chicken
Ginger chicken, 57
Gingerroot chicken wing soup, 136
Glaze(s)
    chaud-froid, 175
    fruit-wine, 70
    honey-mustard, 66
    orange-mustard, 69-70
    tomato-soy, 69
Golden harvest casserole, 179
Grandmother's chicken soup, 142
Gravy
    chicken pan, 22-23
    creamy mustard, 174
    giblet, 21
Great hero, 165
Greek chicken pie, 239
Grilled turkey, cheese and tomato
    sandwiches, 169
Headcheese, mock, 161-162
Hearty beef and chicken soup, 133
Hearty giblet soup, 129
Hearty winter soup, 135
Herb-grilled chicken, 63
Hero sandwich, 165
Hollandaise sauce
    foolproof, 215
    mock, 108
    quick, 213

Indian chicken curry, 240
Indian rice pilaf, 241
Indonesian sates with pepper relish, 243
Italian chicken roll, 184-185

Jambalaya, 82
Johnny Appleseed chicken, 58

Kabobs
    chicken, 64
    Indonesian sates with pepper relish,
      243
    lemony chicken wings and shrimp,
      54-55
    rumaki, 118
Kansas barbecued chicken, 68-69

Lamb, Scottish pie with chicken livers
    and, 105
Last-minute chowder, 135

Layered chicken salad, 164
Legs
    barbecued turkey, 57
    deviled chicken, 66-67
Lemon and sage chicken breasts, 176
Lemon-butter broiled chicken, 65
Lemon-herb marinade, 55
Lemony chicken wings and shrimp
    kabobs, 54-55
Linguine with chicken in garlic sauce,
    40
Liver, chicken
    with bacon and green beans, 216
    brochettes with apple and, 118
    chopped, New York-style, 120-121
    pâté
      Danish, 120
      festive, 121
      fine chicken and, 119
      with port wine aspic, 122-123
      terrine à l'orange, 196-197
    peppers and, 206-207
    polenta with, 89
    with rice, 215
    rumaki, 118
    Scottish lamb pie with, 105
Louisiana turkey royale, 203

Macaroni and chicken salad with tuna
    dressing, 150-151
Macaroni salad with broccoli, turkey
    and ham, 153
Marinades
    lemon-herb, 55
    sweet and sour, 69
    wine, 69
    yogurt, 69
Maryland fried chicken with cream
    gravy and biscuits, 35
Matzo balls (knaidlich), 143
Microwave ovens, 200-204
    chicken and
      cooking tips, 200
      rosemary, 202
      rosso, 201
    defrosting with, 14-15
    heating casseroles with, 88
    turkey and
      Louisiana turkey royale, 203
      speedy loaf, 204
Minced chicken and pork pie, 180
Mock headcheese, 161-162
Mock hollandaise sauce, 108

Mold(s)
  asparagus and chicken salad,
    160
  chicken and avocado salad, 157
  cranberry relish, 31
  creamy chicken mousse, 159
  curried salad Indienne, 158
  mock headcheese, 161-162
  peppery chicken loaf, 163
  turkey and potato salad, 162
  turkey salad, 156
Mornay sauce, 178
Mousse, creamy chicken, 159
Mushroom-herb stuffing, 23
Mushrooms and chicken lo mein, 236
Mustard mayonnaise dip, 123

Normandy chicken, 224

Old-fashioned bread stuffing, 24
Old-fashioned chicken pot pie, 101
Open hot turkey sandwich, 168-169
Orange-broiled chicken, 65
Orange-ginger-soy chicken, 54
Orange-mustard glaze, 69-70
Orange-pecan stuffing, 25
Oriental chicken wings, 117
Oriental-style chicken salad, 152
Oriental sweet and sour chicken
    pie, 104
Oven-fried chicken, 37

Paella, 222
Party dishes, 171-197
  appetizers, see Appetizers
  chicken
    braised, in champagne, 177
    breasts, and mushrooms in Madeira
      sauce, 182
    breasts, champagne sauce, 188
    breasts, lemon and sage, 196
    breasts, stuffed, 178-179
    breasts, with almonds, 183
    breasts, with blueberries in orange
      sauce, 187
    with cheese fondue, 181
    crêpes with artichoke and, 193-194
    golden harvest casserole, 179
    Italian chicken roll, 184-185
    pie with pork and minced, 180
    terrine à l'orange, 196-197

    tetrazzini, with spinach, 190-191
    wings, sweet and pungent, 185
  pickled cranberries, 176-177
  tips for, 172
  turkey
    buffet noodle bake, 191
    coulibiac of, 192-193
    crêpes with cheese sauce and, 195
    ham and, Florentine, 186-187
    stuffed breasts, ballottine, 173-174
    stuffed breasts, galantine, 174-175
    tetrazzini, with green noodles, 189
Pasta
  buffet turkey-noodle bake, 191
  chicken-spinach tetrazzini, 190-191
  chicken-noodle Spanish dinner, 94
  chicken rosemary with orzo, 83
  linguine with chicken in garlic
    sauce, 40
  quick chicken-noodle casserole,
    94-95
  salads, 148
    chicken, 151
    macaroni, with broccoli, turkey and
      ham, 153
    macaroni and chicken, with tuna
      dressing, 150-151
    Oriental-style chicken, 152
  turkey breast tetrazzini with green
    noodles, 189
  turkey noodle soup, 145
Pastry
  chicken, water chestnuts and herb-
    cheese triangles, 113
  chicken-filled pastry boats, 110
  chicken picadillo empañadas, 112
  chicken pillows, 111
  coulibiac of turkey, 192-193
  flaky pie, 107
  for turkey ragout, 77
  see also Pies
Pâté
  chicken, with port wine aspic, 122-123
  chicken terrine à l'orange, 196-197
  Danish liver, 120
  festive chicken liver, 121
  fine chicken and chicken liver, 119
Peach sauce, 116
Pennsylvania chicken and corn
    soup, 141
Peppers
  chicken livers and, 206-207
  chicken with, Mexican style, 229
  grilled, 56

relish of, 243
roasted, 165
scaloppine with, 44
Peppery chicken loaf, 163
Pickled cranberries, 176-177
Pies
  chicken
    bistro pot, 102-103
    Greek, 239
    minced, with pork, 180
    old-fashioned pot, 101-102
    Oriental sweet and sour, 104
    with sausage and leeks, Basque
      style, 106-107
    Scottish lamb and chicken
      liver, 105
    freezing and heating, 103
  turkey
    supper, 107-108
    vegetable amandine, 100-101
Piquant barbecue sauce, 53
Plantation skillet, 84
Poached chicken breast, 161
Polenta with chicken livers, 89
Pollo di Anna, 56
Pork
  Caribbean chicken and squash, 72
  chicken with ham and mushrooms,
    212
  Chinese chicken with ham soup, 144
  macaroni salad with broccoli,
    turkey and ham, 153
  minced chicken and pork pie, 180
  tablecloth stainer with chicken
    and, 230
  turkey and ham Florentine, 186-187
  see also Sausage
Port wine aspic topping, 122-123
Potato
  buffet Russian chicken salad
    with, 155
  layered chicken salad with, 164
  molded salad with turkey and, 162
  stuffing with, 25
Poulet Marengo, 225
Puréed cream of turkey soup, 130-131

Ragout
  chicken
    marinated, 74
    with peas and mushrooms, 75
  turkey
    in puff pastry, 76-77

see also Stew(s)
Relish(es)
  Cape Cod, 30
  cranberry relish mold, 31
  pepper, 243
  raisinberry, 31
Rice
  arroz con pollo criollo, 231
  chicken livers with, 215
  chicken soup with, 139
  chicken and rice deluxe, 78-79
  Chinese fried, and chicken, 209
  fruited brown rice stuffing, 23
  Indian pilaf, 241
  in salads, 148
    curried salad Indienne, 158
    curried salad with turkey and, 154
  turkey casserole with, 219
Rich cream of turkey soup, 130
Roast(s)
  chicken
    with cherry sauce, 218
    with herbs, 22-23
    Indian style, 242
  turkey, 20
    with barbecue sauce, 29
    carving, 19
    facts, 18
Rotisserie cooking
  favorite herb-grilled chicken, 63
  teriyaki turkey, 62
  tips, 59-61
Rumaki, 118


Salad(s), 147-164
  layered chicken salad, 164
  molded, 156-163
    asparagus and chicken, 160
    chicken and avocado, 157
    creamy chicken mousse, 159
    curried, Indienne, 158
    mock headcheese, 161-162
    peppery chicken loaf, 163
    turkey, 156
    turkey and potato, 162
  tips for, 148-149
  tossed, 149-155
    apple and pear slaw, 30
    buffet Russian chicken-potato, 155
    chicken and cherry tomato, with
      avocado dressing, 150
    chicken and Chinese cabbage, 149

Salad, tossed *(cont'd)*
    chinoise chicken, 153
    curried turkey-rice, 154
    garnished chicken-grape, 154-155
    macaroni, with broccoli, turkey and
        ham, 153
    macaroni and chicken, with tuna
        dressing, 150-151
    Oriental-style chicken, 152
    pasta and chicken, 151
Sandwich(es), 165-169
    freezing tips, 167
    great hero, 165
    grilled turkey, cheese and tomato, 169
    open hot turkey, 168-169
    tips for, 166
    tomato salad, 167
    turkey bonanza, 168
Sauce(s)
    barbecue, 29
        piquant, 53
        Southern, 55
    basic tomato, 233
    curry, 125
    hollandaise
        foolproof, 215
        mock, 108
        quick, 213
    mornay, 178
    peach, 116
    sweet and sour orange, 115
    tartar, 41
    tomato and green chili, 157
    velouté, 203
Sausage
    Basque style pie with chicken, leeks
        and, 106-107
    in chicken-noodle Spanish dinner, 94
    in Italian chicken roll, 184-185
    in peppery chicken loaf, 163
    stuffing
        apple and, 27
        carrot and, 24
        corn-, 24
        cornbread-, 26
Sautéed dishes, 34
    chicken
        Athena, 42
        breasts, in champagne sauce, 188
        breasts, in curried chutney, 211
        breasts, with blueberries in orange
            sauce, 187
        with cream sauce, 211
        cutlets, 41

    cutlets, with hollandaise sauce,
        212-213
    cutlets Parmesan, 40-41
    with ham and mushrooms, 212
    lemon and sage breasts, 176
    linguine with chicken in garlic
        sauce, 40
    Madeira, 213
    *see also* Scaloppine, chicken
    turkey
        scaloppine, 43
        schnitzel, 42
Savory chicken wings, 116
Savory lima bean soup, 134
Scaloppine
    chicken
        basic recipe, 43
        herbed, with white beans, 48
        with lemon peel, 44
        in mustard sauce, 45
        Normandy, 46
        with orange sauce, 45
        with peppers, 44
        Sicilian, 47
        and zucchini avgolemono, 46-47
    turkey, 43
Schnitzel, turkey, 42
Scottish lamb and chicken liver pie, 105
Seafood
    lemony chicken wings and shrimp
        kabobs, 54-55
    paella, 222
Sesame chicken wings, 114
Shallow-frying, 34
Slaw, apple and pear, 30
Soufflé topped turkey casserole, 90-91
Soup(s), 127-145
    chicken
        broth, 128
        Chinese, with ham, 144
        corn 'n' chicken chowder, 131
        curried apple and 139-140
        dumpling, 137
        French gumbo with, 138
        gingerroot chicken wing, 136
        Grandmother's, 142
        hearty beef and, 133
        hearty giblet, 129
        hearty winter, 135
        Pennsylvania, with corn, 141
        rice, 139
        savory lima bean, 134
        springtime, 133
    tips for, 141, 143

turkey
    broth, 129
    with egg dumplings, 140
    last-minute chowder, 135
    noodle, 145
    oven, with beef, 144-145
    purée cream of, 130-131
    rich cream of, 130
Southern barbecued chicken, 55
Soy sauce dip, 136-137
Spätzle, 86
Speedy turkey loaf, 204
Spinach
    chicken tetrazzini with, 190
    turkey and ham Florentine, 186-187
Springtime chicken soup, 132
Stew(s)
    chicken
        Caribbean, with squash, 72
        Carolina Brunswick, 78
        marinated ragout, 74
        ragout with peas and mushrooms,
            75
        rice deluxe, 78-79
        tomato, 84-85
    turkey
        boiled dinner, 77
        ragout in puff pastry, 76-77
Stir-frying, 204-210
    Cantonese-style chow mein, 238
    chicken and snow peas in orange
        sauce, 205
    chicken and vegetables, 208-209
    chicken chinoise, 210
    chicken livers and peppers, 206-207
    chicken provençale, 206
    Chinese fried rice and chicken, 209
    mushrooms and chicken lo mein,
        236
    sweet and pungent chicken breasts,
        207
    tips for, 204-205
    turkey with mushrooms and snow
        peas, 208
    velvet sliced chicken, 237
    walnut chicken with broccoli, 235
Stuffed breast of turkey
    ballottine, 173-174
    galantine, 174-175
Stuffed chicken breasts, 178-179
    dinner of, 214
Stuffing
    baked casserole with chicken
        and, 96

casserole with chicken and, 91
    easy herb-celery, 26
    fruited, 28
    fruited brown rice, 23
    mushroom-herb, 23
    old-fashioned bread, 24
    orange-pecan, 25
    potato, 25
    sausage
        apple and, 27
        carrot and, 27
        corn-, 24
        cornbread-, 26
    storage of, 13, 18
    traditional sage, 20-21
    tropical, 28
Sweet and sour dishes
    marinade, 69
    orange chicken wings, 115
    Oriental chicken pie, 104
    sweet and pungent chicken
        breasts, 207
    sweet and pungent chicken
        wings, 185

Tandoori turkey breasts, 67
Tartar sauce, 41
Teriyaki turkey, 62
Texas-style barbecued chicken, 68
Thigh, turkey
    scaloppine, 43
Ticino-style lemon chicken, 234
Tomato and green chili sauce, 157
Tomato salad sandwich, 167
Tomato sauce, basic, 233
Tomato-soy glaze, 69
Traditional sage stuffing, 20-21
Tropical stuffing, 28
Turkey
    baked
        Louisiana turkey royale, 203
        microwave, 200
        speedy turkey loaf, 204
    barbecued, see Barbecue, turkey
    buying tips, 6, 7
    casseroles, see Casseroles, turkey
    cutting up, 10-11
    defrosting, 13-15
    ground
        coulibiac, 192-193
        croquettes, 39
        speedy turkey loaf, 204
    leftovers, 18, 21

Turkey *(cont'd)*
nutritional value, 4
pastry
coulibiac of, 192-193
pies
supper, 107-108
vegetable amandine, 100-101
roast, 20
breast, with barbecue sauce, 29
carving, 19
facts, 18
salads
curried, with rice, 154
macaroni, with broccoli, ham and,
153
mock headcheese, 161-162
molded, 156
molded, with potatoes, 162
sandwiches
bonanza, 168
grilled, with cheese and tomato,
169
hero, 165
open hot, 168-169
tomato salad, 167
sautéed
scaloppine, 43
schnitzel, 42
stir-fried
with mushrooms and snow peas,
208
storage of, 13, 21

stuffed
breast, ballottine, 173-174
breast, galantine, 174-175

Velouté sauce, 203
Velvet sliced chicken, 237
Vinaigrette dressing, 164

Walnut chicken with broccoli, 235
Wine-basted barbecued turkey, 59
Wine marinade, 69
Wings, chicken
barbecued chicken drumettes, 117
curried limas and, 99
gingerroot soup with, 136
Oriental, 117
savory, 116
sesame, 114
shrimp kabobs and lemony, 54-55
sweet and pungent, 185
sweet and sour orange, 115
Wok cooking, *see* Stir-frying

Yogurt marinade, 69

Zucchini
grilled, 56
scaloppine and, avgolemono, 46-47